HiKE iT BABY

100 AWESOME OUTDOOR ADVENTURES
with BABIES and TODDLERS

SHANTI HODGES

FOREWORD BY DR. SCOTT SAMPSON,
host of PBS Kids *Dinosaur Train*

FALCON®

An imprint of The Rowman & Littlefield Publishing Group, Inc.
4501 Forbes Blvd., Ste. 200
Lanham, MD 20706
www.rowman.com
Falcon and FalconGuides are registered trademarks and Make Adventure Your Story is
a trademark of The Rowman & Littlefield Publishing Group, Inc.

Distributed by NATIONAL BOOK NETWORK

British Library Cataloguing in Publication Information available

Library of Congress Cataloging-in-Publication Data available

ISBN 978-1-4930-3390-4 (paperback)
ISBN 978-1-4930-3391-1 (e-book)

♾™ The paper used in this publication meets the minimum requirements of American
National Standard for Information Sciences—Permanence of Paper for Printed Library
Materials, ANSI/NISO Z39.48-1992.

Printed in the United States of America

Hike it Baby hikes are led by volunteers who have no professional training and are not
experts to guide families on hikes. They are people who want to raise a generation to
love the outdoors and they accomplish this by facilitating meetings outside for all to
join. Tips like these have been gathered from collective experience. As with any physical
activity, please be sure to check with your healthcare provider and other experts when
hiking with your children.

The authors and The Rowman & Littlefield Publishing Group, Inc.
assume no liability for accidents happening to, or injuries sustained by, readers
who engage in the activities described in this book.

ACKNOWLEGMENTS

To begin, I'd like to thank the entire Hike it Baby community and other contributing organizations: Adventure Mamas, Women Who Hike, 52 Hikes Challenge, and the individuals who jumped in when I put a call out for the best Hike it Baby adventures. Not only did location ideas stream into my inbox, but fully baked pieces with photos, making the daunting task of writing this book easier. I would especially like to thank Bobby and Maura Marko, Kristin Hinnant (photos and text), Katy Severe, Melissa Hollingsworth (photos and text), Maureen Cooper, Jessica Featherstone, Kiera Wickliffe Berger, Angela Malson (photos and text), Amelia Mayer (photos and text), Jennifer Bradwin and Christel Peters.

A huge shout-out to Kristin Mannion and Vong Hamilton for helping me organize when I realized this was a much bigger project than originally anticipated. To the Hike it Baby leadership team (Jessica Carrillo Alatorre, Corie Reeves, Jessica Featherstone and Bailey Ludlam) who ran everything while I worked on the book. Thank you to my friend Donna Vasquez who took care of Mason and kept him entertained while I worked.

So much appreciation for my editor, Ursula Cary, who guided me from shaping the proposal to writing the final pages. And thanks to the rest of the team at Globe Pequot and FalconGuides.

A much needed shout-out to the first five women who ever went hiking with me that lovely July 2013 day. Also to all of my hike crew and branch ambassadors in Portland who pushed me along to keep the momentum going as Hike it Baby began to grow.

Lastly, so much love and huge thanks forever to my husband Mark Hodges, who held my hand, read my pages, offered me insights, and put me in check when I doubted I could do this. Without him and our spirited, adventure-loving, often-barefoot-hiking son Mason, this book and the whole organization of Hike it Baby wouldn't exist.

CONTENTS

FOREWORD

HIKING IS MY BLISS. For this passion, I thank my mother, who had me trundling on trails as a toddler. By the age of 9, I was signed up as a member of the local mountaineering club. Living in the Pacific Northwest, we hiked coastlines and rivers, mountains and glaciers. There were afternoon strolls on the beach, challenging day hikes to craggy peaks, and backpacking trips to alpine lakes. Perhaps no surprise, then, I sought out a profession that would take me on outdoor adventures to amazing places. Eventually, I settled on dinosaur paleontologist.

Today, in my midfifties, I still crave the trail. If I don't make time for regular hikes in beautiful places, my wife, Toni, sends me outside to rediscover my nature connection (and become a little more human). These days, while on my nature jaunts, I see all too few babies and toddlers—or kids of any age, for that matter. Even walking in my local neighborhood, I'm more likely to come across squirrels than children.

The statistics back up my anecdotal observations. The average American child now spends 7 to 10 hours each day gazing at screens, compared with a handful of minutes playing outdoors. Digital technologies cannot shoulder all the blame here. As parents, we tend to hold deep fears of "stranger danger" (even though child abductions by strangers occur no more frequently now than in the 1950s or 1960s). We also tend to overschedule our children, leaving them precious little time for that all-important unstructured "free" play.

This indoor migration over the past generation has been at least partially responsible for skyrocketing rates of such health conditions as childhood obesity, attention deficit disorder, diabetes, and depression. Some health professionals make dire predictions that this generation of children could be the first in recorded history to have life expectancies shorter than those of their parents.

In response to the trend toward "domesticating" kids, a growing movement has emerged aimed at "rewilding" childhood. In countries all over the world, we see more and more initiatives emerging around forest preschools, nature-based learning, family nature clubs, and the like.

Yet, for all our recent efforts to reconnect kids with nature, babies and toddlers are often—even typically—left out of the mix. I find this omission an odd one. My connection with nature began well before my earliest memory (my mother used to say "in the womb"). Yet, despite the documented health benefits, parents often don't think of the natural world as a place to delight and engage their offspring.

Far too often these days, children reach the middle years (6 to 11 years old) with minimal outdoor experience. For these kids, usually with senses numbed by years of screen time, nature is boring—the place where nothing happens. Yet, those of us who remember free-range childhoods tell a different story, with evenings and weekends spent playing tag, climbing trees, and kicking cans.

No, the time to begin connecting kids to nature is at birth (or, if you follow my mother's example, even before that). If you are a parent or grandparent faced with a crying, inconsolable baby, try stepping outside. Often just the feel of the breeze or the wonder of falling leaves or a starlit night is all that's required to calm a young soul.

Anyone who has spent time with babies knows that they are astoundingly curious. Now imagine how a baby or toddler perceives the world while riding in a backpack on a trail. So many sights, sounds, smells, and feelings to stimulate the senses!

———

I first met Shanti Hodges in Denver's City Park. She and I had communicated via e-mail but had never met in person. Shanti informed me that she would be in Denver for a "Hike it Baby" walk around Denver's largest park, adjacent to where I was working. She kindly invited me to join in.

When I arrived, a group of moms, dads, and youngsters was already gathering. The adults held steaming beverages and wore broad, open smiles. Some of the wide-eyed babies and toddlers sat perched in backpacks. Others were safely nestled in a stroller and ready to roll. And a few others were steadfastly determined to start off, however unsteadily, on foot. There was a buzz in the air as the grown-ups chatted excitedly.

Shanti emerged from the group wearing one of those beaming smiles. She shook my hand and immediately followed it with a hug. It was easy to tell that there was something special about this woman. She was clearly one of those people about whom the term "force of nature" is aptly applied. Shanti introduced me to her son, Mason, too distracted by the smorgasbord of sights and sounds to pay much attention to me.

And then, a few minutes later, Shanti offered a rallying cry and a few short comments, after which we set off.

In the intervening few years since that first meeting, Hike it Baby has exploded into a growing movement of its own. Parents and other caregivers all over the US and beyond are feeling empowered to pack up their kids and discover the great outdoors. Along the way, those fortunate babies and toddlers are having amazing multisensory experiences while developing a meaningful connection to nature.

Thankfully, Shanti has pulled together numerous lessons and insights from her many journeys around the US (and beyond) to share them with you in this marvelous book. Within, you will find essential tips for getting youngsters out into the wild (even if that wild is sometimes an urban park). You'll learn about gear, from clothing and headlamps to packs and tents; how to regulate your kiddo's temperature with layers of clothes; and, perhaps most critical, the need for always bringing plenty of snacks.

To help you find adventures appropriate to your abilities and your child's age, Shanti has also provided a list of 100 adventures spanning the breadth of the US. You should be able to find wonderful, accessible experiences not far from home.

Helping a child foster a deep connection with the natural world is one of the most precious gifts any parent can offer. But the reality is that children are unlikely to grow into nature-loving adults unless we grown-ups value it first. Kids follow our example.

Connecting kids with nature, so the studies tell us, requires two key ingredients: abundant time spent in wild and semi-wild places and a grown-up to share in the journey. So what better way to foster that love of the natural world for the children in your life than to get them outdoors with you to have fun in amazing places? Put another way, the best strategy to getting kids out into nature is to take them there. And the earlier you start the better.

Connecting kids with nature, I would argue, is among the great works of our time, critical for both the health of children and the places they live. If, a generation from now, many more adults are taking their babes and toddlers into nearby nature, much of the credit will need to go to Shanti Hodges. This book is an enthusiastic invitation to join a growing movement. So why not? Hike it Baby!

SCOTT D. SAMPSON, PHD
President & CEO, Science World British Columbia
Author of *How to Raise a Wild Child: The Art and Science of Falling in Love with Nature*
Host & Science Advisor of PBS Kids *Dinosaur Train*

INTRODUCTION

IT'S ESTIMATED THAT CLOSE TO A MILLION WOMEN SUFFER from postpartum depression each year. I was convinced I'd be one of them. At 38, after years of feeling down, I had reached a point where I couldn't even talk to my life coach without crying. She eventually suggested medication and a therapist, and that's when I realized for the first time in my life I was officially depressed with a capital "D." Things turned around eventually, and by 40 years old I moved to Portland, OR, found out I was pregnant, got married, and decided to settle down, all within a year. It was a lot of change quickly after living a fairly adventurous and nomadic life through my 20s and 30s.

As my due date neared, I started to feel the old dark cloud edging back in. Everywhere I looked I saw stories on postpartum depression. People talked about it in my birthing classes and in prenatal yoga. I talked to my doctor about whether I could breastfeed and medicate once I had a child. I was convinced I was doomed to suffer postpartum depression because the memories of my dark place were in the not-so-distant past.

When my son arrived, I was high with the euphoria of newborn love. But I was also weepy, overwhelmed, bleary-eyed, and hormone-whacked. One minute I was laughing at my baby pooping 12 times a day, and the next minute I was sobbing about my sore nipples and how exhausted I was. It didn't help that my husband would just stand there looking at me like I was a stranger. I just sobbed harder.

Three weeks after Mason was born, I found myself sitting in a new mama group inside in the middle of summer. I heard myself complaining about my husband and how he just didn't understand how tired I was and how scared I was of getting depressed. Everything seemed scary. I was scared of people on the street, cars driving too close on the freeway, lead poisoning in our windows, going out for a hike. It felt like pretty much everything in the world was out to get my beautiful new baby. And as I thought and talked more about all of this, I could feel the symptoms of depression lingering darkly around the edges of my newborn bliss.

I remember thinking, "What would happen if I got so depressed I couldn't take care of Mason?" That's when it dawned on me that the one thing that always made me feel a little better was getting outside. Even if I just sat outside in a park and breathed in fresh air, it made a difference. I asked the group of women if anyone wanted to go on a little hike with me. Nothing hard, just a 0.5-mile trail down the street from my house. I had thought about it before, but I didn't want to go alone.

The next week, I arrived at the park armed with a ridiculous amount of stuff for this "little" outing. I brought a day's worth of diapers and wipes, diaper cream, food and water for an army, a carrier (which I had never used), and my trusty BOB stroller. Three women waited there at the trailhead and two more texted to say they were on the way. I am still a bit shocked that they came! We started out, and I bumped along with Mason in the stroller, but eventually we came to a place where it was obvious I needed to ditch the stroller and carry my son. The "veteran" mamas with 3-month-olds helped me adjust my carrier, slide tiny Mason in, and keep hiking. I only made it about another 15 minutes before I got tired and turned around, but it was exhilarating to feel the dirt crunch under my feet for that 0.5 mile. I felt my spirits rising, and I knew I wanted to do it the next week.

The following morning, I woke up with the dark cloud hovering in the back of my mind. I decided to go for a walk. I started in the neighborhood, pushing the stroller, but as I neared the same park, I decided to try stepping onto the trail. I locked up the stroller and asked a stranger passing by if she could help me buckle the back of my carrier, which I'd brought along, you know, just in case. I tried to act nonchalant, like I did this all the time, but my mind raced—did I bring enough stuff? What if Mason had a blowout? What if I needed to nurse? I had only nursed in the privacy of my home at that point and was still struggling with it there so doubted I could do it in public. What if he slipped down in the carrier or I just dropped him? What if a scary homeless dude was on the path? Could I protect myself from the unknown with a baby strapped to me?

As I started walking, I felt the pressure still there in my chest, but with every step, the fears and tears started melting away. It was so silent in the forest. The birds got louder, as did the bubbling water in the stream alongside the trail. Everything was so green and lush in spite of the sweltering July heat. I felt Mason's warm little infant body snuggled up against me. I leaned down and kissed his head and breathed in his new baby smell. I moved so slowly, but with every step, I felt a little lighter, a little calmer.

That day, I doubled the distance I had done with the group. Along the way, Mason wailed with hunger, so I stopped and asked a random couple to un-buckle the carrier so I could sit down on a fallen tree and nurse. I was nervous and not as graceful as I would have liked, but I did get enough milk in Mason to appease him and get back home. And when my husband came home and I announced that I went hiking alone, I felt so proud of myself.

The next week, at my invitation, 10 women showed up to join me. I wasn't alone in feeling the need to commune with nature and "hike it out." As the weeks progressed, my circle of friends widened, and new faces showed up to hike with us. I also noticed something shifting inside me. With every hike, I felt physically stronger, and the dark clouds moved further and further away from me.

That's when I decided to create Hike it Baby. I thought, "Wouldn't it be cool if I could have someone to hike with me whenever I wanted? If I was nervous about going to a trail, I could easily find someone to go with me?" I started a newsletter, then built a website and a Facebook group. By May 2014, Hike it Baby had spread beyond Portland. It was the beginning of a national commu-nity of families helping each other get out on trail all across the country—to date, we have thousands of families hiking together on more than 100 hikes on any given day.

While writing this book in 2017, I met up with a Hike it Baby group in the Gorge at Upper McCord, one of four Hike it Baby outings happening in Portland that spring morning. The hike is slightly challenging because there are a lot of switchbacks, and while it's especially great for a toddler to hike, carrying is doable because it's only about a mile up. It was a beautiful day, and I was joined by nineteen women with babies—three were tandem-wearing (carrying two children) and two were visibly pregnant in addition to baby-wearing.

As we descended from the top and approached a more level, forested stretch, I watched my son, Mason, running and laughing in the shade. I looked around at all of the smiling families surrounding me, and I felt so incredibly happy. The simple act of putting one foot in front of the other in an effort to evade depression, make friends, and spend time with my newborn son got me to that place. I am forever grateful for the community, experiences, and new trails I have discovered through Hike it Baby.

It may be a cliché, but the first step truly is the hardest. Once you take it, you'll notice how quickly the clouds will lift and the path will open in front of you.

Happy hiking,

Shanti

10 Tips to Getting Started on Trail with Your Baby

1. Create a regular hike/walk day for yourself, and commit to doing it.

2. Try to plan at least two hikes per month. (If you plan two, you'll likely make it to at least one.)

3. Pack the night before so you don't use the next morning's chaos as an excuse to stay inside and skip it.

4. Choose a mantra for the trail. As heavier thoughts or stressful things enter your mind, go back to that word and look at the trail, and you will notice stress slipping away.

5. Try to leave the cell phone out of reach so you can enjoy the hike and your child. Take that photo and put it away.

6. Find a hike buddy with a similar-age child. Your buddy will help keep you accountable and get you out there. Put them on speed dial if a beautiful day opens up when you least expect it.

7. Don't let your gear hold you back.

Think used, think simple, think re-purpose. I once put my old cashmere socks on my baby's legs over his clothes and booties to keep him warm on a 30-degree day.

8. Keep it close to home. No need to go on an epic journey to find adventure. Some of my best days hiking were no more than a few miles from my house.

9. Don't get hung up with weather. Rainy day? Carry an umbrella on trail. Too hot? Look for shady trails and water features.

10. Find groups like Hike it Baby (or start one in your area) to help you get out on days you just don't feel like it.

"We have such a brief opportunity to pass on to our children our love for this Earth, and to tell our stories. These are the moments when the world is made whole. In my children's memories, the adventures we've had together in nature will always exist."

—RICHARD LOUV, author of *Last Child in the Woods: Saving Our Children from Nature-Deficit Disorder*

HOW TO USE THIS BOOK

WHILE OUR FAMILY IS ADVENTURE–LOVING, we aren't summiting peaks or traversing the length of the Appalachian Trail (although we will be sharing a story about a family who did it with a 1 1/2-year-old!). We are just getting out there, and we want to share some of the adventures we've found that work for families with young children.

I wrote this book because I believe getting outside with your children regularly is important to your family dynamic, but also in creating a lasting habit in young children that they will carry into life. Taking that outside time one step further and venturing beyond your local park is also what this book is about. I've enlisted the Hike it Baby community to help me by sharing their wild spaces with you so you can expand your family's experiences out there, no matter where you are in the country. So that it's easy to see what each trail has to offer, I've marked each spot accordingly, which means most of the hikes are toddle-waddle approved (good for new little walkers). But keep in mind that you are still headed out into nature, and there's always the unexpected we can't list, like lightning storms popping up in Colorado or a mama bear wandering across your path in Alaska.

While I'd like to say I've been on every single adventure I'm sharing in this book, that wouldn't be humanly possible, considering that would have put us on the road for pretty much every day of Mason's childhood. Instead, I've connected with many amazing families all around me who are part of organizations like the one I founded, Hike it Baby, as well as the other great family-focused organizations like Adventure Mamas, Hike Like a Woman, Women Who Hike, 52 Hike Challenge, and other friends I've met along the way who are like we are: just getting out there through trial and error.

As for the types of trails covered, some are truly wild in the sense that it would be a major undertaking to get to that part of the country, like traveling deep inside Glacier National Park in Montana, adventuring to the middle of nowhere in Utah to Capitol Reef National Park, or backpacking to Second

Beach in LaPush, Washington. And there are other adventures just down the road from your hometown that might be local spots you just keep forgetting about or need that extra push to get to.

No matter where the adventure, each one has been carefully curated and takes into account the fact that you could be carrying a 3-year-old who is throwing a tantrum or that you need to stop and nurse a 9-month-old and change a poopy diaper halfway through the hike. While some of the locations offer a little more challenge, others are simple boardwalks.

As for the terrain, you might see a set of stairs or a brief drop-off that you need to be aware of, or the location could have ticks. I try to warn you about these hazards in the details so you can anticipate them. All of the hikes are doable by most Hike it Baby families and have been tested and approved by the community.

In case you are unfamiliar with the guidelines of the Hike it Baby community, one of the first guiding principles is that we "leave no family behind," and the adventures in this book are no exception. To find these adventures, I surveyed the community nationwide and asked for people to share their favorite spots, insider tips, and amazing photos that help capture why the hike gets a gold star from the community.

While I tried hard to find a location for every state, in the end, some places just didn't stand out strongly enough to make it into the book; one constraint with a book is there are only so many pages. Because I was committed to finding the best hikes I could, I decided that in some states where there was a waterfall or amazing location, we added a few extras; in other states, we just offered a suggestion or two. I made sure that no matter what state you were in, there would always be a Hike it Baby adventure near you. This helps make the book relevant whether you are at home or on the road.

Some of the stories in this book are from my family, but the rest have been carefully curated, taking into consideration what Mark (my husband) and I feel will be fun and supportive in getting families out there with young children. Things we took into consideration were the various stages in our 5 years with our son Mason, from my pregnancy to recovery, to when he was first learning to walk, and then the toddler phase, where he was up and down and all over the place. One thing we can assure you is that hiking with young children is a very different experience than hiking with older kids. Our criteria for choosing trails is rarely reflected in the online guides and in general park information. This is changing as more families get out there with young children, and we are excited to be a part of the change and help you get started.

The best way to use this book is to look at it as a road map to help you find adventures. It's the first step, and from there you can go as far as you'd like, venturing longer on trails on which we start you. In some of the reviews, we tell you about other trails you can find in an area. Elsewhere, we might even suggest heading down the road to another park if we think it can easily be done in a day. The one thing we can guarantee about these hikes is they are all Hike it Baby community member favorites.

Another thing we tried to do with this book is get a little farther out of town than just the hike in the park. It's often easier to find adventures in town through local parent groups, but we wanted to give you a little nudge farther down the trail. In some cases, these locations might be far from urban centers and something you might want to explore on a road trip or when visiting another part of the country.

Making our adventures accessible for most—including families with children or parents who have disabilities, as well as grandparents and other elderly family members—was also an important factor. As I previously mentioned, one of our community's guiding principles and why so many people love getting out with our organization is we "leave no family behind." This means we not only wait for everyone on our hikes and move at the pace of the group, but we also look for trails that really are friendly for many different family needs.

I hope you enjoy the adventures provided by the community and recognize the book as a jumping-off point for raising your little one to love the outdoors. The Hike it Baby community is sharing their best adventures with all of us. Where you take it from there is up to your family. To further research and step beyond this book, you can tap into Hike it Baby communities across the US by joining us at HikeitBaby.com. This is the beauty of finding a community of like-minded families who are excited to share their explorations with toddlers and babies.

At the end of the day, the goal for all of us is to spend more time in nature and to help our children learn that nature is something we must love. As our planet becomes more steeped in technology, making an effort to connect with nature has never been more critical for both you and your children. We hope this book is one of the tools that will help make that happen more easily and regularly. Welcome to our family. We look forward to seeing you on trail!

CAHABA RIVER NATIONAL WILDLIFE REFUGE, ALABAMA, **CAHABA RIVER LOOP**

ACTIVITIES: Hiking, splashing, birding, paddling

LENGTH OF HIKES: 1.4 miles

OUT AND BACK OR LOOP: Both

DIFFICULTY OF TERRAIN: Easy

ELEVATION GAIN: 346 feet

PARKING FEE/PASS: No

TOILETS: No

CHANGING TABLE: No

NURSING BENCHES: No

DOGS ALLOWED: No

BIKES/HORSES/MOTORS ON TRAIL: No

CELL RECEPTION: No

DRINKING WATER AVAILABLE: No

POTENTIAL CHILD OR BABY HAZARDS: The current can be swift after it rains. Always recommend children wear life jackets or flotation devices.

GEAR SUGGESTIONS: Personal Flotation Devices

One of the newest Wildlife Refuges in the country, this site was established in 2002 and is home to the Cahaba shiner, a ray fin fish that's on the endangered species list. But even more spectacular and obvious to the passing hiker are the Cahaba lilies, rare, delicate, spindly looking flowers that grow in only a few areas in the southeast US. The reason for this is that the lilies require a special habitat of swift-flowing water over rocks and lots of sun, and the 200-mile Cahaba River offers this.

The park offers many easy trails for new walkers with limited elevation gain on three easy all-access trails: the Cahaba River Loop, Cahaba Lily Trail, and Tannehill Ironworks Trail. Up your mileage a little bit, and hike through mountain longleaf and loblolly pines filled with woodpeckers, orchard orioles and Kentucky warblers skipping from limb to limb, and you can cover between 2 to 3 miles on the Piper Trail Interpretive Loop or venture farther out to Falling Rock Falls. The falls can be slippery, so beware if you are carrying a little one. Also note that there are sections of the trail that may be better suited for older kids, so you might have to carry a toddler through some of it.

Finished hiking? Swim, kayak, float, canoe, or play on the edges of Alabama's longest free-flowing stream. This wild wetland is best known for having 131 fish species and 13 plant and animal species that are found nowhere else in the world. Love birds? This is a great place to spot belted kingfishers, great blue herons and the occasional osprey or bald eagle.

Keep in mind that traveling through the park is slow going. Expect delays as you travel down a narrow gravel road, with pedestrians and ongoing car traffic. Pullouts can be found up and down the road, allowing you to dip into different trails within the refuge.

WHY IT'S A FAVORITE

"The Cahaba lilies are only found in a few places in the country, and this is one of them. They are absolutely breathtaking to witness and one of the reasons we keep coming back to this park over and over."
—KATHRYN JONES

INSIDER'S TIP

Visit between Mother's Day and Father's Day every year for the best viewing. The weekend to avoid is the last Saturday in May due to a large festival honoring the lilies that grow in the area.

LOUISE KREHER PRESERVE AND NATURE CENTER, ALABAMA, **POND WAY**

ACTIVITIES: Hiking, birding, interpretive trails, playground, nature center

LENGTH OF HIKE: 1.5 miles

OUT AND BACK OR LOOP: Loop

DIFFICULTY OF TERRAIN: Mostly level terrain, with one stream crossing with stepping stones

ELEVATION GAIN: No

PARKING FEE/PASS: No

TOILETS: Yes; handicap-accessible

CHANGING TABLE: Yes

NURSING BENCHES: Yes

DOGS ALLOWED: No

BIKES/HORSES/MOTORS ON TRAIL: No

CELL RECEPTION: Yes

DRINKING WATER AVAILABLE: Yes

POTENTIAL CHILD OR BABY HAZARDS: Snakes and ticks

GEAR SUGGESTIONS: Bug repellent and sun protection

Nestled in a corner of Auburn, AL, a southern college town where football and barbecue reign supreme, lies the Kreher Preserve and Nature Center—120 acres of old-growth hardwood forest. Owned by Auburn University, the preserve acts as an outreach program of the School of Forestry and Wildlife Sciences, providing a source of outdoor recreation and education to the thousands of visitors that walk its trails every year. Park employees host field trips and day camps for children of all ages. There are informative and interactive workshops year-round, like guided hikes and lectures with scientists. Signs and kiosks are scattered around the park, educating both children and adults alike about the native flora and fauna in the area.

The wide, groomed trails are easy for all ages to navigate, especially new walkers and toddlers. The park has all sorts of whimsical and interesting features for kids to explore, like a section filled with fairy houses and faces painted onto trees. An old homestead and vegetable garden provide great spots to teach children about gardening, and a nearby butterfly garden attracts all kinds of winged visitors. There's a pond with tiny docks for turtles to climb onto and separate enclosed habitats nearby for both turtles

and baby alligators. The woods are filled with wildflowers, azaleas, a hidden waterfall, and plenty of shady places to relax.

The park is open year-round, from sunrise to sunset. It's a great place to visit at any time of year, but it's particularly beautiful in the spring, when the leaves start to fill up the canopies and wildflowers are in bloom. Depending on the season, you'll see frogs, turtles, alligators, birds, butterflies, and deer. There's another parking lot just around the corner on Farmville Road that gives you faster access to the old homestead, vegetable garden, and butterfly garden.

To hit all the best features of the preserve, take a 1.5-mile loop through the interior of the park. Starting at the pavilion, take Pond Way through the woods and across a field of wildflowers until you reach the pond. Turn left to take Barn Trace up to the old homestead and vegetable garden, and then turn right on Homestead Trail to wander through the butterfly garden. Turn right at the parking lot and follow Pond Way around the right side of the pond, and then turn left at Hidden Falls Trail to follow the stream to beautiful views of these gentle falls. Stepping stones will take you across the stream, and then take a right onto either Songbird Loop or the next wide, handicap-accessible trail to head back toward the pavilion, passing the turtle and alligator enclosures along the way.

WHY IT'S A FAVORITE

"I take my 1-year-old son to the preserve several times a week. The nature playground is a great place to let him explore and play in the dirt, with several park swings and benches where parents can watch and relax." —KRISTIN HINNANT

INSIDER'S TIP

The best feature of all is the incredible nature playground, a shaded area filled with natural materials to climb on and endless opportunities for kids to get dirty. The playground includes a treehouse, "eagle's nest," slides, logs, tunnels, boulders, balance beams, jungle gyms, a sand pit, and more. There are picnic tables for enjoying an al fresco lunch and a handicap accessible bathroom nearby. There are also benches located around the park for relaxing, enjoying a snack, or nursing.

CHUGACH STATE PARK, ALASKA,
TURNAGAIN ARM TRAILHEAD

ACTIVITIES: Hiking, birding, wildflowers, wildlife

LENGTH OF HIKE: 3.8 miles

OUT AND BACK OR LOOP: Out and back

DIFFICULTY OF TERRAIN: Moderate, rocky

ELEVATION GAIN: 250 feet

PARKING FEE/PASS: No

TOILETS: No

CHANGING TABLE: No

NURSING BENCHES: No

DOGS ALLOWED: Yes

BIKES/HORSES/MOTORS ON TRAIL: No

CELL RECEPTION: Yes

DRINKING WATER AVAILABLE: No

POTENTIAL CHILD OR BABY HAZARDS: Devil's club spring, moose and bear

GEAR SUGGESTIONS: Hiking poles are nice for some but not needed

Winters are long in Alaska, so finding trails that are easy and clear up early in the spring can help give you something to look forward to during the long, dark days of winter. This trail is actually hikable in the winter with micro-spikes and a headlamp during dark months.

Head south on the trail and wind about a mile uphill through a lovely birch forest, then either continue hiking along the Turnagain Arm Trail toward McHugh Creek or scramble up scree to climb Rainbow Peak (not recommended with toddlers).

Rainbow Trail runs along the railroad and highway and was a support route built in 1910. There are beautiful coastal vegetation and tons of wildflowers in the spring. The trail has flat stretches, but expect a little climbing to get your heart rate up, then slow it down when you cross bridges. Be sure to stop at the creek for toddler fun in the summer. Bridges are great motivators for little ones. You can remind them at the beginning that you are going to look for the "troll under the bridge," and then have them hide at the bridge and be the troll. There's a beautiful overlook for pictures and views of the Kenai Mountains all around you.

What Hike it Baby Ambassador Kathy Rumsey likes about this one is that it's a short hike and easy to get to from town. Also, it's just off the highway and less likely to be crowded than the fee lots at McHugh and Potter.

While our suggestion is Rainbow Trailhead, there are multiple adventures off of this one if you want to go farther, including Potter, McHugh, and Windy Corner. The trails leading off the main trail will give you access to McHugh Lake, Table Rock, and several rock-climbing areas as well.

Keep in mind that this is an area where moose are calving and bears are spotted frequently, so carry bear spray and know what to do when crossing paths with wildlife in the area. If you do make it to Windy Corner, look for Dall sheep in the rocks above.

WHY IT'S A FAVORITE

"The Turnagain Trail is great because it has a good uphill climb to get from the trailhead to the main trail, but then a good variety of ups and downs. It's a great hike in the winter when the bears are hibernating and it's easier to see the moose. It's a fun place to try out snowshoeing, too, if there is a fresh snowfall; but the trail quickly gets packed down from many people using the trail. In the fall, winter, and spring, depending on the conditions, you might need micro spikes." —HEATHER HELZER

INSIDER'S TIP

Bears are a pretty common experience in Alaska on many trails. It's important to carry bear spray when on trail and to know how to use it. You can often rent bear spray if visiting or purchase at stores like Cabela's or REI in Anchorage. Most Alaskans own bear spray, so if you are visiting friends, ask to borrow it. You can't travel with it on the plane, so don't purchase prior to your trip.

CHUGACH NATIONAL FOREST, ALASKA, **SPENCER GLACIER**

ACTIVITIES: Hiking, birding, wildflowers, picnicking, horseback riding

LENGTH OF HIKE: 2.6 or 6.2 miles

OUT AND BACK OR LOOP: Out and back

DIFFICULTY OF TERRAIN: Easy

ELEVATION GAIN: No

PARKING FEE/PASS: No

TOILETS: Yes

CHANGING TABLE: No

NURSING BENCHES: Yes

DOGS ALLOWED: No

BIKES/HORSES/MOTORS ON TRAIL: No

CELL RECEPTION: No

DRINKING WATER AVAILABLE: No

POTENTIAL CHILD OR BABY HAZARDS: Cold water

GEAR SUGGESTIONS: Sun hats in the summer

Want an epic but relatively easy, first adventure for both little ones and toddlers? What makes this hike especially engaging in spite of no elevation gain is the wildlife sightings from the train ride you take to get to the trailhead. The hike starts with catching a lift on the Glacier Discovery Train from either Anchorage or drive to Portage (58 miles from Anchorage). The train slowly rumbles past fields where moose and bear can occasionally be spotted ambling through the tall grass. Overhead, eagles swoop in search of mice scampering through the long grass, and if you come in the spring, purple lupines blanket the landscape.

Get dropped off at the trailhead and a US Forest Service park ranger will greet the family with maps and an offer for an interpretive hike. No need to follow the crowds because the trail is a flat, well-marked walk or stroller ride for 1.3 miles around Spencer Lake. Enjoy the picture-perfect Alaskan view with cold, blue icebergs spilling into the bay from Spencer Glacier. It doesn't get more Alaskan than this—unless you bush plane into a hike.

Looking for something more challenging? Hike beyond the lake for 2.3 more miles up Spencer Glacier, and make the whole out and back adventure 6.2 miles. If you want to make the train back, however, walk fast or see if you can catch another train in a few hours. Don't be surprised if you see people from your train who looked like backpackers pulling out dry suits and blowing up pack rafts on the shore of the lake and heading out for an adventure. These 5-pound inflatable kayak-like boats were founded in Alaska and popularized with YouTube videos in the last few years by backcountry adventurers like Roman Dial; Dick Griffith; and the Alpacka Raft inventor, Sheri Tingey.

Toddlers will love how easy it is to run along this trail and around the lake, and parents can rest assured that should their little one tire, the shoulder ride out isn't far. Trains run every few hours to take you back to Portage. But if you are feeling like making it an overnight, grab one of the primitive campsites in the area and train back the next day.

A second option if you are interested in making a full day of this adventure after the train ride back is to drive less than a mile down the road and spend the afternoon in the Alaskan Wildlife Conservation Center. Here, kids will get a close-up view of bison grazing on grass and grizzly bears snacking on salmon; you can even get up close and personal with a porcupine.

A last option is to stay overnight and rent the brand-new, small, rustic Spencer Bench Cabin in the area, but this is hard to come by so make sure you rent it early! The cabin sleeps six and has bunks, a cooking area, and an outhouse. No water or power. Between May 27 and September 18, you will want to rent this cabin through the Alaska Railroad. The rest of the year, go on to www.recreation.gov.

WHY IT'S A FAVORITE

"We went with a few families to Spencer Glacier last year—five kids ages 3 and under and a baby on the way! The kids were so excited about the train ride from the second we choo-chooed into the station until we were dropped off at the whistle stop. Once off the train, we spent time floating between icebergs on the lake before hiking up to the cabin. In August, the mountains are full of wild blueberries. It's the most fun time to hike

with my babies because I love the joy in their faces every time they spot a good berry. We spent the night in the cabin and were witnesses to one of the most amazing Alaskan sunsets. The next morning, we hiked down to the whistle stop." —GEORGIA KUBIK

INSIDER'S TIP

Remember that Alaska in the spring and summer means long days. In June, nighttime comes well after midnight, and the sun only sets for maybe 2 to 3 hours. It's not uncommon to see families on trail with babies at 9 p.m. in the summer; so if you find yourself in Alaska, adopt the local way and soak up every second of daylight that you can to get the most out of your time there.

TONTO NATIONAL FOREST, ARIZONA,
BOYCE THOMPSON ARBORETUM

ACTIVITIES: Birding, hiking

LENGTH OF HIKE: Main trail is 1.5 miles

OUT AND BACK OR LOOP: Loop

DIFFICULTY OF TERRAIN: Easy

ELEVATION GAIN: No

PARKING FEE/PASS: Adults $12.50 / children 5–12 $5

TOILETS: Yes

CHANGING TABLE: Yes

NURSING BENCHES: Yes

DOGS ALLOWED: Yes

BIKES/HORSES/MOTORS ON TRAIL: No

CELL RECEPTION: Yes

DRINKING WATER AVAILABLE: Yes

POTENTIAL CHILD OR BABY HAZARDS: Rattlesnakes in the summer

GEAR SUGGESTIONS: Water, hat, sunglasses

Recognized as one of the most beautiful arboretums in the country, Boyce Thompson, located in the shadow of Picketpost Mountain, is a new parent and toddler delight with 2 miles of trails that are mainly flat and gentle. Beautiful views line the 1.5-mile main trail, and numerous varieties of butterflies flit about, which makes this a delightful spot for the ever-awestruck toddler. With a number of resting points, it's easy for nursing moms or new little hikers to slowly make their way through the park. The entire park is family friendly for everyone from baby to grandma.

Look for the Children's Garden with fountains and easy-to-follow interpretive signs that cater to younger kids. The gardens loop around from trail to trail, so you can make it a short hike or connect the various parts of the trail and get in some distance. Regulars at the arboretum suggest planning on a minimum of 2 hours to walk the trails. Take a picnic, and your family can make a day of it.

Flowers are plentiful, cacti and succulents dot the landscape, and water can be found throughout the park at various times of year. Surprisingly, visitors report that this park is doable even in the hot summer sun, thanks to resting spots and shade. Venture into the central mission, where older kids and adults can enjoy an exhibit about the area. Or meander down the trails and capture snapshots of the hundreds of plants and desert birds.

Spring and early summer are when the sandy landscape especially comes alive with wildflowers. Look for the state flower, the saguaro, in May and June. Poppies, red flax, and verbena are just a few of the blooms you'll find over the 100 acres of native vegetation. Beyond that, there are 200 acres of exhibits with desert plants from around the globe.

The numerous varieties of flowers also bring in birds and other small animals like squirrels, javelinas, raccoons, foxes, and the occasional mule deer. Look in the flowers or up in the trees for black-tailed sparrows, curve-billed thrashers, verdins, northern mock-

ingbirds, black phoebes, Cooper's hawks, Gambel's quail, broad-billed hummingbirds, Abert's towhees, song sparrows, and great-tailed grackles.

Being that this is desert and a fairly remote location (it's about an hour outside of Phoenix), keep in mind that rattlesnakes, tarantulas, and scorpions are also a part of the landscape. They usually scatter at the sound of people, but be watchful of kids around rock piles, where critters and slithering friends can hide. If you see a rattlesnake, simply take a step back and let it pass.

But more dangerous than the animals of the desert is dehydration. Bring lots of water when you hike, because even though this is a developed reserve, it's still a desert! Another thing to note is that dogs are welcome on leash, and the park provides filled water bowls throughout the trails to help remind people to stop and water their four-legged friends as well.

WHY IT'S A FAVORITE

"Boyce Thompson is a wonderful place to hike in the desert and get away from the urban centers in Arizona. The trails are all stroller-accessible and perfect for a new mom carrying a young baby, yet interesting enough and diverse enough for bigger kids (up to grade-schoolers). There is something for kids of all ages." —JILL CRAVEN

INSIDER'S TIP

If you are up for an additional challenge and are a more experienced hiker, after touring the arboretum, you can travel 0.5 mile west down the road and hike Picketpost Mountain. It's steep, not toddler friendly, and there's a 2,000-foot elevation gain, so it will take about 2 to 3 hours one way. We advise this one only if you are comfortable carrying your baby.

COCONINO NATIONAL FOREST, ARIZONA,
WEST FORK OF OAK CREEK CANYON

ACTIVITIES: Hiking, photography, birding, splashing

LENGTH OF HIKE: 5.2 miles

OUT AND BACK OR LOOP: Out and back

DIFFICULTY OF TERRAIN: Easy

ELEVATION GAIN: 500 feet

PARKING FEE/PASS: $10/day parking fee

TOILETS: Yes

CHANGING TABLE: No

NURSING BENCHES: Yes

DOGS ALLOWED: Yes

BIKES/HORSES/MOTORS ON TRAIL: No

CELL RECEPTION: Spotty

DRINKING WATER AVAILABLE: No

POTENTIAL CHILD OR BABY HAZARDS: There are 13 stream crossings

GEAR SUGGESTIONS: Bring water shoes and a change of clothes if you get wet splashing in the streams.

When Hike it Baby ambassador Jill Craven tells friends about her pick for a first hike postpartum, she suggests the West Fork of Oak Creek Canyon. "I grew up hiking this trail, and then after college, I returned with my best friend and her 1-year-old. It was her first hike postpartum, and they were just testing out their carrier. On that hike I was also with my 5-year-old niece, who ran along the trail and also played in the shallow parts of the creek. And just recently in 2017, I took my infant with friends and their infant in our carriers. It is a hike that both parents and kids (of all ages) can enjoy."

Located just 10 miles from Sedona, this hike is a good day adventure with some manageable elevation gain and lots of shade. The high slot canyon walls of orange Coconino sandstone and the numerous creek crossings less than a mile from the start of the trail help keep the hike cool. Depending on the age of kids you have, it's a perfect out and back hike just to get to the first creek crossing if you have a new walker. Go the distance and you are looking at 12 miles out and back, but you can go as far as the toddler will allow and still feel the beauty of the hike, turning around when your family feels ready.

Most of the terrain is pretty flat, but the creek crossings will need some navigation with small children. Older siblings will be fine as the crossings aren't deep, but be aware that the rocks can be slippery when wet. There are definitely parts of the trail where you have to hike down rock surfaces, but even these can be negotiated while wearing a baby.

The biggest perk for kids is playing in the water as you are hiking across the creek. There are several good water holes along the trail, and, depending on the age level of the children, you can hike long or short to get to a good water hole. The wildlife is fairly standard on this hike. Expect to see butterflies, birds, squirrels, lizards, and snakes. The crowds most likely have scared away any other wildlife that may have traditionally been found on this trail. There are ruins from an early 20th-century settlement that have long since been abandoned, but a fireplace and some floor stones are still visible as you hike through.

Locals suggest visiting this spot in the summer and arriving early in the day because of the many stream crossings and crowds. The water crossings are surprisingly cold and not as pleasant in the dead middle of winter, even in Arizona. This hike has become increasingly popular as it's now a regular feature on "best hike"-type articles in local magazines and newspapers.

While there are not a lot of hazards on this hike, be aware that at certain times of year, there are high levels of ticks hatching. Also there are a few cliffy areas that are unmarked, and the area can be very crowded in peak season. Look out for mountain bikes and dogs!

If you want to beat the crowds, consider doing this one as an overnighter. There are a number of overhangs that offer shelter for camping. The farther out you go, the less people you will see. There are also side canyons you can duck into to get away from the masses.

WHY IT'S A FAVORITE

"West Fork of Oak Creek Canyon in Sedona is a peaceful and cool escape from Phoenix. I grew up taking this hike as a teenager with my parents, siblings, and family dog, Molly. It is a hike that has something for all ages. It is beautiful all year-round and is a must-see in each season. The fall color is tremendous, the winter snow is peaceful and beautiful, and in the spring and summertime, the water in Oak Creek provides the fun addition of splashing and swimming to the hike. Often, I feel like I'm walking through the Arizona Highways magazine. As a parent, I have enjoyed taking my daughter in her carrier, and I look forward to when she can hike it herself." —JILL CRAVEN

INSIDER'S TIP

Go early. This hike has become increasingly popular over the last 20 years. If the parking lot is full, you can park on the highway for free, just outside of the parking lot.

LAKE CATHERINE STATE PARK, ARKANSAS, **FALLS BRANCH TRAIL**

ACTIVITIES: Hiking, splashing

LENGTH OF HIKE: 2 Miles

OUT AND BACK OR LOOP: Loop

DIFFICULTY OF TERRAIN: Easy

ELEVATION GAIN: No

PARKING FEE/PASS: No

TOILETS: Yes

CHANGING TABLE: No

NURSING BENCHES: No

DOGS ALLOWED: Yes

BIKES/HORSES/MOTORS ON TRAIL: No

CELL RECEPTION: Yes

DRINKING WATER AVAILABLE: No

POTENTIAL CHILD OR BABY HAZARDS: Ticks and mosquitoes during their seasons

GEAR SUGGESTIONS: Extra diapers, shoes, and clothing for after playing in the creek and waterfalls

Nestled in the Ouachita Mountains on the 1,940-acre Lake Catherine, you'll find a favorite Hike it Baby trail called Falls Branch Trail. While rivers and lakes are popular destinations for fishing, floating, and tubing, few have hiking trails and can achieve the trifecta of water access, varied hiking terrain (moderate climbs, rocks, and bridge crossings), and a loop that can be managed even with toddlers in tow like this one can. During the rainy season when water is flowing over the falls, they are an awesome sight to see and even more fun for the kids to play under. It's best to visit when there has been lots of rain—usually late spring is good—so there will be water flowing over the double falls and the creek water will be running and clear, which helps reassure that it is safe for kids to splash and swim in.

However, this is not a year-round falls, so expect it to be dry in the fall. But this is still an easy destination with the trail being under 2 miles to navigate and a good hike year-round for families.

While most of the trail and park is relatively friendly for young children, there are a few elevation changes along the trail that include steps, rocks, or drop-offs to the creek. If you want to add a bit more hiking in the day, continue to Slunger Creek Trail. This is a paved path, so it's good for strollers if you want to get a little more outside time and nap your baby or toddler in a stroller. There are also good benches to stop and nurse on this little trail, and it is an excellent alternative trail if you have a child or adult with a walker or wheelchair.

"Fall Creek Falls trail is just about the right length for most," says local ambassador Stefie Gold, "and the falls make a great reward not too far from the end." Start off the hike winding through the pine forest of the park and cross Little Canyon Creek several times. Then arrive at the falls. After a break at the falls, pause to take in the view of the lake and travel across the cool swinging foot bridge that will keep toddlers from complaining about being tired or wet.

WHY IT'S A FAVORITE
"Even though Arkansas is landlocked, we locals love water. What's great about this trail is it's only a short 1 hour and 15 minutes from the center of Little Rock. In summer months, Arkansas heat and humidity can be a challenge all across the state, but there is no reward for hiking greater than a dip in the cool water just below the falls." —STEFIE GOLD

INSIDER'S TIP
Pack a picnic, and either before or after your hike, plan to take a break at the picnic area that is conveniently located near the car and the trailhead. This is also the state park campground, which has hookup sites, a group primitive tent area, and yurts and is close to Lake Catherine. There is also a full ADA-compliant cabin right on the waterfront for families needing wheelchair accommodation. This hike is close enough to Hot Springs, AR, and Little Rock, AR, to make an easy day hike, but it can easily be combined with camping at the campground for more of a weekend adventure.

FOSTERING A LOVE OF NATURE

PATTY FLANAGAN-LINDERMAN

For Patty and her husband, Chris, hiking has been one of their greatest passions together over the last 27 years as a couple. It was no surprise when they became foster parents in 2014 that they would introduce their new daughter-to-be to the woods and the joys of hiking. What came as a surprise to them, though, was how healing and grounding it was for both themselves and their new little one.

MiyMiy was placed with them first as a foster child when she was just 3 months old. Although she was too young to understand what hiking was all about, they noticed right away how much she loved being wrapped tightly to their chests as they wandered through the woods. Patty said she noticed how her little body relaxed more than usual, and she would stare around in wonder at the sunlight streaming through the leaves and laugh as raindrops landed on her face. Eventually, they moved her on to the frame carrier and were happy that she would nap easily in the pack, which provided the family many hours of enjoyment as they hit the trails regularly.

Now at 3 1/2 years old, MiyMiy has gone through three pairs of hiking boots and can pretty much outrun them on any trail she encounters. Patty and Chris have also noticed how hiking with a child has changed how they engage with nature. They had been longtime mountain climbers, and most hikes were for training with the goal being to reach the summit. Now, with a little one in tow, they have slowed down their pace and are noticing more and stopping to examine things they used to rush by to get to the top of a mountain. "I could never have imagined taking the time to watch a slug progress across a trail or play 'follow the leader' with a butterfly before having a child to follow on trail! We are fortunate to live within a couple miles of a state park where there are many trails, and we certainly get out more often even though the distance we travel has shortened."

Camping has also become a regular family activity, and they are working their way up to backpacking. One of their short-term goals is to hike the Wonderland Trail in Washington (an 80-mile trail around Mount Rainier) once MiyMiy is able to go the distance without needing to be carried. Patty says that so far she seems as comfortable in a tent as she is at home, and when she knows they are going camping, she's the first to jump in the car and patiently wait for the adventure to begin.

"She has not only found her 'forever' home with us," says Patty, "but we love that we've helped her discover where to go and what to do whenever she is feeling less than whole in her life."

FAVORITE TRAIL: DASH POINT STATE PARK, WA
This is an easy, meandering trail system in Federal Way, WA, that offers lovely lush Northwest forested trails and ends up down at the beach on the Puget Sound. "We recently moved and are now within walking distance to the Dash Point State Park trail system," says Patty. "This is definitely our daughter's favorite, as it is where we go on a regular basis. We also love to go out to Long Beach and camp and hike around Cape Disappointment State Park."

LOVE, SWEAT,
AND TEARS

ANNIKA MANG

WAS THIS REALLY A GOOD IDEA? I wasn't so sure anymore. I was stuck 90 minutes from home and a mile up a steep trail with a whiney 3-year-old and a 25-pound 2-year-old who just wanted to jump in and out of the hiking carrier every 15 minutes. But let me start at the beginning.

My husband was away camping with a friend and so, of course, I needed to find something really fun to do with the kids. With this in mind, I had re-solved to take the girls by myself on the Ptarmigan Cirque Hike in Kananaskis Country—a beautiful 3-mile hike with 700 feet of elevation gain. I knew that my 3-year-old could hike it herself, as she had tackled harder hikes the past summer but taking both kids by myself to conquer this trail was proving to be mentally exhausting. It didn't take long before I began to question if this truly was "fun."

I thought about turning around pretty early on, but my stubbornness pre-vailed, and we kept going in hopes that our overall moods would change. We slowly made our way up the trail as I told stories about volcanos and bribed the girls with blueberries. We hiked this trail last year as a family, so I knew that the forested trail would soon open up to a beautiful hollow filled with al-pine flowers and expansive views. I asked some hikers coming down the trail about how far it was to get to the Cirque, and I did not receive the answer I was hoping for. We still had quite some ways to go up the trail. Feeling a little, but not entirely, defeated we continued to trudge, the girls' tired little legs struggling to navigate over the big roots and rocks.

Next we met some hiking angels. They told us we only had to go up a little farther around the bend and then, voilà, we would be above the tree line! When hiking with littles, there is nothing better than news that you are farther up the trail than you thought you were.

My littles walked as if there were lead in their shoes, but I, on the other hand, found a new burst of energy. We were close to our destination! I pulled out more blueberries and ran ahead of them on the trail, urging them to move their little feet. It took quite a bit of coaxing, but we finally made it—we had reached the Cirque!

The girls were jumping with excitement since they knew that this was where we would have our treat. I brought out the apple sauce and cookies to munch on while we happily soaked in the views and watched the ground squirrels run around us. The challenge to get up to this spot was well worth the effort.

My oldest turned to me and said, "Mom, this is the best day ever. I am having so much fun." Talk about living in the moment. Then as she took a bite of her cookie, she added, "And you know what the best treat is? It is being together as a family." My heart immediately melted, and I knew my decision to take on this trail, was the right one.

We stayed for quite a while and played volcanoes while searching for special rocks. The kids were sad when it was time to leave. Nature really is the best playground. Once we were packed up and ready for our descent, I tried to put my 2-year-old in the carrier for a nap. After a couple of aggressive bum drops in the carrier and blood-curdling screams, I knew that I would have to wait until we reached the car for naptime.

I was so happy that I decided not to fight her opposition to sitting in the carrier (although I'm sure her screams would be a good wildlife deterrent!). The two girls held hands as they skipped their way down the mountain. Their spirits were high as they relished in the experience of being together and accomplishing something difficult.

The way down was slow but manageable. They drew in the dirt, slid on their bums, and jumped off pretty much any rock they could find. But they were happy, and we were having such a great time that it felt like we reached the car in no time at all.

In the end, I can say without hesitation that I am so happy we did this hike together. The quality time and our ability to work out the challenges brought us together in the kind of bonding experience that is hard to find anywhere but in the outdoors. Needless to say, I am SO looking forward to our next adventure.

Annika Mang is the founder and writer at BorntobeAdventurous.com and the mother of two adventurous toddlers.

10 THOUGHTS ON
ADVENTUROUS PARENTING

1. **SURROUND YOURSELF WITH A LIKE-MINDED TRIBE.** You are the company you keep—be intentional, and spend time with people who invite you to be your best, most epic self. Building community isn't a passive process. Putting yourself out there requires courage and vulnerability, but it's so worth it.

2. **RECOGNIZE THAT EPIC IS SUBJECTIVE.** Challenge and adventure look different for each of us. Take it at your own pace and in your own style; encourage your family to do the same.

3. **THE STRUGGLE IS REAL...AND IT'S PART OF THE PROCESS.** Embrace challenge as one of the greatest teachers of all. What makes an epic hike epic is working hard, pushing past perceived boundaries, adjusting when things don't go according to plan, and reaching heights you never thought possible—often it's uncomfortable. You'll model important values for your kids, such as patience, perseverance, and passion, as a result.

4. **INVEST IN YOURSELF.** Enroll in a climbing class; get first-aid training; take a

wilderness course. As you begin to feel more confident in your skills, you'll become more comfortable bringing your family along. Plus, you'll demonstrate that learning is a lifelong priority.

5. **FIND INSPIRATION.** Instagram, Pinterest, blogs, magazines, and books are all great resources to keep you stoked.

6. **SET SPECIFIC AND MEASURABLE GOALS.** By setting goals, you'll have a clear concept for where you'd like to see yourself in the future. Try setting goals as a family, and then keep one another accountable.

7. **FAILURE IS PART OF THE PROCESS.** Don't be discouraged by failure. It's important to dream big. Reflect on shortcomings, and use them as an opportunity to grow.

8. **STAY PRESENT.** Make it a point to put the camera away from time to time and focus on being fully present and engaged in the activity at hand.

9. **REMEMBER THAT WE WERE ALL NEWBIES AT ONE POINT.** Everyone started as a beginner. Be patient with yourself and make sure your family does the same. Laughter and light-heartedness are often the best antidotes when you're feeling awkward and newb-esque.

10. **BECOME AN ADVENTUROUS PERSON.** As you foster independence and passion in your children, be sure to develop those same values within yourself. It's healthy and exciting to prioritize personal adventure.

Justine Nobbe is a mom of one and the cofounder of Adventure Mamas Initiative (AMI) along with her best friend, Stephanie Feller. AMI is a non-profit organization that uses adventure to support women's maternal health. They have grassroots-led groups all across North America. Join them at adventuremamas.org.

HIKE IT BABY **AMBASSADOR**

THE ROMANIAC

ANKA TRIFAN

If you're struggling with a fussy child who never seems to sleep, you're not alone. When Anka Trifan's first son was born, she and her husband, Ezechel, found that hiking became their saving grace to keeping the calm in their household. "Our child had almost two personalities," she says. "Indoors he was very demanding, and then we would go outside and he was an angel. I felt like we lived outside more than we lived inside the first year or two of his life. That's how we got so into hiking."

Anka wasn't a stranger to hiking prebaby, as she tells stories of climbing huge hills in her town just to get home after school. Looking back, she says that was probably pretty good training for all of the hiking she's gone on to do since Apollo was born, including an all-day 17-miler called Aneroid Mountain that involved assistance ropes to get up, which she and Ezechel did with Apollo when he was just 2 years old.

"How did we not hike more when we didn't have kids? Probably because we weren't forced to," Anka says. "What we quickly found was that Apollo would only nap when we were on the go outside hiking, and he only slept well at night if we spent time outside in the day."

Hiking became such a staple for Anka's family that she even earned a nickname in the Hike it Baby community, "the Romaniac," because during the quarterly Hike it Baby 30 Challenges, she would rack up tons of miles, and she and Ezechel would climb amazing peaks around Oregon and Washington that most families would only dream about.

Anka says hiking has become so much a part of the Trifans' lives that they have now made it an annual tradition to spend the whole day hiking on Mother's Day. "It's a better gift than anything my family could get me. We're busy people and even more so now that we have a second child. When we're outside, we have meaningful conversations and really connect with each other, and our kids are happy."

Life with a second child is proving to be both easier and harder than with one. The good thing is that she is a better sleeper and napper than her first. The bad news is that Anka says she is "sassier."

"She has no shame when it comes to screaming her head off or throwing herself on the floor when she wants something," Anka says. "But she loves hiking and the outdoors just as much as our son does. We also have gone camping a lot more since she came around and from a much earlier age than with our first. I guess we finally got an idea of what the heck we're doing."

The best and most unexpected payout Anka said she has found from getting on trails with her 4-year-old son from such a young age is that she can see the impact on him and how this translates to the bigger world. "Recently, we were on a random walk to the park when my son decided, all by himself, to pick up every piece of trash he was finding along the sidewalk and trail and not just that, when we got home, he wanted to separate it into trash and recyclables. That really melted my heart! Well done, son!"

FAVORITE TRAIL: HURRICANE RIDGE, WA

"You're on the top of the Olympic Peninsula range, and you can see all the way to Canada. There are amazing wildflowers and deer everywhere just walking around with you like you're in a Disney movie," says Anka about the easy 3.2-mile trail that spans Hurricane Ridge just outside of Port Angeles. The first 0.25 mile of this trail is paved, making it wheelchair-accessible and walker- and toddler-friendly. "At 18 months, Apollo hiked a bunch of the switchbacks on that trail by himself, and we were like, 'Look at him go!'"

EASTERN SIERRAS, CALIFORNIA,
BARNEY LAKE TRAIL

ACTIVITIES: Hiking, horseback riding, splashing, birding, camping

LENGTH OF HIKE: 8.8 miles

OUT AND BACK OR LOOP: Out and back

DIFFICULTY OF TERRAIN: Moderate

ELEVATION GAIN: 1,519 feet

PARKING FEE/PASS: $10

TOILETS: At Mono Village Resort

CHANGING TABLE: No

NURSING BENCHES: No

DOGS ALLOWED: No

BIKES/HORSES/MOTORS ON TRAIL: Horses allowed

CELL RECEPTION: No

DRINKING WATER AVAILABLE: Available at Mono Village Resort

POTENTIAL CHILD OR BABY HAZARDS: Some narrow areas with dropoffs

GEAR SUGGESTIONS: Sturdy hiking shoes, camping or backpacking gear, hiking poles, sun protection, bug spray, water filter system, bear canister if camping

Escape the chaos of the big city and venture to Barney Lake, a well-trafficked but pristine hike that's just challenging enough to get your heart rate moving and takes you deep into the Sierras. This is probably not the easiest toddler hike if you are planning on doing the whole hike, but for parents with new babies and those comfortable with carrying older kids, you will be rewarded with a high alpine lake and mountains jutting up out of the water high into the sky.

What makes this location perfect for families with toddlers is you have a beautiful alpine village at 7,000 feet to explore and head up from there. Since we all have those days when we can't get the toddler to hike forward, there's a perfect fallback with Buckeye Hot Springs, boating, fishing, a tent/RV campsite, and a resort. This hike is close enough to civilization to consider this one for a first backpacking adventure with a baby and toddler.

The trail is fairly trafficked, and hikers start early here. Consider leaving before 8 a.m. and getting in some distance. The farther you go, the less busy the trails get. Camp out overnight and you can wake up to silence other than birds chirping at Barney Lake and the beautiful early morning alpenglow. Overnight trips in this area (Barney Lake) with toddlers and infants are great because the crowd starts to leave early evening, so you get this area to explore by yourself. Splash in the water, wade, throw rocks. It also becomes very private for nursing mothers. And at night you get to hear all the animal noises, and stargazing is amazing without any city lights to disturb the darkness.

Hike it Baby mama Xenia Pyne reported that the highlight of her backpacking excursion was waking up to the view of Crown Point, a granite peak that towers over the lake. When you camp out, you can take day hikes from this point to Robinson Lake, Crown Lake, and Peeler Lake. These lakes are pristine, with the first one offering a deep turquoise color and a clear view of rocks on the bottom of the lake. The hikes up to these lakes are advanced, so be prepared to climb, but the incredible views are worth the grind. If elevation isn't your thing, stick to circumnavigating Barney Lake and you will enjoy pine trees, wildflowers, and a grove of aspen trees. It's easy to find shade to pitch your tent, so don't worry about bringing a shade structure.

Some of the hazards to consider in this area are ticks, bears, snakes, and fallen trees. There are some cliffy areas that are unmarked as well, so if your little one is a runner, consider bringing a harness.

WHY IT'S A FAVORITE

"I love this location because there are many options for outdoor activities even if you are not planning on backpacking at Barney Lake. Buckeye Hot Spring is a great find nearby and worth checking out." —XENIA PYNE

INSIDER'S TIP

If you want to avoid the crowds, plan on visiting late in the summer, especially when the school year has begun. Also, make sure to grab a pastry at Nugent High Sierra Bakery in Bridgeport to take out on trail for a tasty breakfast treat with camp coffee. If you overnight it, make sure to visit the ranger station, and check on permits.

HENRY COWELL REDWOODS STATE PARK, CALIFORNIA, **REDWOOD GROVE LOOP TRAIL AND SAN LORENZO RIVER TRAIL**

ACTIVITIES: Hiking, photography, birding

LENGTH OF HIKES: 1.2 miles

OUT AND BACK OR LOOP: Lollipop (loop with an out and back stick)

DIFFICULTY OF TERRAIN: Easy

ELEVATION GAIN: 30 feet

PARKING FEE/PASS: $10

TOILETS: Yes

CHANGING TABLE: No

NURSING BENCHES: No

DOGS ALLOWED: No

BIKES/HORSES/MOTORS ON TRAIL: Horses are allowed on the portion of the trail at the end (after crossing the bridge)

CELL RECEPTION: Spotty

DRINKING WATER AVAILABLE: Yes

POTENTIAL CHILD OR BABY HAZARDS: There's a river and railroad tracks run near the trail

GEAR SUGGESTIONS: Swimsuits

If you find yourself in Santa Cruz, don't miss this state park just a mere 20 minutes away from downtown. While there are longer hikes, the redwood loop is easy at less than a mile and is something most anyone can walk with ease. The ground is also soft, so this is a great place to let your new little walker get her hiking legs on. You might hike it fast if you're babywearing and on the move. But why rush it? We suggest taking an hour or two to stand in awe of the huge forest.

The tallest tree in the park is around 1,500 years old, stands 277 feet tall, and is about 16 feet wide, which means it would take a few family members to wrap your arms all the way around this one! Keep your eye peeled for banana slugs and black-tailed deer. In quieter moments (if this ever happens with a toddler around) or early in the morning, you might spot coyotes and, if very lucky, the rare bobcat.

The nearly flat and wide trail takes you through a wonderful grove of huge picture-perfect redwoods. These skyscraping redwoods inspired some of California's earliest redwood preservation efforts. Don't worry about bringing along a tripod to get that family picture among these greats. Extremely friendly volunteers are all around offering interesting insights and ready to snap your picture.

What makes this special is not only the opportunity to walk among the 40 acres of big trees, but also the fact that you can play in the river traveling through the park. This is a special treat especially on a hot summer day. Keep an eye out for steelhead trout in the river. And if you really want to get the story on the fish, stop at the visitor center and check out the freshwater aquarium with an exhibit called "A Fish Tale" showing the life cycle of eggs from fry (young steelhead) to release.

While toddlers will love the giant trees, the train that goes chugging by is sure to get a big smile and some Thomas the Train enthusiasm. As you hike, you can hear the train approach and then in some spots pass overhead. Wave to the train riders and then ride the train yourself later. You can take a train all the way to the Santa Cruz beach, but make sure you buy tickets ahead of time.

Really enjoying the park? Consider staying overnight. Reservations are required, and this is definitely one of those places you need to plan months ahead of time to stay, but it is well worth the commitment.

Another option is to enjoy this park and then head another 30 minutes north on Rte. 9 to Big Basin Redwoods State Park, where you will find another short play toddler trek through the giant redwoods.

WHY IT'S A FAVORITE

"Big trees always make a place feel peaceful and relaxing to me, and this park is no exception, even if it's filled with kids. The thick redwood needles and the lush undergrowth soften all the sounds. There is so much to do in this park. It's easy to spend the entire day (or the entire weekend if you can manage to snag one of the campsites) walking among the huge trees, wading the river, watching for banana slugs and other creatures in the undergrowth, even riding a steam train in the woods. If that's not enough, you can take another train over the hill and down to the beach in Santa Cruz." —RYAN IDRYO

INSIDER'S TIP

This is a popular park. The parking lot is big, and it can get full on summer weekends. If you plan to swim, note that the river gets wider the farther downstream you go, and there are some nice swimming holes. Look on the map for Garden of Eden, Cable Car Beach, and Big Rock Hole.

JOSHUA TREE, CALIFORNIA, HIDDEN VALLEY

ACTIVITIES: Hiking, camping, rock climbing, historic remnants

LENGTH OF HIKE: 1 mile

OUT AND BACK OR LOOP: Loop

DIFFICULTY OF TERRAIN: Easy

ELEVATION GAIN: 200 feet

PARKING FEE/PASS: Yes

TOILETS: Yes

CHANGING TABLE: No

NURSING BENCHES: No

DOGS ALLOWED: No

BIKES/HORSES/MOTORS ON TRAIL: No

CELL RECEPTION: No

DRINKING WATER AVAILABLE: No

POTENTIAL CHILD OR BABY HAZARDS: Cacti, snakes, scorpions, poking bushes

GEAR SUGGESTIONS: Water, sunscreen, hat

Joshua Tree is a perfect hiking location for families with young kids for so many reasons. The landscape looks like it's straight out of a Dr. Seuss book between the spiky Joshua trees, cholla cacti, and the giant granite boulders that look like pebbles tossed in the sand and then supersized. The only drawback to this area is that it can get pretty hot, so it's definitely not a summer spot to hit. What is amazing about this park is you can hike in 70- to 80-degree weather in the middle of the winter.

The main trails, like many national parks, are very well marked and have nice plaques along the way explaining animals, plants, and petroglyphs. Why we chose this hike was because, while it's only 1 mile, there are so many side adventures you can do like climbing on rocks and investigating the desert along the way that's more or less doable by new little walkers.

This is a lollipop hike with a short lead-in through to the loop, and then it travels around a little rock hill, then heads back toward the parking lot. There's a short, not-to-be-missed offshoot trail that leads to a petroglyph wall as well.

What you will like about this hike is how much flat, wide-open terrain there is, allowing children to run free without concern. Keep an eye out for spiky things, however, and make sure you point them out to little ones so they can learn to identify them quickly. There are a few cacti in this desert that will reach out and grab you as you pass by, so steer your littles away from these. Most are fairly easily spotted.

Toddlers and little kids will also love how easily they can climb the round granite boulders. Keep an eye on them because they can get pretty high quickly if you turn your back. Joshua Tree is a popular climbing spot, so also look out for rock climbers dangling

high on the walls or bouldering mats on the ground and people scaling the walls rope-free like Spiderman.

There are a few other noteworthy hikes nearby that are super easy for toddlers to hike on their own two feet. Check out Barker's Dam, which has a dammed-up pond in the middle of the hike and a dam and is about 1.5 miles long. And go to Ryan Campground and hike out 1.2 miles to the Ryan Ranch Ruins, which are the leftovers of an old adobe house from the 1800s. This is a great spot for pictures, especially at sunset.

WHY IT'S A FAVORITE

"Mason is a fairly timid child and gives up easily when it comes to climbing things. The round grippy rocks in this park make it easy for every kid to succeed when climbing. You actually have to watch your kids a bit because they can climb too high quickly! The path is fairly easy to follow here, and the hike is just short enough to get through without a toddler meltdown."
—SHANTI HODGES

INSIDER'S TIP

Junior Ranger hikes happen often in this park so check for times on these. They usually start at 10 a.m. and are out of Barker Dam. If you want to camp for the weekend and didn't set yourself up ahead of time, plan on being there by Thursday morning to get a weekend campground. Also, there are a number of campgrounds outside of the park, like Joshua Tree Lake Campground, that are easy-to-get spots most of the year and are a quick drive into the park.

TAHOE NATIONAL FOREST, CALIFORNIA,
LOCH LEVEN LAKES

ACTIVITIES: Hiking, water play

LENGTH OF HIKE: 2 miles

OUT AND BACK OR LOOP: Out and back

DIFFICULTY OF TERRAIN: Rough trail in places

ELEVATION GAIN: 216 feet

PARKING FEE/PASS: No

TOILETS: No

CHANGING TABLE: No

NURSING BENCHES: No

DOGS ALLOWED: Yes

BIKES/HORSES/MOTORS ON TRAIL: No

CELL RECEPTION: No

DRINKING WATER AVAILABLE: No (plenty available for purification, though)

POTENTIAL CHILD OR BABY HAZARDS: This is a summer-only hike. High elevation means easy sunburns. Bears, snakes, and standard Sierra wildlife.

GEAR SUGGESTIONS: Hiking poles, life jackets if swimmimg

With this adventure, we offer up two trailhead options to get you out there. Both are not far from San Francisco with a big reward for the trek out. The first trailhead to Loch Leven Lake is easy to get to as it's right off of the I-80 freeway; however, there's a steep climb in the beginning and you can hear freeway noise on the hike. The second hike requires at least a 30-minute drive in on a dirt road with potholes. As long as you are comfortable with this option, we would recommend this route because it's an easier trail for kids.

The hike is just 2.5 miles and leads to a beautiful set of lakes (middle and high Loch and Salmon Lake). The hike starts out in a meadow that is wildflower filled in June and early July. Then it travels through an old-growth fir forest and crosses over some granite outcroppings.

This is a popular hike for families from Sacramento and San Francisco, but even if the trailhead looks crowded, there is a lot of room to spread out. The lakes offer a good base for exploring, so consider camping out.

The trail is only open for use from June through November because of snow blocking access in the winter. Summer is the best time to come anyway so you can enjoy the high mountain lakes. At 6,800 feet, these can be chilly for much of the year; but in the summer, they are warm enough for swimming. They also have small islands that are fun to swim out to, so bring a life jacket for your little one. There are also some great rocks to jump off of, and the water is clean and clear.

Dogs are welcome, so expect that. For wildlife, there is the possibility of bears, but these sightings are rare with so many people around. If you camp out, just like most places, don't leave food out overnight. There are a lot of birds and frogs in the area. Fishing is generally good, and camping is dispersed throughout the basin. Campfire permits are required for fires, but backpacking stoves, BBQs, and lanterns are okay.

WHY IT'S A FAVORITE

"This is a relatively short hike to a beautiful set of lakes with the harder trailhead being only a couple minutes off a main highway. Even though the trailheads may look crowded, there is a lot of room to spread out and it doesn't feel like there are a lot of people around. The lakes offer a good base for exploring." —RYAN IDRYO

INSIDER'S TIP

If camping, consider setting up at Salmon Lake for fewer crowds. Don't be afraid to take the dirt road and get the mellower hike in. Even though it may seem like more of a haul, it's worth it! These back roads can be a little confusing, so make sure to really check your GPS and look at a topo map with dirt roads before you head out.

YOSEMITE NATIONAL PARK, CALIFORNIA,
SENTINEL DOME

ACTIVITIES: Hiking, climbing, camping

LENGTH OF HIKE: 2.2 miles round trip

OUT AND BACK OR LOOP: Out and back

DIFFICULTY OF TERRAIN: Moderate

ELEVATION GAIN: 400 feet

PARKING FEE/PASS: Yes

TOILETS: Yes, at trailhead

CHANGING TABLE: No

NURSING BENCHES: No

DOGS ALLOWED: No

BIKES/HORSES/MOTORS ON TRAIL: No

CELL RECEPTION: Unknown

DRINKING WATER AVAILABLE: No

POTENTIAL CHILD OR BABY HAZARDS: Steep cliffs

GEAR SUGGESTIONS: Sun hat, hiking poles are useful.

Looking for stunning views of both Yosemite Falls and Half Dome on a trail hike instead of a pavement "highway" that most of the tourists are on? This is a short venture that is not accessible in the winter because the road is closed, so you will want to check road conditions and make sure all snow has melted before venturing in.

It's a short out and back that will put you at just over 2 miles with 400 feet of elevation climb, but it will be well worth it for the amazing views. Right on the dome, there's the sad remains of the famous tree from Ansel Adams's photos. The dead, twisted tree at the top was one of the most well-known trees in the world and photographed by many. Sadly, it died from drought in the 1970s despite people hiking in water to try and save it.

From here, you can also hike to Glacier Point, or Taft Point is also accessible from the same parking lot if the hike wasn't long enough for you. If you do this hike, try to get to the dome when the sun is in the east or overhead. You can get a good look at the middle section of Yosemite Falls, which is completely hidden when you see it from the valley.

While this hike might be a carrier hike for some families, it is walkable for a confident 4-year-old with the short distance. "We did this one when our little guy was a baby, but I'm pretty sure he'd like the challenge of the final ascent now at 4 years old," says Hike it Baby ambassador Ryan Idryo.

The trail itself is well marked and well trod. There are many interesting sections with rocks and trees that will keep your toddler interested. When you come to the end, the climb will be a challenge for a hiking toddler. But it's pretty short, so bring a carrier for this section and expect to go slow if you are carrying.

Another thing to consider with a little one on this hike is that it's very exposed at the top and can be windy and sunny. Ryan says this initially upset his 9-month-old, but once they got him over the fear of the whipping wind, all was well. A piece of advice: Keep a close watch on a walking kid in the steep sections.

As the parking lot serves two semipopular trails, it is frequently full in the summer and you have to park where you can. This isn't a drive-up viewpoint, nor is it in the valley, so it will be less crowded than the most popular locations.

May through October is a good time to visit Yosemite, but keep in mind that there are around 4 million people visiting this park a year with the peak time being between June and August. Consider hitting the shoulder months like April, when snow is melting and the crowds haven't come yet.

Camping requires planning, so if you are unable to get a spot right away, keep calling back until you can secure a cancellation.

WHY IT'S A FAVORITE

"The top of Sentinel Dome has an amazing view. You can see out of Yosemite Valley into central California as well as deeper into Yosemite and all of the surrounding mountains, and some of the Valley's key sights—Yosemite Falls, Half Dome, Nevada Falls, Cloud's Rest, and North Dome. Some of the views are similar to Glacier Point, but this area feels a lot wilder because you didn't just drive up to it. There are lots of places to explore and plenty of room to get a little space to yourself." —RYAN IDRYO

INSIDER'S TIP

There's a huge Jeffrey pine tree along the trail. If you stick your nose into the cracks in the bark, it smells just like butterscotch. Heading to the dome, the tree is on the left side about 2/3 mile from the trailhead, just after a thick fallen tree also on the left side.

SAN BERNARDINO NATIONAL FOREST, CALIFORNIA, **ERNIE MAXWELL SCENIC TRAIL**

ACTIVITIES: Hiking, biking, climbing, fishing, camping

LENGTH OF HIKE: 4.6 miles

OUT AND BACK OR LOOP: Out and back

DIFFICULTY OF TERRAIN: Easy–moderate

ELEVATION GAIN: 600 feet

PARKING FEE/PASS: $5

TOILETS: Yes

CHANGING TABLE: No

NURSING BENCHES: Yes

DOGS ALLOWED: Yes

BIKES/HORSES/MOTORS ON TRAIL: No

CELL RECEPTION: Spotty at best

DRINKING WATER AVAILABLE: No

POTENTIAL CHILD OR BABY HAZARDS: A few steep cliffs on one side of the trail, but trail is pretty wide in most parts.

GEAR SUGGESTIONS: Carrier, water, snacks, comfortable shoes, layers (since it can get cold quickly in the mountains), sun protection

Looking for a beautiful getaway from the hustle and bustle of Los Angeles and all of the suburbs around? Venture out east to Ernie Maxwell Scenic Trail in the San Jacinto Mountains for a mellow "hiking-only trail." No need to worry about mountain bikers or horses because the trails are separated (not that we don't love bikes and horses, but this allows a toddler to run ahead more freely). You can also find bouldering and fishing in the area.

While there are various ways to approach hiking this area, Hike it Baby ambassador Vanessa Wright highly recommends starting from the Tahquitz View Drive (south side) entrance because the first leg of your hike is uphill. Then take a rest at Humber Park and have snacks. This will end the hike with a downhill, and you see the spectacular views toward the top of the mountain, making it a great "Yay, I did it!" moment, instead of starting with the pretty views and ending with a hike up a mountain to get back to your car.

Humber Park is a great turnaround point, as you feel you are being rewarded for your efforts, instead of a very nonclimactic turnaround point you would get if you turned around at Tahquitz View Drive, which is just a dirt road.

Some of the beautiful views you can expect to see on this hike are Suicide and Tahquitz Rocks as you pass through a field of small boulders and a forest of oak and manzanita dropping 600 feet and ending at Tahquitz View Drive. Also look for Marion Mountain, an impressive 10,362-foot peak.

If you would like to make that hike a bit harder, you can go up Devil's Slide Trail to Saddle Junction. This moderate-to-hard trail adds another 4.9 miles and over 1,600 feet of elevation to your hike, but it has even more breathtaking views of the local mountains and valleys below. Lake Fulmor, about 10 minutes outside the small town of Idyllwild, is a beautiful 1-mile easy toddler waddle-friendly loop.

This is Southern California, so hikes can get hot. Fortunately, this hike has a mix of exposed and tree-covered trail to offer. Consider going early in the morning so you can enjoy cooler conditions. Visit in the spring for amazing wildflowers or in the fall for incredible displays of yellow, orange, and red leaves. Check the conditions in the winter before you head out because they are known to get snow. Expect to see a mix of manzanita and oak trees and squirrels, birds, or even the occasional deer.

Why we give this one five stars is the gentle elevation gain and wide path that make this a toddler-friendly trail for new walkers. It's also easy to find parking right at the trailhead. It can get busier during peak times and on the weekend, but you should still be able to get on trail fairly easily. Don't forget to get an Adventure Parking Pass, which is $5. You can find it at the ranger station and many stores throughout town.

WHY IT'S A FAVORITE

"What we like about this trail is it's safe and easy enough for little kids to walk the entire thing. On our last trip there, my toddler enjoyed pointing out different birds, bugs, and flowers she saw. This trail has become one of our favorite hiking trails in Southern California because of the gorgeous views and scenery." —VANESSA WRIGHT

INSIDER'S TIP

Though both sides of the trail have parking, we highly suggest parking along the south entrance off Tahquitz View Drive, which means your journey will start uphill and end downhill instead of the other way around. This way you get to enjoy the spectacular views as a reward for your hard work toward your turnaround point instead of right at the beginning of your hike. Once you reach your destination of Humber Park, you can stop for a break and picnic lunch before heading back down.

GREAT SAND DUNES NATIONAL PARK, COLORADO, **MONTVILLE NATURE TRAIL AND MOSCA PASS**

ACTIVITIES: Hiking, sandboarding, splashing, fishing, biking, ranger talks,

LENGTH OF HIKES: 1 mile or 7 miles

OUT AND BACK OR LOOP: Out and back

DIFFICULTY OF TERRAIN: Easy

ELEVATION GAIN: Little

PARKING FEE/PASS: Park fee

TOILETS: Yes

CHANGING TABLE: No

NURSING BENCHES: No

DOGS ALLOWED: No

BIKES/HORSES/MOTORS ON TRAIL: No

CELL RECEPTION: Spotty

DRINKING WATER AVAILABLE: Yes

POTENTIAL CHILD OR BABY HAZARDS: Heat exposure near summer

GEAR SUGGESTIONS: Sun hats in the summer, extra water on hikes

Welcome to the tallest sand dunes in North America. These 30 square miles of Sahara-like expanse with five dunes jutting up over 700 feet tall into the sky offer a never-ending sandbox that will delight those toddlers who can spend hours in one at home. Bring a shovel and bucket for constant digging entertainment, and expect to shake sand off of everything for days after you get home.

There are two choices for trails in this park. Keep it simple and toddler friendly by walking the 1-mile well-trafficked Montville Nature Trail with no elevation gain. Toddlers and new walkers can easily complete this one. From there, if you want to push on or if you are babywearing a little one and aren't as worried about distance, you can continue for the moderate 7 miles out and back with some elevation gain up Mosca Pass Trail, reaching 1,459 feet at the summit. This is all uphill on the way out and down on the way back and offers great views of the sand dunes. Keep an eye out for bighorn sheep on the rocky hills as you meander through ponderosa pines and aspen forests.

Another highlight of this park is a stream that in the springtime is no more than 2 to 3 inches deep and very wide between the dunes and the campsite. The Albanese family said this was their kids' favorite activity. "We also hiked up the sand dunes but had to carry our kids most of the way." Remember, walking on sand is twice as hard as walking on dirt, so make sure you plan accordingly when you head out with your little walker.

Visit for the day or overnight it. The campsite is 0.25 mile from the dunes, with an easy downhill walk. Remember, you have to get back up later in the day, so bring snacks to bribe little ones back to camp. Evenings can be chilly even in May, so dress accordingly. Expect mosquitoes in June around the campsite and no-see-ums (tiny biting gnats) early in the spring.

WHY IT'S A FAVORITE

"The water is all snow melt so it's cool but not so cold because the sun warms the shallow water. This was our kids' favorite activity. They spent hours just running around and playing in this stream. We felt very safe having them do that because it's so shallow."
—JESSE ALBANESE

INSIDER'S TIP

You know a park is truly all family friendly when wheelchair options are made available in the least likely places. If you are traveling with a family member in need of an all-access wheelchair, the park has a big, sand-friendly wheelchair so the whole family can head into the dunes.

UNCOMPAHGRE WILDERNESS, COLORADO, **OURAY PERIMETER TRAIL**

ACTIVITIES: Hiking, birding, caves

LENGTH OF HIKES: 4.2–5.8 miles

OUT AND BACK OR LOOP: Loop

DIFFICULTY OF TERRAIN: Moderate

ELEVATION GAIN: 1,150 feet

PARKING FEE/PASS: No

TOILETS: No

CHANGING TABLE: No

NURSING BENCHES: Yes

DOGS ALLOWED: Yes

BIKES/HORSES/MOTORS ON TRAIL: Horses in some areas

CELL RECEPTION: Yes

DRINKING WATER AVAILABLE: No

POTENTIAL CHILD OR BABY HAZARDS: There are some very narrow and rocky parts. Put toddlers/younger children in a carrier pack, if possible, through these areas.

GEAR SUGGESTIONS: Carrier pack, bug spray

The Ouray Perimeter Trail is located in an old mining town and is an exciting day trip for families interested in getting in a good, lengthy hike. Expect to see butterflies, mountain goats, maybe a bear, and lots of birds. You will also find old mining tunnels, ropes, and bridges, because silver mining was big in this town in the 1800s. There are two versions of this hike, depending on if you choose to take a shortcut, which shaves off about a mile. The hike will take around 3 to 4 hours to complete, depending on if you opt for the ice park shortcut. Ouray Ice Park is a man-made ice climbing venue in the Uncompahgre Gorge that's considered to be one of the premier ice climbing spots in the world. Every January, the Ouray Ice Festival attracts elite ice climbers from around the world to this area. While this is one of the main hikes people visit in the area, from this trail you can access a number of other harder and longer trails off of the Ouray Perimeter.

This may not be the ideal hike for a new walker, but we couldn't pass up adding this to the book because of its uniqueness and beauty. This hike is iconic Colorado with amazing views into a deep canyon and some narrow sections that you will just want to hold a hand to venture through.

The trail starts off with a steep uphill climb (plan to carry here), but don't worry, it gradually flattens as you hike along. In the beginning, you will see high mountain peaks all around you, starting with Mount Abrams (12,801 feet) and Hayden Mountain (11,475 feet). To the southwest is U.S. Mountain (13,036 feet), and to the west are Whitehouse Mountain (13,452 feet) and Twin Peaks (10,798 feet).

There are moments on this hike where it will feel "risky" with narrow ledges and high bridges, but this is not a razor-thin hiking trail. The trail isn't crowded, and you will never feel like ants marching along. The narrow sections will keep you on your toes and add to the excitement and fun. Keep in mind, if you do have a fear of heights, this might not be the trail for you.

Your first breathtaking site on this hike is the Cascade Waterfalls. Spray from the falls can be a little cold if it's not a sunny, warm day and you get too close. Obviously, you will want to keep kiddos back from the falls because it's powerful and definitely not swimmable! While you can hike this trail at any time of the year, we would recommend the summer so you can enjoy the mountain chilliness of the waterfalls and streams.

Cascade Falls can be pretty crowded because many people just hike to the falls from the access point downtown, but don't worry about the whole trail having this feel. There's only a small section where you will notice the masses. Take a moment at the falls and then head on because there is a lot more fun coming up on the trail.

The waterfall is followed by the baby bathtubs, then continue hiking and you'll enter a beautiful meadow, cross the Million Dollar Highway, and you'll have views for days. From here you can take the left fork and go out to the ice park bridge and dam or you can take the right (the ice park shortcut) and still see part of the ice park. Remember that at certain times of year, mosquitoes can be fierce.

That's not the end of the adventure, though. Keep hiking and you get to Box Canyon. Megan said one of the highlights of their hike was the tunnel at Box Canyon. "Our 3-year-old kept asking to go through it again and again. He loved running through

the open meadows, and he had fun "oooohing and aaaahing" at the waterfall, but the tunnel was the best."

There is a little walk over a bridge, then you go through the tunnel and go left, where a new offshoot was just completed in summer 2017.

Note that there are multiple areas where the town has provided a "registration" area so they can keep track of hikers entering the different areas of the trail. It's best to sign in to all of the registration logs. They just ask for your name, number in your hiking party, ZIP code, and a few other things. This allows emergency services to quickly locate hikers in case of an emergency.

WHY IT'S A FAVORITE

"The Ouray Perimeter Trail is truly one of the most incredible and FUN hikes my husband and I have been on (especially with kids). Ouray is considered the "Switzerland of the US," so as you can imagine, the views are breathtaking. But it's not only the views that make this trail worthwhile. It's as if every mile you hike, the trail leads you to another amazing site or attraction to see. Our kids especially loved being able to go through a cave on the hike!" —MEGAN MOUNTAIN

INSIDER'S TIP

The parking is rarely full. If it is, you can also park at the visitor center. Go to the Ouray hot springs at the end of your hike (there are fees to get in and they vary by age). There is also a fun playground and green space/park at the end. You can walk into the hot springs entrance area and buy fish food to feed the fish in the pond (a quarter for a bag). Don't miss Mouse's Chocolates and Coffee. "Their turtle sundae is amazing, and their chocolates are great for bribing little ones to get through the hike."

DAWSON'S BUTTE RANCH OPEN SPACE, COLORADO, **DAWSON'S BUTTE RANCH OPEN SPACE TRAIL**

ACTIVITIES: Hiking, wildlife viewing

LENGTH OF HIKE: 5 miles

OUT AND BACK OR LOOP: Loop

DIFFICULTY OF TERRAIN: Very easy, gently rolling terrain

ELEVATION GAIN: 400 feet

PARKING FEE/PASS: No

TOILETS: Yes

CHANGING TABLE: No

NURSING BENCHES: Yes

DOGS ALLOWED: Yes

BIKES/HORSES/MOTORS ON TRAIL: Bikes, horses

CELL RECEPTION: Yes

DRINKING WATER AVAILABLE: No

POTENTIAL CHILD OR BABY HAZARDS: Be aware of mountain bikers or horses, and snakes

GEAR SUGGESTIONS: Snacks, water, baby carrier if you have a young baby/toddler, sunscreen

Dawson's Butte is a beautiful trail in an 828-acre open space near Castle Rock, CO, halfway between Denver and Colorado Springs. The actual butte is a flat-topped, 7,474-foot mountain overlooking the gently rolling terrain, patches of pine-shaded areas, open meadows, and beautiful views. This is the perfect trail to get your little hiker trained to hit the bigger peaks of Colorado. The terrain and access make it a great year-round trail as you can snowshoe in the winter, and the provided shade in the summer offers a nice escape from the strong, high, desert Colorado sun.

One of the reasons this is a great trail is that during the colder seasons, many Colorado trails can be muddy or icy and not allow much distance. This is not the case with Dawson Butte. Early season sun exposure and easy-to-follow and generally even trail make this a perfect one to hit up.

Megan Mountain said her 3-year-old completed his longest hike ever on this trail. Consider doing the full loop, or just hike the trail a little ways and do an out and back. There are nice wooden benches in different areas throughout the trail, making it an excellent first hike back for a postpartum mama wanting to get back out there. There are also picnic tables at the parking lot under nice shaded trees.

Colorado has a lot of wildlife close to civilization, so you might spot elk, bears, mountain lions, and many other wildlife species who call this area home. Look for pine trees, open meadows, and in the spring a colorful display of wildflowers.

While this is generally not a crowded trail, it still sees a steady flow of visitors and there is a lot of horse traffic. This also means horse poop, which can get a bit stinky in the summer months. Little kids should be made aware of horses and be cautious when approaching. There is ample parking for hikers and horse trailers, so don't worry about visiting it on a sunny early summer day when it seems like everyone and their grandmother is on the trails in Colorado.

WHY IT'S A FAVORITE

"The wide-open trails and meadows provide endless opportunities for fun and imaginative play! It is so fun to watch our 3-year-old run around in his superhero masks and capes. We love this trail because he can often run ahead a good ways and we can still see him and assure his safety. We have seen beautiful Clydesdales on this

trail and we've even seen a donkey! Thanks to its gradual, meandering trail, this is also a great trail for out-of-town guests who may not be acclimated to the altitude. Our favorite Gramma KK joined us on this hike one beautiful spring day, and fun was had by all!"
—MEGAN MOUNTAIN

INSIDER'S TIP

If this hike still hasn't burned off your little one's energy, be sure to check out Philip S. Miller Park 15 minutes down the road in Castle Rock. There's a nature play area that kids absolutely love.

NORTH CHEYENNE CAÑON PARK, COLORADO, **COLUMBINE TRAIL**

ACTIVITIES: Hiking, splashing, nature center, waterfall

LENGTH OF HIKE: 3 or 8 miles

OUT AND BACK OR LOOP: Out and Back

DIFFICULTY OF TERRAIN: Moderate–strenuous

ELEVATION GAIN: 1,902 feet

PARKING FEE/PASS: No

TOILETS: No

CHANGING TABLE: No

NURSING BENCHES: No

DOGS ALLOWED: Yes

BIKES/HORSES/MOTORS ON TRAIL: No

CELL RECEPTION: Yes

DRINKING WATER AVAILABLE: No

POTENTIAL CHILD OR BABY HAZARDS: Gravel, rocks, waterfalls

GEAR SUGGESTIONS: Sunscreen, hats

Looking for water play and a trail that can adjust to the mood of your child? If you're feeling like a quick out and back, there's plenty to see depending on where you enter this trail. Take a quick easy 3-mile hike if you are new to getting out there, or bump it up and move on to the more advanced hikes and get 8 miles in.

The Columbine Trail is located in the 1,600-acre North Cheyenne Cañon Park. Deep within this park, you might find the occasional black bear or mountain lion, but you are more likely to see mule deer and little birds like the kingfisher, American dipper, and broad-tailed hummingbird. This trail is beautiful with mountain views in every direction and treelines with leaves in the fall and streams to splash in during the summer months when the trail gets hot.

The trail is broken up into three sections: lower, middle, and upper. The entire trail weaves in and out through the canyon of Cheyenne Cañon Park. It starts at the Starsmore Discover Center and ends at the base of the famous Helen Hunt Falls. Each section of the trail has its own individual parking lots, so if you are looking to limit the length of your hike you can adjust accordingly by parking nearby. Lower Columbine is the easiest section to hike, is more toddler friendly, and allows for more exploration for younger kids. It's scenic, has tree cover, and runs along a flowing creek.

This trail gets a little more challenging for little walkers as you go on, so expect to carry them through chunks of the trail where it climbs. If you have a good hiker who listens, there shouldn't be a problem letting them up and down for sections that are walkable. Be aware of your little walker, and stay close as you start to head up to Upper Columbine, where it becomes a bit more narrow with a steeper incline. There is also loose gravel, so you can start to lose traction if not wearing hiking shoes with tread.

Because all of the trailheads lead off the main road, you can start at different points depending on the length you would like the hike to be. The Lower Trailhead, located behind the Starsmore Discover Center, is a great place to finish with your kids when the hike is over. The middle section is the toughest with the most climbing. The Upper Trailhead has views of the mountain ranges, the canyons, and the city.

Along the bottom of the 1.5-billion-year-old granite canyon, you will find North Cheyenne Creek. Visitors can drive, hike, and bike from the entrance of the canyon up to Helen Hunt Falls if the hike isn't happening that day. You can either park here and hike or drive to this after your hike for an additional viewing moment in the area.

WHY IT'S A FAVORITE

"I really love the gradual transitions of this hike. Lower Columbine is a very mild trail, and as you enter Middle to Upper Columbine, it gets a bit more difficult as you are inclining, but not too intense. Also, there are beautiful views as you make your way up. The trees and mountain views are some of the best in this part of Colorado." —KRYSTAL WEIR

INSIDER'S TIP

Locals suggest visiting this hike in the end of September and early October, when the temperature starts to cool down a bit. Otherwise, be prepared to be on a hot, exposed hike.

Questions to Ask Yourself Before Heading Out

One of the reasons the Hike it Baby community works so well is because we are first and foremost conscious of safety on trail when we gather together. We watch each other's children, and we are clear in suggesting if a hike is carrier-only or if it can be toddler-led. Whether hiking with a group or on your own, here are some key questions to ask before choosing a trail.

1. **WHAT'S YOUR CHILD'S MOOD ON HIKE DAY?** You may have a carrier-only hike planned, but if your child is not interested in being carried, you might need to modify and look for a more toddler-friendly trail. "Toddler-friendly" means trails that are wide where kids can run without risk of steep terrain drops.

2. **WHAT ARE THE POTENTIAL HAZARDS ON TRAIL?** Is there cell service? Is there a good turnaround point that you can note? Have you been on this trail before? Is it open and exposed, and could weather come in quickly? Are there bears, moose, mountain lions, or rattlesnakes? Understanding the wildlife in your area or trails you visit elsewhere is important. Animals shouldn't be a reason not to hike in an area, but you should be prepared if you do meet up with them on trail.

3. **HOW COMFORTABLE ARE YOU WITH HIKING?** Did you hike a lot pre-baby? Now that you have a baby, the experience will be different, so think about what adjustments you may need to make in packing your gear and expectations of yourself. No matter how fit you were prebaby, having a child in the mix can throw off your balance and strength.

4. **WHAT KIND OF CARRIER DO YOU HAVE?** Make sure you have a good age-appropriate carrier for your child. Make sure he/she can't arch out of the carrier or slide out of straps. Protect your lower back with a carrier that has a strong waist band. You don't necessarily need a frame carrier to keep your lower back protected. Consider checking out some baby-wearing resources (Babywearing International is a good one), or visit a local store and try on a lot of carriers before you commit to one. Ask Hike it Baby

communities for suggestions. If there isn't a Hike it Baby branch in your area, check out our national Facebook page where members discuss carrier suggestions.

5. **DO YOU HAVE GOOD FOOTWEAR?** Sneakers are comfy for flat trails, but as you get into steeper trails and are hiking on unstable, muddy, root-covered, rocky terrain, it's important to make sure you have proper footwear for the trail. Sneakers will often slide out on steep, loose terrain.

6. **DO YOU KNOW THE TERRAIN ON THE TRAIL?** Have you been on it before, or are you with someone who knows it? A preliminary web search on the trail can help, but keep in mind that guides and reviews are not often considering a parent carrying a 15- to 35-pound child. Before heading out for a "family-friendly" hike, make sure the website is considering your family dynamic. Again, relying on local family hike groups is a great way to find appropriate trails, especially if you have children of different ages hiking.

7. **WHAT'S THE FORECAST?** In places like Colorado, weather can start out sunny and 70 and drop to freezing temps or with lightning storms by the end. What's the terrain like? Are there open spaces where lightning can hit? Is there tree protection if a sudden hailstorm comes in? What about wind? Keep an eye out for snags on the trail. These are dead, overhanging trees that can fall on windy days. In Oregon, we have a lot of rain, which can change a stable trail to a muddy mess of a path quickly. Know your weather patterns, and take them seriously when you have a kiddo. Again, this is not to worry you but is a reminder to be more conscious of weather and consider potential backup plans if the weather shifts.

8. **DO YOU HAVE A FIRST-AID KIT AND A LIGHT?** These are critical pieces of gear, even if you're only heading out for an hour. Your first-aid kit may contain only Band-Aids, a safety pin, gauze, and first-aid tape, but these items will allow you to mend cuts and take care of small issues until you get help. Adventure Medical Kits makes great compact kits filled with anything you may need on the trail for a day hike. These weigh no more than a disposable diaper and can fit in the palm of your hand. If a hike takes longer than expected and you end up in the dark, you'll get back to your car a lot faster (and safer) if you have light. I personally carry a tiny LED keychain on my keys, or you can bring a small headlamp or pen light.

9. **DOES SOMEONE KNOW WHERE YOU'RE GOING?** Make sure you always let someone know your planned route and when you expect to return home. Consider purchasing an emergency beacon ($200–$300) if you plan on hiking farther out. With these, you can send a message in the case of a serious emergency. If you will be in cell range, you can set your smartphone with a "find me" option so you can be located.

THE OUTDOORSY CONVERT

KRYSTAL WEIR

Growing up in Texas, Krystal never really thought of herself as a hiker or an outdoorsy person. Then her husband, who is in the military, was stationed in Colorado Springs, and they moved from Indiana to Colorado. With two kids, ages 3 and 5, and no idea how long they would be living in the area, Krystal felt she should be making the most of her time in the mountains. Nervous about exploring alone when her husband was at work or away, when she heard about Hike it Baby, she signed up and joined a hike right away. "My daughter took to getting outside immediately, but it's been a bit of a challenge with my son."

The group offered tips on everything from how to get her son interested and out on trail to what to pack in her bag. "I learned to look for trails that are more interesting for an older kid so he could explore and forget about how far we were going."

As Krystal got out there with the group, she also started shooting more photos. She was already a portrait photographer, but on trail, she said her photography started to change. "I became more aware of the landscape and our relationship to everything around us."

Krystal documented the hikes she went on and captured her children playing with others in rain, snow, or shine. Her work got on the Hike it Baby radar, and within a few months, her photos were regularly featured on the Hike it Baby Instagram account and website.

"I do credit Hike it Baby all of the time for inspiring me to get outdoors," Krystal said. "I've met some great friends through the community, and I love that we have our appreciation for getting outdoors in common. It helped that we moved to a place where you want to get outdoors. That's also been a motivation!"

Krystal's incredible pictures of red sandstone trails cutting through canyons and dreamy shots of her children digging up handfuls of mud and splashing in puddles have helped inspire the community nationwide to adventure more. But beyond that, she hopes she is also inspiring those who never get to the mountains. She said, "I have family members who will never see this. So when I shoot, I think as a person who wouldn't be able to see what it looks like from the top of a mountain."

While Krystal's passion for the outdoors is growing increasingly by the day, she says her husband is a reluctant outdoors enthusiast.

"I think with being in the military, outside time is often work for him, so he doesn't get as excited, but he's coming around," Krystal said with a chuckle. "And while it can be a challenge to get him on to trail, it's just naturally happening more and more."

Where she notices the biggest difference is in her daughter. "My youngest is where I see the biggest change. I notice a difference in her. She loves to be outdoors. I think she's becoming so much more comfortable with every hike. At first she was terrified of bugs, but she's coming out of that now as we spend more time outside."

FAVORITE TRAIL: COLUMBINE TRAIL, CO
"There are three levels to this trail: lower, middle, and upper. What's great about it is that it's a simple trail, but there are different challenges throughout the different sections. It starts really safe and flat and becomes more challenging, but the views are so pretty as you go up from middle to upper. I'll admit I still haven't made it to the top, but that's a goal for me."

THE MORE THE
MERRIER

AMELIA MAYER

EXACTLY A MONTH AGO TODAY, after the birth of my last child, I was cata-pulted into the job title of Mom-of-Five-Kids. It's not that I wasn't expecting child number five, but I was admittedly shocked by the amount of directions I was suddenly being pulled in. I thought it would be just like adding another one on, but I spent the last month with my head spinning, wondering how in the world I was going to do this with our new addition. I yearned for some nor-malcy and anything to prove to myself that I could handle this challenge, too.

I find my greatest opportunities for self-discovery and growth come from being outside. But with this new child, I found I was suddenly more than ever finding obstacles to actually getting out there (poopy diaper, another poopy diaper, a baby needing nursed, older kids fighting, and lots of gear to put on everyone). With baby five, for the first time I understood why people just stayed home. Even a simple walk seemed daunting, and actually making it to the trail felt simply impossible.

But, I also have been a parent long enough to know better. I know there is great happiness and peace to be found outside, and it's worth the (some-times immense) struggles.

And so outside we go, armed with diapers and wipes, jelly beans, and more than enough snacks to feed our small army. I can handle a lot of things, but hangry kids isn't one I want to tackle right now.

We stand out (big surprise), and I get plenty of comments about how my hands are full. And they're right—I'm certainly busy right now. But, like it al-ways has been for me, whether with two kids or five, everything seems so much less stressful out on the trail. Maybe we all feel the reality that the walls are no longer holding us in, and nature invites us to be free and fully our-selves. I feel a sigh of relief happen physically in my own body and watch my kids do the same.

So, bottom line—how do we do it? Right now, I feel a lot more comfortable bringing my husband or a friend with me. Soon enough, I'll be doing it on my own, but I like being able to laugh with someone over the army we are.

- Bring snacks. And lunch. And dinner. And more snacks. I wish I were kidding.

- Tandem baby-wear. I have three girls ages 3 and under. It's a pretty good bet I'll be carrying at least two at some point. While I insist that a kid on the back and one on the front evens out the weight, it looks (and feels) pretty badass. We moms need to feel that every once in a while.

- Let kids share the load. My older two (and sometimes three) wear back-packs and are expected to carry their extra layers and water. They insist on carrying their own snacks, too.

- Remain positive (this is super hard for me at times when we go toddler-pace), and don't stress the small stuff (and the small hikers).

- Sing. It's pretty awesome to hear all my kids singing as we hike. Something about the knowledge that we really are in this together.

- Go small. I always seem to bite off a little more trail than I mean to, so I am working on this one. But, baby steps, kid steps, and ANY steps are still hiking steps. And that is the whole point of all this.

My kids need steps in the dirt. I desperately do, too. There is nowhere else we connect as a family better than we do outside. And so I work hard to get out. All of us. Because truly, more is merrier.

Amelia Mayer lives in Yellowstone National Park with her husband, five young children, and their lab, Katmai. Check out her blog, Tales of a Mountain Mama (www.talesofamountainmama.com).

TRAIL HAZARDS:
BE PREPARED NOT SCARED

WHEN PEOPLE THINK ABOUT GETTING OUT HIKING with a baby or toddler, they often immediately think about the bugs, animals, and other dangers that come with it. People ask me all the time about trail hazards I am concerned with, like ticks, rattlesnakes, poison oak, stinging nettles, and so on. Being aware and ready for any trail hazard is not being an overly paranoid parent; it's smart hiking. Luckily, I haven't been touched much beyond a round of poison oak and a lot of mosquito bites, but nature has its hazards no matter where you are in the country. If you are headed out for a hike, remember that you are the visitor, so tread respectfully and pay attention to everything around you.

BUGS

MOSQUITOES are nasty little vampires that require our blood to complete their life cycle. Not awesome. They can spoil a fun hike with their dive-bomb technique and tendency to roam in packs, so make sure you are ready for them. It's smart to leave a small bottle of repellent in your car if you hike a lot in marshy areas or near rivers and lakes. There are also bug nets you can wear on a hat or put over a frame carrier.

According to experts, you can use up to 30% Deet on a small child (although we wouldn't recommend for infants). However, within most Hike it Baby groups, I have found people are not that interested in chemicals on their babies. If this is you, consider trying some of the natural repellents out there. Here are a few we like: California Baby, Honest Company. Also in the last few years a company called Thermacell has developed a little electronic device that can protect you when hiking or sitting outside for a 15-foot radius.

Creepy crawly **SPIDERS** are on every trail. Make sure to familiarize yourself with what spiders are in your area, and when you set a blanket down for baby to play, just keep an eye for spiders crawling on the blanket. Spiders are good at attaching and staying attached to fabric. Shake your clothes and blankets out well before packing them into your bag or stroller. Spider bites can be quite serious. If you or your little one gets bitten by a spider, make sure you seek medical attention immediately if you see any swelling or change in your skin. Also, try to take the spider with you to the doctor; that will help a lot (make sure you kill it first!).

TICKS are much harder to notice because their bite isn't necessarily felt while hiking, like a mosquito or a horsefly. When hiking in an area where there are ticks, make sure you check yourself and your baby after a hike, and look especially in the folds of your baby's skin and behind their ears! You will notice a dark spot on the skin if a tick has burrowed in, and they can be quite small.

A tick bite is not what's most concerning to people; it's the Lyme disease that can be found in the ticks. If you or your child is bitten, don't panic. If there is Lyme disease present, you have a few weeks to take the antibiotics to clear the disease. Some of the symptoms of a tick bite that is infected include: fever, chills, headache, fatigue, joint and muscle aches, and rash.

If you suspect your child was bitten by a tick, visit a doctor right away to get tested. If you are unsure, it's worth a visit for ease of mind. Also, remembering to check your kids after every hike is important, especially when they are smaller and may not be able to vocalize how they are feeling.

ANIMALS

Encountering wild animals on the trail is a very real probability in many parts of the country, but this shouldn't stop you from getting out there. Know what animals are out there, whether **SNAKES, MOOSE, BEARS, OR COYOTES**. A little bit of research and talking to local rangers can help you learn how to manage animals if you come across them. If you are in areas where there are bears, carry bear spray and know how to use it. In states like Alaska and Montana, there are classes available to teach you how to use bear spray. Most animals are more scared of you than you are of them and will leave you alone or run the other way at the sight of a human. Again, hiking with a group can help minimize risk during an animal encounter. The forest is their home, so do your best to respect it and the animals living there.

RATTLESNAKES are more of a concern in desert areas, but we have had reports all over of hikers seeing or hearing these on trail. If there are rattlesnakes in your area, please be aware of them, and pay attention when you are in areas where you are walking over rocks. Rattlesnakes like to curl up against warm rocks in the sun. These little slithery guys are super common in eastern Oregon (Pendleton), Santa Cruz, and Santa Clarita! They are good about rattling for warning, so just keep an ear (and eye) out. Chances are they will see you first and slither away.

PLANTS

POISON OAK & POISON IVY. As a hiker, you are bound to encounter one or the other of these plants. Not everyone is allergic to them, however; experts say the more exposure you have to them, the more chance you have for a reaction to them. This can change over time, too. As a teen, I used to mountain bike through patches of poison oak in Eugene, Oregon, and never thought twice about it. As a 30-something, I walked through a patch of poison oak in the mountains above Malibu, of all places, on a trail and battled a rashy, oozy mess for a few weeks. My reaction was strong enough to require medication.

Poison ivy is supposed to be worse than oak, but both can make you feel miserable! If you have a lot of poison oak in your area, I would suggest keeping some Tecnu on hand at home so you can shower as soon as you get home from a hike. Wash with cold water first, use Tecnu, and then switch to warm water. Also, if you hike with your dog, be sure to bathe him regularly, since the oil he brings in can transfer to your clothes or furniture even weeks after you hike.

STINGING NETTLES don't have a long-lasting sting, but they can cause little welts. If you feel a sort of prickly feeling on your skin and see some raised bumps, there's a good chance you brushed up against stinging nettles. These are mainly found all over the Pacific Northwest and Alaska.

Cow parsnip is very common in Alaska and can create a rash on skin if you rub up against it. Get to know this plant if you are in the Anchorage area. Don't worry about getting this on clothes, though, since it's not an oil like poison oak.

Devil's club can usually be found near water and is very distinctive. It has big green leaves and long spikes on the limbs. Look for this along rivers' edges throughout the Pacific Northwest and Alaska.

WEATHER

Weather can shift fast in places like Utah or Colorado, causing lightning or flash floods. Make sure you are ready with a light layer to protect you from the rain or wind. If you

see lightning starting, make sure you are in a place where there is protection, like a stand of trees. Get off an empty hillside immediately if there are no trees around you and there is lightning.

My family and I were hiking in Hawaii a few years ago when a flash flood hit. One second my husband and I were walking next to a dry river, and seconds later it was full! This woman who was coming down from the waterhole we were headed to said she had been going to that place for 20 years and had never seen that before! So if you know there are flash floods in an area, be aware if any rain is happening in higher country above where you are hiking. This can happen in places like Colorado and Utah, areas where it's very dry but storms come in fast.

PEOPLE

For better or for worse, we have been taught to fear people on trails, thanks to scary media popping up about what can happen when you are in a remote place. Just remember that most remote trails are not that interesting for those who might do a person wrong. Breaking into a car? That definitely happens at certain trailheads. Random abductions...very rare. This is not to say you shouldn't consider safety when at a trailhead, and be aware of people around you. Going with a few people or making sure someone knows when you are returning is a good idea. Pick trails that are heavily trafficked if you are nervous about being alone, or better yet, plan a Hike it Baby hike and people will show up and join you and your baby.

BLUFF POINT STATE PARK, CONNECTICUT, **BLUFF POINT TRAIL**

ACTIVITIES: Hiking, fishing, paddling, horseback riding, biking

LENGTH OF HIKE: 3.6 miles

OUT AND BACK OR LOOP: Loop

DIFFICULTY OF TERRAIN: Easy

ELEVATION GAIN: 190 feet

PARKING FEE/PASS: No

TOILETS: Yes

CHANGING TABLE: No

NURSING BENCHES: Yes

DOGS ALLOWED: Yes

BIKES/HORSES ON TRAIL: Yes

CELL RECEPTION: Yes

DRINKING WATER AVAILABLE: No

POTENTIAL CHILD OR BABY HAZARDS: Hiking near water

GEAR SUGGESTIONS: Studded shoes or other traction in winter

One of the last remaining undeveloped parts of Connecticut, this 806-acre park is pretty no matter what time of year you go. Hike next to the Long Island Sound, and when you get out to the farthest point of the loop, look off in the distance for a lighthouse. You will be able to see pretty far out into the water. Take the main trail, which runs for about a mile all along the coastline to the beach. This is a dog-friendly walk, but remember to bring a leash. Do the whole loop for around 3.6 miles.

If you are a sunset lover, this is your spot. They are breathtaking year-round. It's especially nice that there is so much tree coverage for the paths, because the wind coming off the water can be bitter in winter. The path is a wide dirt road covered with honeysuckle in the summer, so make sure to breathe deeply when you pass through. This is a really nice hike for groups and if you have elderly or family members in a wheelchair or using a walker, although it is a bumpy dirt road, so don't expect pavement.

Regardless of season, the views are phenomenal with leaves changing in the fall, frost-covered grounds in the winter, and warm breezes in the summer. Animal-wise, there are deer, ducks, and whatever you could expect to find in a salt marsh. The birds are plentiful, with over 200 species, several of which are uncommon species of gulls, shorebirds, and land birds. The area is surrounded by the Poquonnock River to the west and a tree-filled coastal reserve to the east, which keeps the trail cool on a hot day. The only way to get out to the point is to walk or bike the 1.5 miles.

This area is a family favorite, so expect to see a lot of toddlers. The wide trail makes it easy to use a stroller or wagon around this park, thus an influx of families. If you want to get off the beaten path, there are other trails shooting off the main thoroughfare that are more single track. If you choose to venture onto these trails, keep in mind there may be mountain bikers, so don't allow your toddler to run too far ahead.

As you head back to your car, you might notice Sunset Rock, a giant boulder on the side of the trail that was once a place of Sunday worship for locals who lived in little cabins on the beach. These cabins were wiped out at some point in history by a hurricane. Also, if you want to catch a little piece of history and take the time to look for it, you might find the remnants of a structure that burned down in the 1600s that was the former home of Governor John Winthrop Jr., the son of John Winthrop Sr., who was the first governor of the Massachusetts Bay Colony.

WHY IT'S A FAVORITE

"We like going here when we visit my husband's family, because kids of all ages enjoy it, as well as parents and grandparents. Older kids can mountain bike, smaller kids can use strider bikes pretty easily, and parents can use strollers or carriers. If the loop is too long for your outing, it's just as easy to do an out and back, and you can choose to be near the water or be more in the trees." —LINDSAY FROST

INSIDER'S TIP
Yaktrax could be helpful in winter for extra traction. The trail is very popular and any snow gets packed down quickly. The area has a large free parking lot. Keep an eye out for the trail that connects this park to Haley Farm State Park, which has even more beautiful trails to explore.

BRANDYWINE CREEK STATE PARK, DELAWARE, **INDIAN SPRINGS TO HIDDEN POND TRAIL**

ACTIVITIES: Hiking, picnicking

LENGTH OF HIKE: 2.25 miles

OUT AND BACK OR LOOP: Loop

DIFFICULTY OF TERRAIN: Easy

ELEVATION GAIN: No

PARKING FEE/PASS: $8

TOILETS: Yes (limited hours)

CHANGING TABLE: No

NURSING BENCHES: Yes

DOGS ALLOWED: Yes

BIKES/HORSES/MOTORS ON TRAIL: No

CELL RECEPTION: Good

DRINKING WATER AVAILABLE: Yes

POTENTIAL CHILD OR BABY HAZARDS: Ticks, poison ivy, rocky trail terrain, close to a river

GEAR SUGGESTIONS: Baby carrier, water, insect repellent (Delaware is a high tick/lyme disease state.)

With miles and miles of flat trails to explore and ranger-led tours, this is a great park for toddlers. The hike starts behind the park office. Head down on the Indian Springs Trail (yellow markers). Once down by the river, the best return is via the Hidden Pond Trail, making the loop about 2.25 miles.

Less than 0.5 mile into the hike, you'll come to a large, flat, "climbing rock" that's perfect for toddlers to play around on. It's just high enough to make them feel like they are adventuring, but not so high as to give you a heart attack if they fall. This is usually a required Hike it Baby stop on hikes in this park, so be sure to stop and let your little one climb. Continue on and you'll find another required stop that's down by the river: a really cool "peephole" tree that is the size of a toddler.

Delaware has very minimal elevation compared to the rest of the country. There are some rocky trail surfaces and minor elevation changes on this hike, but nothing that requires trekking poles on this trail. Corey Heacock says her toddler has hiked the entire trail on his own legs, so if you have a hiker in training, you should do great on this trail.

If you get rained out, there is a nature center, but the report back is that while it's not super exciting, it's still nice to have available if the weather shifts. Outside of the nature center, there are benches and picnic tables that can be used for picnicking and changing a baby. If you need to change a baby or nurse midhike, there's another bench by the river about halfway through the hike.

If you like great blue herons, this is a great hike to spot them. Also, keep your eyes open for white-tailed deer, squirrels, chipmunks, and in the summer there are lots of monarch butterflies migrating.

The hike ends at an open field with a picnic table, so plan to take a break there at the end. Don't worry if you forgot water. There's a water fountain available both inside and outside the nature center. Just note that the one outdoors is turned off in the winter.

WHY IT'S A FAVORITE

"The Indian Springs Trail was the first I hiked after moving to the Wilmington area, and I consider it to be our hiking base. Between the rocks, the river, and the seasonal changes, the trail is always exciting for my son." —COREY HEACOCK

INSIDER'S TIP

Head up to the hawk watch parking lot. The views from up there are some of the best in Delaware.

HIGHLANDS HAMMOCK STATE PARK, FLORIDA, **CYPRESS SWAMP TRAIL**

ACTIVITIES: Biking, birding, camping, geo-seeking, hiking, museum, picnicking, wildlife viewing

LENGTH OF HIKE: 0.5 mile

OUT AND BACK OR LOOP: Loop

DIFFICULTY OF TERRAIN: Easy

ELEVATION GAIN: No

PARKING FEE/PASS: $6

TOILETS: Yes

CHANGING TABLE: No

NURSING BENCHES: Yes

DOGS ALLOWED: Yes

BIKES/HORSES/MOTORS ON TRAIL: No

CELL RECEPTION: Spotty

DRINKING WATER AVAILABLE: Yes

POTENTIAL CHILD OR BABY HAZARDS: Wildlife, swampy areas, insects, narrow boardwalks

GEAR SUGGESTIONS: Child carrier or harness, insect spray, sunscreen/ sun protection, snacks, water, camera

One of Florida's oldest parks, this 9,000-acre expanse offers a labyrinth of trails throughout the park and has everything from botanical gardens to boardwalks to view the wildlife and landscape.

The park was first developed in 1931 during the Great Depression as part of a Civilian Conservation Corps project. The park protects large tracts of pine flatwoods, hydric hammock, cypress swamp, and baygall and is known for being home to 1,000-year-old oaks.

Large wildlife includes deer, black bears, and the rarely seen but present Florida panther. Smaller critters include armadillos, turtles, and otters. Look out for many varieties of birds, including red-tailed hawks, pileated wood-peckers looking for red carpenter ants, and sleeping owls high in the trees. Catwalks and elevated boardwalks traverse cypress swamp, and visitors may observe alligators, birds, and other wildlife.

These narrow boardwalks make up a good portion of the trail through the swampy areas. They are open on one side, giving a bit of thrill walking along the cypress trees and dark water and might make a parent of a little one nervous, but it's worth the walk. "On the sections of trail where it went to the open, narrow boardwalk, we chose to carry. I wouldn't pass up taking the boardwalks. They were a bit intimidating from a mom's standpoint, but it was worth taking the extra precautions and taking the trail slow to see. They really do feel more adventurous and provide a one-of-a-kind experience. It would be easy for a little one to slip off the side, but don't let that deter you—it's a must-see," says Abby Czachur.

Most of the trails within the park are shorter in distance and are worth checking out the different aspects of the Florida environment. While we rec-ommend one here to get started on, this park offers many toddler-friendly options that are easy to evaluate when your family visits. The Cypress Swamp Trail takes you through part of a picturesque Florida swamp dotted with large old cypress trees. The majority of this trail and others outside the narrow boardwalks can be comfortably walked in tennis shoes by most ages of chil-dren. This trail, like many in the park, is mostly shaded, but it's always recom-mended to bring sunscreen or sun protection while hiking in Florida.

There is also sand everywhere and three playgrounds that you might hap-pen upon when exploring. For nursing moms, or if you are bringing an elderly family member, some of the trails have benches, so inquire with the park at-tendants about which trails you will find these on.

Consider checking this hike out near the end of winter when it's cooler out and not very buggy. In late fall, winter, and early spring, you will avoid excessive heat and insects. Different times of the year can affect water levels and provide different scenery in the swamp. But there can also be closures if stormy, so keep that in mind.

If you are having one of those days with a toddler meltdown, consider tak-ing the tram tour through the park. There is a fee ($5 adults/$3 kids) for this, but it's a great way to not miss out on all the park has to offer.

WHY IT'S A FAVORITE

"In the heart of Florida, Highland Hammock gives the truest sense of what the real Florida is in all its natural and wild beauty. The stillness of the area was breathtaking. It was quiet and so very still, which was amazing to watch my daughter take in. The boardwalks only have a simple railing on one side, making it more adventurous." —ABBY CZACHUR

INSIDER'S TIP

Bugs are fierce here. Bring lots of repellent or risk being "bugged" for the entire hike. The hike is also hot and humid, so bring water to hydrate. Lastly, keep an eye out for rattlesnakes. They are nocturnal but are always present in this park. If you are lucky enough to find yourself in the park close to dusk, be on the lookout for fireflies magically lighting up the forest.

BLACK BEAR WILDERNESS, FLORIDA,
BLACK BEAR WILDERNESS AREA TRAIL

ACTIVITIES: Hiking, camping

LENGTH OF HIKE: 2 miles or 7 miles

OUT AND BACK OR LOOP: Loop

DIFFICULTY OF TERRAIN: Moderate

ELEVATION GAIN: 45 feet

PARKING FEE/PASS: No

TOILETS: No

CHANGING TABLE: No

NURSING BENCHES: Yes

DOGS ALLOWED: Yes

BIKES/HORSES/MOTORS ON TRAIL: No

CELL RECEPTION: Yes

DRINKING WATER AVAILABLE: No

POTENTIAL CHILD OR BABY HAZARDS:
Ticks, poison oak, stinging nettles, lots
of roots and uneven ground, possible
alligator presence

GEAR SUGGESTIONS: Hiking poles

If you are looking for a hike that feels like a real hiking boot–wearing adventure, check out the Black Bear Wilderness, a 1,600-acre reserve in northwest Seminole County that features a variety of wetland habitats within the floodplain of the St. Johns River. Check out the 2- or 7-mile version of the Black Bear Wilderness Loop Trail, much of which runs along the river.

The park is home to animals like the white-tailed deer, barred owls, coyotes, swallow-tailed kite, American alligators, and river otters. And if you are quiet, you might even spot the park's namesake: a Florida black bear. Keep an eye out for musk turtles, which might cross your path. You might even catch a whiff of them before you see them because these turtles will release a foul musky odor from scent glands on the edge of their shell if they feel threatened or nervous.

Being that it's such a large piece of land and close to other public lands, this is one of the most diverse parks you will find in Florida and can feel more like North Carolina than the typical swamplands of Florida. This is not to say you won't find the typical Florida fauna and flora, but expect trees and a combination of boardwalk and more of a trail-like feel.

The site is located on a floodplain of the St. Johns River, so during the rainy season, this park might be closed due to flooding. Also, hurricanes have been known to affect the park for periods of time, so make sure to check on whether or not it's open.

Crystal Osborn suggests a combo of carrying and letting kids walk, but remind your little ones not to get too far ahead (there are alligators) and that there are lots of tripping hazards with many exposed roots on the trail. This is a very kid-friendly park, though, because there is about a mile of boardwalks (14 boardwalks traverse the terrain) for kids to run on if they are new little walkers and need a stable surface to negotiate the trail. There is even one floating boardwalk that is fun to venture on. You can choose to do the 7-mile loop and stop at the primitive campground, where you will find a concession stand to grab a quick snack.

Speaking of camping, you can opt to stay overnight and make a little more of an adventure out of this park. Camping is reported to be a little crowded, so expect this to have more of a "parking lot" backcountry type of feel with tents close together instead of a remote experience.

A few things to be aware of: bugs and snakes. They are plentiful, so bring lots of spray and watch where children are walking. The park is home to pygmy rattlers and cottonmouths, both of which are venomous. Snakes are nocturnal, though, so chances are you won't see them. But keep in mind they are present on the trails, as they most likely hide in holes and under rocks.

WHY IT'S A FAVORITE

"Black Bear Wilderness Area is very different from your normal Florida hiking trails. With the more intense terrain and different habitats you walk through, it makes for an enjoyable hike for the whole family. Also, it's a good length. Completing the 7-mile loop is a wonderful workout but not too long that you overexert yourself for a single day hike." —CRYSTAL OSBORN

INSIDER'S TIP

The best time to visit is winter because it will be nice and cool. Also, depending on the GPS in your vehicle, it might take you down a dirt road and you might think you're lost. Keep going! You're not lost. It'll be on your right as you approach.

LEAVE NO TRACE
WITH LITTLE ONES

IT'S HAPPENED TO ALL OF US. Your toddler picks a wildflower and brings it over with a huge smile, presenting it to you with adoration, a gift that he or she insists you must have. Do you scold? Do you ignore? They are so proud of this beautiful trophy they've just given you. How do we build "Leave No Trace" principles into little ones? It starts with simply being aware ourselves how we are impactful and then trying to adjust and use each experience as a learning moment with our kids.

I know it's hard to be zero-impact with a toddler who is newly discovering nature. Here are a few tips:

1. When you arrive at a trail, point out things to your little one like the trashcan at the trailhead. Show her how you put trash in the can before you head to the trail and when you return from your hike. Make a game out of it like you might do at home.

2. Encourage children to stay on trail by singing songs. My husband went to Canyonlands with our son when he was 3 and they learned the fun rhyme "Don't bust the crust, stay on the trail" from a ranger. This became a regular phrase we used with him every time he went off trail, no matter where we were.

3. Help children learn from a very young age that the forest is a place we protect by pointing out the connectedness when you can. Show how ants carry leaves to their homes and how spiders weave webs and catch things. Show them raindrops dripping off of leaves. Look for little details of connected life and plants, and share them over and over with your kids.

4. It's so hard to discourage a child from picking a pretty flower or even a weed. If they bring you the flower, thank them, and use the experience as an opportunity to explain what happens when you pick things and how much you love seeing the flowers alive. Have them point out flowers to you in that moment that they love and agree with the beauty of it living.

5. Bring a trash bag or use a snack bag to pick up little pieces of trash on trail. Make a game out of it, and encourage your child to join in, no matter how young. Practice the game "Leave or Litter," and talk about what stays on the trail and what goes in the trash.

6. Be aware of protected water. Some creeks are sensitive habitats for animals, so respect this and help explain this to your child by talking about the life that is forming in the water. Talk about how mud puddles are great places to enjoy water fun and help them understand the difference between creeks, ponds, lakes, and oceans.

7. Sticks and stones are fun to play with on trail, and you might have a hard time getting your little one to leave them behind. We keep a small collection of sticks and stones in our car so if we are somewhere that it may not be a good idea to take them, I remind my son of the ones we have in the car already, and he quickly forgets about taking the new ones.

8. Consider your influence on your toddler and how your behavior is mimicked by your child and others around you. When you take photos and share them on social media, be conscious of how those will be shared. Be aware of what you are doing with your child in that photo (like picking wildflowers). While you can't stop someone from visiting a spot, you can be aware of the photo you share and the messaging that goes along with it.

THE CONFIDENT HIKER
DINEO DOWD

Growing up in South Africa, Dineo Dowd didn't have a lot of opportunity to hike, so it wasn't until she was in her twenties that she discovered her passion for the trail. "Hiking in South Africa is so much different than in the US. You have to get professional guides because it's not easy to follow the trails and it's not safe. It's not suggested that you hike alone, especially for women," Dineo says.

She first discovered Hike it Baby in Salt Lake City, where she joined the group and started heading out on trails. "When I first started hiking with my daughter, I had a fall on a trail when I was alone, and that made my husband nervous." She also said it took a toll on her confidence as well, and she didn't trust her footing after that fall. Then she joined the group and started getting out more, slowly regaining her confidence. "My husband could see that the more we went on trails together, and he would comment on it and how proud he was of me getting back out there." Through the group, she learned about the best carriers and shoes and realized she could hike alone with her daughter if no one showed up for a hike she planned. "Now I understand that I need to listen to my body and know what gear I need to bring for every condition that can happen out there."

Since joining Hike it Baby, Dineo's family has since moved to Madison, Wisconsin, where she is now an ambassador and has made a whole new group of friends. "It was a lot easier on my daughter to move cities knowing Hike it Baby was there. This is one of the only groups that I feel like my family fits in. It's also one of the few places I found families that had the same interests as us. And what I especially love is how Hike it Baby pushed us over the years to get out more than I ever imagined and explore nature and meet new families every day."

Gaining confidence, finding community, and discovering new trails are big reasons why Dineo has been such an active member and ambassador in Hike it Baby over the last few years. But she also says that at the most basic level, it helps her mental self and the challenges that come with parenting. "I have noticed that since I now get outdoors and hike every day, my mood has improved, I'm happy, and I'm excited about life. Now when I'm having a tough day, all I have to do is pack up and go hiking to figure it all out. Once I hit the trail, I forget all my problems, and I try to enjoy nature and take a lot of pictures so I have something to take home and look back at how wonderful my day was."

She's been so inspired by her adventures with her daughter over the last 2 years that she just wrote a children's book called *Adventure Day*. The idea stemmed from an afternoon when they were hiking and her daughter was so excited about that particular hike that she couldn't stop talking about it for days afterward.

"With my daughter, I can see she's such a happy baby on trail. Recently, she's stopped napping when we hike because she likes to point at the birds, flowers, the sun. She gets excited when I tell her we're going hiking, because she already knows she is going to see so many things out there and have fun. If we have other toddlers with us, she's fine with hiking all the way. It's amazing to see her slowly building her confidence on the trail."

FAVORITE TRAIL: PARFREY GLEN, WISCONSIN
This is Dineo's favorite trail because it's short and toddler-friendly. It's a small hike that may take 30 minutes or less, but it is well worth a visit if you are exploring the area. It gives a small, engaging taste of canyon country in the midst of America's geologically challenged Midwest. Summer or winter, it is a beautiful route.

Hiking with New Walkers

One of the first things I often hear from parents who head out hiking with new little walkers is, "How do you do it? My kid is so slow it's painful." I'm not going to lie, little legs travel slow and the toddler mind works in mysterious ways. One minute he is running down the trail at full speed and you're freaking out that there might be a drop-off around the bend, and the next minute he's on the ground screaming and kicking because you wouldn't let him pick a flower. Don't despair, though. We all feel your pain. Here are some of the tried-and-true Hike it Baby tips that we've found can help keep the trail experience fun and moving forward.

1. **KEEP IT SHORT.** Don't try to pull off an 8-miler your first time hiking. Work your way up. Some kids do well in carriers while others need time to adjust to them, especially if you start hiking with your child when they are already past 12 months. Babies who are raised to sleep on hikes and are used to the constant movement of you on the trail will grow into toddlers who love to hike.

2. **SNACKS FOR THE WIN!** Always bring things your kiddo likes. Squeezie packs, small packages of nuts or raisins, fruit leather, precut apple, Ritz crackers, or Annie's Cheddar Bunnies. These have worked for us. Keep something like a lollipop or a little chocolate in your pocket for those extreme meltdowns. Ideally, you don't want to have to pull this out, but you never know.

3. **TRAIL GAMES MAKE IT FUN.** This only works with older kids, but having a little notebook and a pencil or downloaded fun sheets with activities where they can identify things on the trail can help move a kiddo along. This will most likely only work with 3- to 5-year-olds, but you can try with younger ones. If they can mark off the things you are looking for as you move along, that will keep them excited to get to the next spot.

4. **PICK A MAGICAL DESTINATION.** We have a trail we like to hike in Portland called Lower Macleay. It's an urban trail and only about 1.5 miles, but toward the end of the out and back, there's an old broken-down stone house we call the "Witch's Castle." It was once a bathroom for the trail in the sixties or seventies, but the city found it too costly to keep up midtrail with limited park resources, so now it's just a cool, moss-covered old building with the roof removed. If your little one begins to visualize that the trail has magic, they will be more interested in getting to that destination.

5. **TAKE A REST.** Make sure the trail has lots of visual stopping points. While you may want to get your workout in, a long, flat road might be boring for your kiddo. So if you are stroller hiking with them, for example, and trying to get some miles in, take the time to stop and let them out to throw rocks, spot birds, and take in a view even if it's a flat landscape. Also, hiking around sunrise and sunset with beautiful skies can be really exciting for a child as they watch the colors change from day to golden sunset.

6. **BUGS, SLUGS, AND UGHS.** These are easy distractions. Look for crawlers and creepers on the trail, and get your kiddo to count them. Let them know when they find 10, the hike will end. Get super excited when you find one, and make an even bigger deal when she finds one. You can also substitute with similar things in your area, such as spiders, snakes, snails, or worms.

7. **CRAB WALK, BACKWARD WALK.** Toddlers like walking every which way but straight on a trail. Giddyup like a horse (this works great if a toddler or baby is fussy in a carrier on your back) and even "neigh" for them. This gets a laugh. Walk sideways like a crab and put up your pinchers then walk backward. Flap your wings like a bird and tell them it's time to fly.

8. **UPS AND DOWNS ARE GREAT.** There's no reason to train a toddler to walk distances. Make sure you always have a soft carrier on hand to pop out of a pack so you can put your kiddo up if they are just not moving forward. Let him know you will carry him for 10 minutes. Then put a timer on, and when it rings, that's time for more walking. Kids who are forced to hike will never love hiking. Encourage them to love it by making it easy.

ARABIA-DAVIDSON NATURE PRESERVE, GEORGIA, **MOUNTAIN TOP TRAIL COMBINED WITH MOUNTAIN VIEW TRAIL**

ACTIVITIES: Hiking, biking, wildflowers

LENGTH OF HIKES: 0.5 mile (Mountain Top) and 1.8 miles (Mountain View)

OUT AND BACK OR LOOP: Out and back (Mountain Top) and loop (Mountain View)

DIFFICULTY OF TERRAIN: Easy and moderate

ELEVATION GAIN: 175 feet

PARKING FEE/PASS: No

TOILETS: Yes

CHANGING TABLE: No

NURSING BENCHES: No

DOGS ALLOWED: Yes

BIKES/HORSES/MOTORS ON TRAIL: No

CELL RECEPTION: No

DRINKING WATER AVAILABLE: Yes

POTENTIAL CHILD OR BABY HAZARDS: Steep granite, but navigable for a toddler. Avoid during rain as the rock becomes too slippery. Avoid during peak sun in summer as the heat reflects off the rock.

GEAR SUGGESTIONS: Shoes with nice tread for the granite

Every spring a rare plant called diamorpha blooms all along the Mountain Top Trail in Georgia. For just a few weeks, the landscape turns from green to a blanket of red, and then almost overnight the tiny white flowers open up. These flowers are just a few inches tall, covering the landscape for what seems like a moment, and then it's all gone. This awesome display is thanks to Mother Nature and the perfect environment of granite and hot sun that is found on the Mountain Top Trail in the Arabia-Davidson Nature Preserve.

It's important to also note this plant is on the endangered species list (one of five listed in the area) and occurs thanks to pools of water known as solution pits that have formed all over the granite monadnock landscape due to 40 million years of earth movement. If you are interested in geology, then this hike is a perfect fit for your family as granite monadnock is a formation that was formed by pools of magma cooling and hardening in the earth's crust. After years and years of erosion, it was the only thing that remained. These formations are grippy under the feet and easy to hike with a toddler because of the smooth, gently sloping surfaces.

When you take this trail and arrive at the top of the mountain, you will be privy to beautiful views. It's mostly flat, making it a great spot to let the little ones run around while you enjoy a picnic lunch. For a longer hike, you can add in the Mountain View Trail, which travels along a lake at the base of the mountain.

As you lunch, be on the lookout for hawks high above and butterflies down low. Another cool animal fact for this area is that there is a program called AWARE (Atlanta Wild Animal Rescue Effort) located at the base of Arabia Mountain. This nonprofit rescues sick or injured wild animals, rehabilitates them at their facility, and returns them to the wild.

Warning with little hikers: Don't try to hike the mountain when it is wet (while raining). Even on dry days, there are areas of the rock where water trickles down. These areas are easy to avoid but can be very slippery if stepped on. Also be aware that there are some cacti at the top of the mountain. They aren't too prevalent, and usually the dogs are the ones who tend to run through them, so be aware if you bring a four-legged friend.

The small parking lot keeps crowds to a minimum. Free parking is a plus, but occasionally that means it's full. If the parking lot is full, there are other parking areas with boardwalk access to this trailhead. There are also other trails throughout the preserve, each with a different kind of beauty to enjoy.

WHY IT'S A FAVORITE

"When you reach the top of the mountain, it is almost like you've reached a foreign landscape with beautiful solution pits full of all kinds of life. The best time to visit is in spring, when the diamorpha is in full bloom. You can watch the clouds reflecting off the pools of water and enjoy the great view from the top. It's just so wild and free compared to the hustle and bustle of the city, and yet it is so close to the city center."
—MELISSA HOLLINGSWORTH

INSIDER'S TIP

The parking lot is right next to the AWARE Wildlife Center in the southwest area of the park. Time the hike on a Saturday or Sunday so you can attend the free tour of the animal rescue facility at 1 p.m. Donations are appreciated.

CLOUDLAND CANYON STATE PARK, GEORGIA, **WEST RIM LOOP**

ACTIVITIES: Hiking, camping

LENGTH OF HIKE: 2 miles or 5 miles

OUT AND BACK OR LOOP: Loop

DIFFICULTY OF TERRAIN: Easy–Moderate

ELEVATION GAIN: No

PARKING FEE/PASS: $5

TOILETS: Yes

CHANGING TABLE: No

NURSING BENCHES: Yes

DOGS ALLOWED: Yes

BIKES/HORSES/MOTORS ON TRAIL: No

CELL RECEPTION: Spotty

DRINKING WATER AVAILABLE: Yes

POTENTIAL CHILD OR BABY HAZARDS: Steep drop-offs are fenced, but the fence is such that a toddler could crawl through it.

GEAR SUGGESTIONS: Carrier or hiking harness for the section of trail near the cliff if your toddler likes to run off or climb through things.

With minimal effort and toddler in tow, there are two amazing places in this park where your family can catch the highest view in Georgia without much effort. The first is along the edge of the loop of the West Rim Trail. The second is near the visitor center. What we love about this trail is you can park fairly close and spend a little time walking out to the viewing area. If you come for the trail, don't miss the second viewing spot near the visitor center. If you can time your visit for fall, even better; the hills are ablaze with color.

If you just do the first section of the West Rim Trail, you are looking at 2 miles and it's relatively flat and wide in places. However, caution is advised near the fences as ambitious toddlers can crawl through them easily.

It goes without saying that the canyon cliffs are dangerous. If you're interested in hiking the full portion of the West Rim Trail (5 miles), there is a section with steep gullies, cliff walls, and no fence. It's very easy for an adult to stay safe on this section because it's flat and wide; however, don't let children wander unattended ever. This section is not fenced, and even where fences are provided for the canyon walls on other parts of the trail, these are still not very toddler friendly. The trail is wide enough in these sections to stay far enough away from the fences, but keep your eyes on little ones or plan on using a harness.

If you go the distance and opt for the 5 miles or go to the waterfalls (6.2 miles), this is a lollipop loop with the first section being flat; then expect stairs as you hike through the canyon. Adding the Waterfall Trails means, in total, you are looking at 1,400 feet of elevation change as you hike this trail and an estimated 1,200 steps. We only suggest this if you are an experienced hiker and are comfortable carrying your little one for this distance, as this suggestion is not for new walkers.

For the easiest exit on the hike if your toddler gets tired on the way out, you can start off by parking at the farthest parking lot near the loop of the West Rim Trail. This will allow you to complete the loop without having to go down and back up out of the canyon.

WHY IT'S A FAVORITE

There is so much to see and do in this little spot. There is a sense of wildness here, and yet the park itself is fairly built up, allowing you to explore with comfort nearby. Even though it may be a drive for us to get there, we keep returning every year. There is something about the trail and the views that keep calling us back."
—MELISSA HOLLINGSWORTH

INSIDER'S TIP

The yurts are amazing and worth an overnight. Stay a couple nights and take the time to explore the other trails and see the waterfalls.

CUMBERLAND ISLAND NATIONAL SEASHORE, GEORGIA, **RIVER TRAIL**

ACTIVITIES: Hiking, camping, kayaking, historical tours

LENGTH OF HIKE: 0.8 mile

OUT AND BACK OR LOOP: Out and back

DIFFICULTY OF TERRAIN: Easy

ELEVATION GAIN: No

PARKING FEE/PASS: National park fee (free parking)

TOILETS: Yes

CHANGING TABLE: No

NURSING BENCHES: Yes

DOGS ALLOWED: No

BIKES/HORSES/MOTORS ON TRAIL: Potential for wild horses. No bikes on River Trail.

CELL RECEPTION: Yes

DRINKING WATER AVAILABLE: Yes

POTENTIAL CHILD OR BABY HAZARDS: Ocean

GEAR SUGGESTIONS: Bug spray, sunscreen

Arriving at Cumberland Island feels like you're no longer in Georgia. Live oaks with hanging Spanish moss and saw palmettos cover the landscape. There are wild horses all over the island and a beautiful white sand beach where sea turtles can be found nesting at certain times of the year.

This is why Hike it Baby ambassador Melissa Hollingsworth insisted on this magical place. "The beach—I mean, it's the beach—so that's always amazing with a toddler. But besides being able to spend 4 hours playing in the sand, there's lots of shade under the oak trees and the potential to look for sea turtle nests in the right season, so that just adds to the adventure."

Melissa suggested the River Trail as a great starting point, but this can be combined with other toddler-friendly hikes on the island, like the Dungeness Trail. Another trail to look for is the Parallel Trail. The end of this hike offers ruins and is a good place to view the wild horses. The horses are very accustomed to people. As long as you keep a respectful distance from them, they will keep their distance from you.

But that's not all of the wildlife you'll find on this amazing island. Also look for horseshoe crabs, many species of birds, and deer catching some shade under live oaks with brilliantly colored hanging moss.

Keep in mind this is the South, and it's incredibly buggy in summer. If you know the climate, you will expect it. If you are new to the area, be aware of mosquitoes, swarming gnats, and ticks. While the insects are annoying, you can look at it as just a little bit of the challenge that comes with nature.

The reason we like this adventure is that crowds are limited to the number of ferry tickets sold per day (and they do sell out!), so you will not find the island overrun in the summer months like many other places. That said, weekdays are better for limited crowds. There is plenty of parking at St. Marys for your car, and the only cars on the island are the guided tour shuttle buses, which means you can sit back and relax as you journey from hike to hike.

Want to get around more easily? Consider bringing a bike and trailer. Not all of the trails and roads allow bikes, so be sure to plan accordingly.

If you decide to camp, plan to book months in advance. There are wagons to help you get your things to camp; however, the best thing is to bring your own wagon. Pack it before you board the ferry and then wheel it directly off the boat and straight to camp. No need to wait for more wagons to become available. There is a 0.5-mile walk to camp, but that's what adds to the fun!

There are flush toilets and showers; wood and ice are delivered two times a day on the ferry. There is no store available, though, so you must bring all food and supplies to the island. On that note, be sure to store food properly. The raccoons are very people savvy and know what they are doing when it comes to finding food. They are sneaky but actually really fun for the kids to watch as they scurry around camp.

WHY IT'S A FAVORITE

"Besides the amazing scenery and the beautiful beaches, I think my favorite part is the fact that, for the whole day, weekend, or week that you are there, your whole world becomes the island. Because you don't have immediate access to your car, there is no question of where you are supposed to be. There is no temptation to rush back to your hurried life, to get sidetracked on an errand you didn't need to run. Your only agenda is to enjoy the time with your family in this beautiful place until the boat returns to pick you up."
—MELISSA HOLLINGSWORTH

INSIDER'S TIP

Before you head out to the island, look for the amazing playground on the mainland within walking distance of the visitor center. Use it to get the wiggles out before your ferry ride or to convince your kids to get back in the car after your return trip.

PROVIDENCE CANYON STATE PARK, GEORGIA, **CANYON LOOP TRAIL**

ACTIVITIES: Hiking, camping

LENGTH OF HIKE: 2.45 miles

OUT AND BACK OR LOOP: Loop

DIFFICULTY OF TERRAIN: Easy–moderate

ELEVATION GAIN: 100 feet

PARKING FEE/PASS: State park pass $5

TOILETS: Yes

CHANGING TABLE: No

NURSING BENCHES: Yes

DOGS ALLOWED: Yes

BIKES/HORSES/MOTORS ON TRAIL: No

CELL RECEPTION: Yes

DRINKING WATER AVAILABLE: Yes

POTENTIAL CHILD OR BABY HAZARDS: The trail is fenced on the rim, however, ambitious toddlers could get through in some sections.

GEAR SUGGESTIONS: Change of clothes to let the little ones splash in the creeks at the bottom of the canyon

While it's not the size of the Grand Canyon, Providence Canyon is a type of topography that really shouldn't exist in this state and looks more like something you would expect to find in Arizona or Utah. This is why the crumbling red sandstone landscape has been nicknamed "the Little Grand Canyon of Georgia." Interestingly, the area is actually a result of human intervention with nature.

The topography formed in the early 1800s, shortly after the first settlers arrived. They saw the flat ancient seabed as a perfect landscape to farm, so they removed all trees and vegetation and began harvesting crops. What they didn't understand was that the natural landscape was holding the crumbling terrain together. This shift in the geology by human impact led to a dramatic erosion, and within 50 years, deep ditches, up to 5 feet deep, were cut into the land. From there, this led to 16 different canyons forming, some as deep as 150 feet today.

Take some time to explore the canyon floor. Along the trail, you'll find Georgia pines and salamanders. But what will stand out more than anything is the cross-section of the clay that is truly spectacular. It's only in Providence Canyon that you can see the striations of the Georgia red clay, exposing the colors of iron ore, manganese, kaolin, mica, and sandy clays. Remember, this is a fragile landscape, so it's important to stay on trail because the area is still heavily eroding daily.

What your toddler will love are all of the great little puddles and a shallow creek for splashing. Bring waterproof shoes for the canyon floor. The creek at the bottom is only an inch or so deep in most places, but it is muddy.

Keep in mind that there is a lot of heavy erosion near the edge of the cliffs, so stay away (there are fences all around to remind you). The path is far enough away from the fences that it is very safe. However, if you have a particularly ambitious toddler, make sure you keep an eye on him as there are places he could climb through.

If you are an experienced backpacker, consider staying overnight and head into the backcountry if you are feeling adventurous. This is by permit only and there are no designated sites, so you will truly be on a full adventure.

WHY IT'S A FAVORITE

"I always love stumbling upon a place whose natural surroundings are so different from everything around it. Providence Canyon is exactly that. There are a lot of little canyons to explore on the valley floor. I love the juxtaposition of the old cars in the forest. Beautiful cross-section of the Georgia clay that you can't see anywhere else." —MELISSA HOLLINGSWORTH

INSIDER'S TIP

It is very hot in summer. Also, it can be crowded during good weather on a weekend. Parking may be difficult if you arrive late in the day during that time. But, it's practically empty during the week.

LA PEROUSE BAY, HAWAII,
LA PEROUSE BAY

ACTIVITIES: Hiking, splashing, snorkeling, paddling

LENGTH OF HIKE: 4.6 miles

OUT AND BACK OR LOOP: Out and back

DIFFICULTY OF TERRAIN: Easy

ELEVATION GAIN: No

PARKING FEE/PASS: No

TOILETS: Yes

CHANGING TABLE: No

NURSING BENCHES: Yes

DOGS ALLOWED: Yes

BIKES/HORSES/MOTORS ON TRAIL: No

CELL RECEPTION: Yes

DRINKING WATER AVAILABLE: No
Potential Child or Baby Hazards: Sunshine, the ocean, tripping hazards

GEAR SUGGESTIONS: Shade for carrier, umbrella, plenty of water, sand toys

La Perouse is hardly a Maui secret, but it does take an adventurous spirit to seek it out and go beyond the first mile of trail. Located at the dead end of a bumpy dirt road past the famous "Big Beach" and through the Ahihi Kinau Reserve, look for the horse corral and the stone monument to park your car and begin your journey down a trail that goes through lava beds that formed two centuries ago when Haleakala last erupted. This area is called Keone ʻoʻio Bay by the Hawaiians and got the name La

Perouse Bay from a French explorer named Captain Jean-François de Galaup in 1786. De Galaup is said to be the first Westerner to land on Maui.

You have two choices in the beginning of this hike. You can take the shoreline trail for a shorter adventure, or follow a slight detour around some ancient Hawaiian ruins. In the first 0.25 mile on the shoreline, keep an eye out for a blowhole that will delight a toddler. Just make sure they keep their distance because the force of water could snatch a little one right off the rocky shoreline. This is also a great place to stop for sunsets.

The longer version of this trail that ends up at Kanaio Beach is exposed and much of it is made of volcanic rock, so it can be pretty hot. Bring sunscreen, hat, and consider a frame carrier with a sunshade. Also consider doing this hike either early in the morn-

ing or late in the day when it's cooler. Later in the day, it will also be quite windy as it's often the case in Maui. If you need to cut the hike short, the first sandy beach is at 0.5 mile into the hike. There you'll see reef fish and sea turtles frolicking in the water. Come early in the morning, and you will most likely spot dolphins snacking on small schools of fish for breakfast. If you're able to push on, you'll come to a shaded grove of ragged trees and the remains of rock walls. Be on the lookout for packs of wild goats grazing, and you might even spot pygmy deer in the area.

Once you get past the first mile of the trail, expect the crowds to thin out as most tourists will just hike a little ways out and call it a day, turning around to head back for the sandy beaches that are easier to access and cold poolside drinks. (But this is not you. That's why we are sharing this fun adventure.) Journey on and you'll be rewarded with beautiful views and a relatively empty sandy beach to chill out on, a rarity in this part of Maui.

Visit this trail between November and February and you are sure to see whales spouting off the coastline when you stop and look for them.

"My boy loves to climb, so the boulders are everywhere on this hike. These also could make great nursing benches if you needed to stop," says Hike it Baby Maui ambassador Tommy Barton.

One thing to keep in mind is that lava rock is sharp, so be careful of little walkers stumbling off of the trail or venturing out onto the rocks. Also, lava does have plant life growing on it (that's why you will see so many goats out there grazing), so while you will see many trails deviating off of the main trail, try to stay on the main one so as not to disrupt any growth that is happening in the lava rocks.

WHY IT'S A FAVORITE

Our family loves this hike because it has everything, including several beaches, forest, shrub land, and lava rock. Taylor, our wild boy, always yells, "Goat go BAAHH BAH BAAAAAHHHH!" when we see the goats running by. The rock scrambling and tide pools are great, and, of course, there are epic vistas of the South Shore." —TOMMY BARTON

INSIDER'S TIP

Bring headlamps, and hike this trail at the very end of the day into the night for the ultimate easy-to-get-to total stargazing experience with no crowds. Hopefully, the little one falls asleep in your frame pack from the sound of the waves crashing on the sand, so the parental units get a romantic semi-alone evening in the "wild."

KANEOHE, HAWAII, LIKEKE FALLS

ACTIVITIES: Hiking, splashing

LENGTH OF HIKE: 1.5 miles

OUT AND BACK OR LOOP: Out and back

DIFFICULTY OF TERRAIN: Moderate

ELEVATION GAIN: 425 feet

PARKING FEE/PASS: No

TOILETS: No

CHANGING TABLE: No

NURSING BENCHES: No

DOGS ALLOWED: Leashed

BIKES/HORSES/MOTORS ON TRAIL: No

CELL RECEPTION: Decent

DRINKING WATER AVAILABLE: No

POTENTIAL CHILD OR BABY HAZARDS:
Muddy in areas, roots, and muddy rocks

GEAR SUGGESTIONS: Bug repellent,
sunblock, water, snacks, comfortable shoes

Occasionally it's fun to throw in a "locals only" hike, and when it comes to Hawaii, this can be a good thing because so much of the island and many of the trails are overrun with tourists. If you decide to adventure on this one, note that it's not well marked and not going to be one you find in most guidebooks for a few reasons. First of all, depending on where you park, you might need to climb under the road through a little culvert. Secondly, because it's definitely a short, very easy hike, most people looking for an adventure in Hawaii are going to seek out a longer journey, leaving this one for those with little kids.

The story behind this hike is that it was built by a man named Richard H. Davis in the '60s. The waterfall was man-made as a result of the highway being built through the area, causing the waterfall to form. Apparently when Richard, who was a member of a local hike club, discovered this newly formed waterfall, he decided to make this trail his pet project. He built and maintained it until he passed away in the '80s. The trail is a bit rough these days in part due to nature taking it back, but you can still see evidence of Richard's trail work in the stone paths through various parts of the trail. Likeke is actually the Hawaiian word for "Richard," so the falls were actually named after him.

Maureen Cooper and Andrea Sauka-Hazelbaker submitted this one because they felt like it's a great off-the-beaten-path short hike for toddlers, with the reward of the Likeke waterfall to splash in at the end on a hot day. Although this one is muddy in areas and there are tree roots and rocks to negotiate, both you and your toddler will enjoy the adventure of it all.

The hike starts out on a little road where you will pass a chain link fence. Then follow it past a graffiti-covered water tank. Walk about 0.5 mile up the trail and you will come to a large tree carved with more graffiti, including an arrow pointing in the direction of the waterfall. Pass through a tunnel that's been formed through a messy bush of trees. When the trail starts to get a little wet with water flowing on it, you'll know you're close to the falls.

You can expect your toddler to walk most of the way, but have a backup carrier if he or she decides it's not going to happen. The trail is pretty wide for the most part, but expect some uneven footing as you get closer to the waterfall. Also, the lushness of this hike means mosquitoes are plentiful, so juice up with bug spray.

WHY IT'S A FAVORITE

"With this trail, I liked that there aren't too many steep drop-offs to get to the waterfall, so I was more comfortable letting my son wander around on the trail. Also, it is a shorter hike but with a great reward!" —MAUREEN COOPER

INSIDER'S TIP

Park at the Ko'olau Golf Club near the First Presbyterian Church. The church asks that on Sundays hikers park after 11:30 a.m. Don't wear white on this hike as you will get muddy!

It's possible to hike through the nearby 400-acre Ho'omaluhia Botanical Garden if a longer hike is desired.

BOISE NATIONAL FOREST, IDAHO,
MORES MOUNTAIN INTERPRETIVE TRAIL

ACTIVITIES: Hiking, biking, camping, birding

LENGTH OF HIKE: 1.9 miles

OUT AND BACK OR LOOP: Loop

DIFFICULTY OF TERRAIN: Easy

ELEVATION GAIN: 575 feet

PARKING FEE/PASS: $5

TOILETS: Yes

CHANGING TABLE: No

NURSING BENCHES: Some

DOGS ALLOWED: Yes

BIKES/HORSES/MOTORS ON TRAIL: No

CELL RECEPTION: Spotty

DRINKING WATER AVAILABLE: No

POTENTIAL CHILD OR BABY HAZARDS: No

GEAR SUGGESTIONS: Bug spray

An easy out-of-town adventure just above Boise and past Bogus Basin ski area, Mores Mountain Interpretive Trail starts at about 6,600 feet and is a spectacular day trip that offers lush meadows of wildflowers in the spring and summer (as late as July), including sticky cinquefoil, scarlet gilia, sulphur buckwheat, lupine, and several species of penstemon. As you hike, you'll find breathtaking views of the Sawtooth Mountain range to the east and Oregon's Blue Mountains to the west.

Keep your eyes on the lookout for wildlife as this area is also home to numerous birds and butterflies. There's a good chance if you're looking for it, you'll spot a redtailed hawk diving for dinner in the deep purple lupine-filled meadows. You're not likely to see mountain lions or bears, but they are out there.

Vehicle access to the Mores Mountain trailhead is generally permitted from June to October, depending on weather and snow conditions, but check local reports. A rough winter can make driving to the trailhead more difficult in a two-wheel drive. From Boise, travel along Bogus Basin Road (FS Road 297) for approximately 20 miles. Continue past the ski area and Nordic Ski Center. The final 3 miles are on a gravel road. Turn right (east) at the campground sign and travel just over a mile to the Shafer Butte Campground and picnic area.

The hike itself is toddler friendly and very walkable with a trail that skirts the top of Mores Mountain and numerous shaded benches along the way, making it perfect for new parents. One thing to keep in mind, however, is that the hike is fairly exposed. Be aware of weather and don't plan to hike this if thunderstorms are expected. Hiking boots and a lightweight rain jacket are recommended in the summer.

WHY IT'S A FAVORITE

"Mores Mountain, located 20 miles north of Boise at 6,600 feet elevation, is a perfect destination for hiking, biking, camping, and picnicking in a scenic mountain setting with an abundance of wildflowers from mid-June through August and some rich-colored

butterflies. Black bears, mountain lions, elk, and deer, also call this area home."
—ANKA TRIFAN

INSIDER'S TIP

Interested in camping out? There are seven overnight spots that are walk-in and fairly close together with limited vegetation screening each spot, so expect to be friendly with the neighbors. Also, be sure to bring water as there is limited, if any, water onsite.

STARVED CREEK STATE PARK, ILLINOIS,
ST. LOUIS CANYON & WILDCAT CANYON

ACTIVITIES: Birding, hiking, camping, fishing, picnicking, paddling

LENGTH OF HIKES: St. Louis Canyon (1.5 miles) & Wildcat Canyon (1.0 mile)

OUT AND BACK OR LOOP: Out and back

DIFFICULTY OF TERRAIN: Moderate

ELEVATION GAIN: 514 feet

PARKING FEE/PASS: No

TOILETS: Yes

CHANGING TABLE: Yes

NURSING BENCHES: Yes

DOGS ALLOWED: Yes

BIKES/HORSES/MOTORS ON TRAIL: No

CELL RECEPTION: Yes

DRINKING WATER AVAILABLE: Yes

POTENTIAL CHILD OR BABY HAZARDS: Lots of stairs

GEAR SUGGESTIONS: Baby carrier if you have a little one. We ended up carrying our 3-year-old and 20-month-old due to all the stairs.

If you're a lover of waterfalls, then this is one park you shouldn't miss. In 14 of the 18 canyons at Starved Creek State Park, you'll see some of the most spectacular waterfalls in Illinois. The most impressive falls found in between the carved-out St. Peter sandstone are St. Louis, French, Wildcat, Tonty, Ottawa, and Kaskaskia Canyons. Of course, the best time to see waterfalls is in the spring, when the snow and ice melt or after a heavy rainfall. But visit in the winter and you'll get to see them frozen. St. Louis Canyon is the biggest and most popular, and for a reason. It's a must-see; and if you have time, don't miss Wildcat Canyon.

Hike it Baby ambassador Brandi Rondinelli said what her family loved most about this 2,600-acre park with 13 miles of trails was the free-range aspect of the area. "We could go right in the water and sit under the waterfall and enjoy every part of the canyon."

The water is a big draw during the sweltering hot Illinois summers, with never-ending pools that are safe for toddlers to wade in. Visit on a weekday if possible, because you will find crowds no matter where you go. Roughly 2 million people visit Starved Rock State Park every year. For perspective, that's actually more than the number of people who live in the entire state of New Mexico! Plan to stay for the day so you get the most of this beautiful location.

While there are numerous short hikes, we're suggesting not missing these two if you visit the park. Expect both to be toddler friendly, but they will require some carrying. The trail to Wildcat has a 125-foot waterfall with three different views you can take in. Toddlers and pre-K kiddos can do this hike down, but it will take a long time with little legs. If you want to see more of the park, consider carrying because the many short hikes can quickly add up to a lot of miles. For older kids over 5 years old, many of the hikes are very doable. The railings on all of the hikes and stairways are very sturdy, and it's clear this park took young children into consideration when developing the trails.

Wildlife is plentiful, from fish (anglers can find bullhead, white bass, walleye, catfish, and crappie), frogs, toads, turtles, and salamanders around the water, to birds flying above and in the trees. Look for the easy-to-spot eagles, bitterns, herons, owls, turkeys, pheasants, and woodpeckers, as well as many others. On land you'll find badgers, beavers, coyotes, gophers, raccoons, foxes, otters, and deer. If you go in the spring, look for a wildflower called mayapples. These grow to about knee high and have a little umbrella of green with a white daisy-like flower underneath.

One thing you'll notice about the canyons at Starved Rock State Park is that they are big and the views are amazing. Make sure you take time to just sit and take in the vastness of it all. There are a few benches scattered throughout the park, but expect to sit on rocks and logs in the bottom of the canyon if you have to nurse.

The best time to visit is end of summer/fall or spring for optimal weather. In spring you can expect the waterfalls to be at their all-time high with running water. When it comes to gear, runners are fine, but hiking sandals are even better if you plan to go down in the canyon, because it's sandy and you will be walking through water.

Interested in the history of Starved Rock State Park and how it got its name? According to legend, in a tribal meeting, Chief Pontiac of the Ottawa tribe was stabbed by a member of another tribe. In an act of vengeance, the Illiniwek warriors, whose leader was the offender, were trapped on a rocky point by the Potawatomi and Ottawa tribes and eventually they died of starvation. Thus, the name Starved Rock. The rock was declared a national monument in 1960.

There's a big parking lot near the building for the main trail and smaller gravel parking lots to the other trails. Go on a weekday and it won't be too busy. There are always plenty of people in this park but also a lot of space.

WHY IT'S A FAVORITE

"There are so many beautiful things to see at Starved Rock, and you don't want to miss a single one, so give yourself plenty of time to explore it all! That said, it's definitely a place we will visit annually because there is so much to see and just not enough time."
—BRANDI RONDINELLI

INSIDER'S TIP

There are no wheels of any kind that will work in this park, so leave the stroller at home. There are many stairs to get down to all of the canyons. Bring only what you need and leave the rest behind so you don't end up dragging a 65-pound backpack up 150 stairs.

SHAWNEE NATIONAL FOREST, ILLINOIS, RIM ROCK RECREATIONAL TRAIL

ACTIVITIES: Hiking, splashing, canyons

LENGTH OF HIKE: 1.7 miles

OUT AND BACK OR LOOP: Loop

DIFFICULTY OF TERRAIN: Easy

ELEVATION GAIN: 360 feet

PARKING FEE/PASS: No

TOILETS: Yes

CHANGING TABLE: No

NURSING BENCHES: Yes on top of trail

DOGS ALLOWED: Yes

BIKES/HORSES/MOTORS ON TRAIL: No

CELL RECEPTION: Excellent

DRINKING WATER AVAILABLE: No

POTENTIAL CHILD OR BABY HAZARDS: Bluffs near trail

GEAR SUGGESTIONS: Water, sunscreen, bug spray

Located between the Mississippi and Ohio Rivers, in southern Illinois, the Shawnee National Forest is 280,000 acres of woodlands, hills, and lakes to explore. Amazing features like Garden of the Gods wilderness area features ancient sandstone cliffs, and formations are what draw people to the area. This is where you can also find the less-visited Rim Rock Trail and the opportunity for your family to experience something akin to the slot canyons of Utah, minus the tight squeeze. It may not be Grand

Staircase Escalante, but any visiting child will stare up in awe at the high sandstone walls and peer into the narrow hallways carved out by years of erosion.

This area was designated a national recreation trail in 1980 because of its beauty and history for both Late Woodland Native Americans and settlers who stored supplies and resting animals in the natural cool caves. Wooden walkways lead through the forest, and eventually you can cross down into the "Pounds," which is an Old English term for "some sort of enclosure." The Rim Rock Trail is one of a few in the area that were man-made over 1,500 years ago by the Late Woodland Native Americans. This is also what makes the area historically significant.

This area is known for its spectacular show of spring woodland flowers along both its upper and lower trails. The upper trail is paved and less strenuous for hikers. The lower trail has a dirt surface and leads along the base of the bluffs before looping back to the parking lot.

Keep an eye out for Ox-Lot Cave at the beginning of your hike, a natural shelter that was historically used by both Native Americans for food storage and early log-

gers who kept their horses and oxen in the cave. If you are near the cave, you'll understand why this was a perfect storage place, because the cool air can be felt rising from the opening and you can hear the water trickling from the base of the bluffs.

As you wander through the forest, expect to see twisted ancient cedar trees, remnants of a stone wall that was erected at some point in history by man, enormous beech and poplar trees in the canyon, and Fat Man's Misery, a rock face with a big crevice to pass through.

While the official information on the National Forest Service website doesn't mention it, there is a trail that heads down to the bottom of the bluffs. The trail is a set of stairs that runs through a rock passage. The path then winds around the bottom of the bluffs, passes a creek, and has a few overhangs of the bluffs that were fun to explore. Hike it Baby ambassador Jessica Featherstone said her daughter, Sky, loved exploring the rock passage and seeing if she fit under the bluff overhangs. "There is plenty of light in the slots we traveled through, so it wasn't scary for our daughter, but it's a great first for little ones to be in slots or a cave-like environment."

Also keep in mind as you hike this trail there is some signage confusion and many report ending up on Pounds Hollow Lake Road, which means you hike the highway back to Rim Rock. There are no signs telling you which way to go on the trail. Just note that if you get to the beach area, you've gone too far.

Visiting in the winter months? The trail tread may be slippery during or after rain or snow. Use caution when descending the wooden staircase and stone steps leading to the canyon floor and Ox-Lot Cave. Also, if you visit in icy months, be aware that large icicles form along the bluff walls and can fall.

WHY IT'S A FAVORITE

"We took a frame carrier and a Kiddo Gear harness (this allows kids to walk but be attached to you) because of the cliffs. Most of the time, we walked the bottom sections and played in the little creek. Bugs were present, but a bit of bug spray kept them away. We went during an incredibly busy weekend, so there were crowds, but it still was worth the visit." —JESSICA FEATHERSTONE

INSIDER'S TIP

Since it's a shorter hike, you're able to head along the top path and the bottom path. The top path is interesting due to the history of the area and a great spot to have a picnic lunch. This is also somewhat wheel-friendly. As you drop into the canyon, plan to carry your little one for a bit. There are also a lot of stairs, so be ready to feel a bit of burn as you hike out of the canyon. Only take down what you want to carry up.

THRU-HIKING WITH BABY:
GO THE DISTANCE AS A FAMILY

You don't need to be a backpacking expert to distance hike with your little one, but here are key components that will make your experience safer and more enjoyable.

1. **BECOME A PRO IN THE SKILL PRIOR TO ADDING A BABY IN THE MIX.** If you already have kids, this will be a little more challenging, but not impossible! Many backcountry skills, such as cooking, filtering water, and pitching a tent, can all be practiced at home. However, we definitely recommend practicing those skills in the backcountry many times until you are comfortable with them first before bringing baby.

2. **BE FLEXIBLE.** Your child's needs are more important than the trip's agenda. This is especially true when it comes to inclement weather.

3. **INVEST IN ULTRALIGHT EQUIPMENT.** A baby is a pretty lofty luxury item! It's helpful to walk quickly while baby naps in the pack, and efficiency is definitely impacted by pack weight. Pare down in every other way possible, from sleeping bags to your tent, and you'll be thankful for every ounce you don't have to carry!

4. **ACQUIRE WILDERNESS MEDICINE EXPERIENCE.** We highly recommend a Wilderness First Responder course. While it is lengthy and costly, the skills you learn will give you a priceless peace of mind to be able to respond to a medical emergency in the backcountry if needed.

5. **MAKE THE TRANSITION FROM HOME TO TENT AS SEAMLESS AS POSSIBLE.** Practice sleeping arrangements and a soothing routine in case your child gets anxious by new surroundings. Also, get her used to being worn in a carrier, around the house, out to errands, and, of course, hiking on the trail. She'll get accustomed to life on the trail much easier if she's familiar with how it works!

Bekah and Derrick Quirin hiked the entire Appalachian Trail in 2017 over a six-month period with their one-year-old daughter, Ellie. Read their full story on the next page.

A TODDLER ON THE
APPALACHIAN TRAIL

BEKAH AND DERRICK QUIRIN

DECIDING TO THRU-HIKE THE APPALACHIAN TRAIL (AT) didn't happen overnight for us. We had been dreaming of thru-hiking for almost 10 years. We just never imagined that the best time in life to do so would be after we had our first baby, Ellie.

From the time our daughter was two months old, we started hiking regularly as a family. But hiking wasn't anything new for me and Derrick. In fact, the outdoors had been the center of our entire adult education and career. This meant it probably didn't come as a surprise to those around us when we announced that we had decided to thru hike the Appalachian Trail with Ellie on a six-month backpacking trip.

Derrick and I both graduated college with a degree in Outdoor Leadership, then took the same career path guiding hiking trips for families in the southeast and backpacking trips for inner-city youth. Not only did we have prior backpacking experience, but a large amount of that experience involved taking care of others while out on the trail.

This was definitely a key component for us to thru-hike with a one-year-old. Backpacking skills were second nature to us. Other than walking, we were able to focus on Ellie and her needs rather than on how to backpack. We were also medically trained for wilderness emergencies as Wilderness First Responders.

When we decided we were going to thru-hike with Ellie, the first thing we did was scoure the internet for resources on how to distance hike with a baby. To our surprise, there was very little information. We pieced together what we could and made up the rest as best as possible. We knew we had a pretty tight time frame in which this would be possible.

We wanted to wait until Ellie could sit up, so she could sit in the Deuter Kid Comfort 3 backpack. And we wanted to complete the trail by the time she gained too much independence to be carried in a pack for multiple hours every day. Not to mention before she gained too much physical weight, too.

We left when Ellie was 12 months and finished when she was 18 months, which was a perfect window of time. After deciding on a time frame, we honed in on her nutrition, diaper, and clothing needs. Ellie was breastfed the entire thru-hike, which helped meet her nutritional needs perfectly. In addition, she would eat little bites of our food, which were freeze-dried and pre-packed in advance.

A few things to note when journeying so far with a baby: We didn't pack any separate food for her. Diapers were a constant battle, and we still don't have a great solution! The wet and humid Appalachian Trail climate meant cloth diapers were nixed immediately, but we also aren't a fan of disposable diapers. We mostly used gDiapers, which have a composting insert in a cloth cover. We had the option of burying the inserts, but preferred to pack them out instead.

Ellie's clothes were minimal, but we made sure she had enough to stay warm at any point during the seasons. Then other than a toddler toothbrush, that's all we had for Ellie. Her toys were sticks and rocks, and some of her first words were "backpack" and "blaze."

Now that we're back home, we're so thankful we got to take Ellie with us on our AT thru-hike and wouldn't have it any other way. The reward of spending that quality time with her on the trail was undeniably one of the most remarkable experiences of our lifetime. But I'm not going to lie, it was hard! Long-distance hiking with your baby is possible—and even enjoyable—but it's not necessary to do a thru-hike in order to have an adventure with your baby.

Bekah, Derrick and Ellie Quirin live in Roanoke, VA, and are ambassadors for Hike it Baby. They hiked the entire Appalachian Trail in 2017 over a six-month period, doing what's called a "flip hike," which means they started at a mid-point on the trail, hiked the southern portion and came back to that same point to hike the northern portion. Two sections put together to make the full 2,190 miles.

ALL ACCESS FAMILY
LINDSAY FROST

Just like most parents-to-be, Lindsay Frost and her husband were over the moon when they found out they were expecting their first baby in 2013. She says they floated along for the first couple of months, basking in the idea of their little baby, and even went on a "babymoon" trip to Jamaica.

When they returned from that trip, they were all set to attend the gender ultrasound, where they would also do the anatomy scan. Their excitement quickly turned to fear when the doctor came in to inform them that something wasn't right with their baby. The doctor threw around a big word they had never heard of but have been unable to forget ever since: omphalocele. This meant their son's organs were born outside of his body, so he would need surgery immediately upon birth.

Once their son, Cameron, was born, they spent 17 days in the NICU, and eventually they went home with their son on oxygen, which is typical for many kids in Colorado, where they lived. However, their son turned out not to be "typical." By the time he was a few months old, they found out he had some chromosomal issues, which meant he would not be off oxygen anytime soon and would most likely have issues walking and suffer health issues throughout his life.

Luckily, at this time, when she was feeling a bit panicked about her life and the future normalcy of their lives, Lindsey stumbled onto Hike it Baby online. Her family had always been very outdoorsy when she was growing up in western Colorado, so it was in her blood to get out there. She and her husband had already ventured out a couple of times on the trails with Cameron to see how difficult it would be to handle a frame carrier, the oxygen tank and cannula, and then a feeding pump and NG tube.

When she showed up to that first hike and found that there was a good-sized group of parents and kids ready to get out on the trail, she was a bundle of nerves because she was going to be the only one with a baby who had a feeding tube hanging out of his nose. Not far into the hike, she could feel some of the nervousness and stress melting away as she chatted with the mom leading the hike, who said her son had also been on oxygen until recently.

As they talked, she sensed something wet on her pant leg and realized that the plug on the end of her son's NG tube had come undone and the contents of it were spilling down her leg. The mom she was hiking with didn't bat an eye and simply said something along the lines of, "Oh don't worry, they'll wait up. Let's stop and take care of this. How can I help?" Since then, Lindsay and her son have gone on hundreds of hikes with the community, and she has found the courage to hike on her own.

While her parenting dreams may have taken quite a turn from what she expected, she has become an advocate to help others with children experiencing disabilities get on trail across the country. "Nature therapy in the form of hikes is my favorite of the therapies we do for our son, so we make sure to schedule it in regularly."

FAVORITE TRAIL: SUTTON TRAIL, OURAY, CO
This trail gives the hiker a beautiful view of the town of Ouray, followed by a very unique perspective of Bear Creek Falls and the Neosho Mine and cabin, which most people usually only see from their cars as they drive over Red Mountain Pass. It's 4.3 miles round-trip, and Lindsay hiked it with her son in his frame pack, along with her mom.

LOSING A CHILD ON TRAIL:
KNOW WHAT TO DO

Losing a child is every outdoor parent's worst nightmare. Something distracts you momentarily, and you turn around to find your child nowhere in sight. Calls are unanswered. A hasty search of the immediate area yields no sign of him or her. You don't know where your child is—and chances are your child doesn't know where he or she is either. Does your child know what to do?

First, lay the family's ground rules for hiking safety. Write down your few most basic rules, then teach them to your children. Talk about it often so it's familiar to everyone. Rules will vary among families, but here are mine:

1. Kids must remain in sight at all times. Running ahead is okay only if they can look back and still see me.

2. An adult always brings up the rear.

3. Kids must stay on the trail at all times unless accompanied by an adult.

Second, have a casual conversation with your kids about what they must do if they ever get lost. Start this conversation young—I started around age 3 with mine—and revisit the topic often. What you teach them to do will vary depending on the approach you use. There are books, videos, and programs that teach these principles and can be very helpful if you are not sure what to say. All of them have the same basic principles.

If lost, your child should:

1. **STAY PUT.** Once they realize they are lost, they need to hug a tree, make a nest, or whatever imagery you choose to use to convey the idea they need to stop walking, sit down, and wait for help to arrive.

2. **CALL OUT LOUDLY AND OFTEN FROM WHERE THEY HAVE CHOSEN TO WAIT.** This can be "Help!" but the key is to repeat it every few minutes as long as they are able. Because this can get tiring, some parents choose to outfit every child with a safety whistle that either goes around their neck on a lanyard or in a pocket before every hike. The sound of a whistle will carry much farther than a child's voice. If they have one, let them practice blowing into it at home in the backyard to get comfortable with it. Then, once on trail, instruct them, if lost, to blow on it every few minutes.

3. **STAY WARM AND DRY WHILE YOU WAIT FOR HELP TO ARRIVE.** You can make sure your children always have a pack with extra layers on them when they hike, or stuff a plain old black garbage bag in a pocket before a hike for them. Precut a hole for their head, and they can use it like a poncho as they sit on the ground. This can be practiced ahead of time at home, too. You can also show them how to cover up with leaves or pine needles to stay warm. Reiterate that it might feel like a really long time until help arrives, but assure them rescuers are coming.

We can sometimes feel hesitant to bring up topics like this with our little ones because we don't want to inadvertently cause fear of the outdoors. That is totally understandable! Just remember that how you approach the topic will be key—explain it as calmly as if you were explaining table manners. But also remember that by talking about it ahead of time, you will actually be reducing fear and anxiety for them if they ever do get lost, because they will know what to do.

As with all emergency preparation, the hope is that your kids will never have to actually use the skills you have taught them! But if they do, you will have given them tools to stay calm and act appropriately while, at the same time, making it easier for rescuers to find them.

Here are two helpful resources:

Lost But Found Safe and Sound (National Association of Park Rangers DVD and program that can be purchased at www.anpr.org).

Hug a Tree and Survive Program (National Association for Search and Rescue program found at www.nasar.org/hug_a_tree_program).

Alana Dimmick is a park ranger-turned-homeschooling mom of three. With her park ranger husband, Curt, they are raising her kids in some of America's most beautiful places. Alana loves hiking, camping, photography, books, coffee shops, farmers' markets, gardening, and backyard chickens. She is a Hike it Baby Ambassador in western Washington (see bio on page 192).

TURKEY RUN STATE PARK, INDIANA, TURKEY RUN

ACTIVITIES: Camping, fishing, hiking, nature center, swimming

LENGTH OF HIKE: 1–3 miles

OUT AND BACK OR LOOP: Loop, with several intersecting trails

DIFFICULTY OF TERRAIN: Moderate

ELEVATION GAIN: 856 feet

PARKING FEE/PASS: $7 in-state/$9 out-of-state

TOILETS: Yes

CHANGING TABLE: No

NURSING BENCHES: Yes

DOGS ALLOWED: Yes

BIKES/HORSES/MOTORS ON TRAIL: No

CELL RECEPTION: No

DRINKING WATER AVAILABLE: Yes

POTENTIAL CHILD OR BABY HAZARDS: Very rugged terrain, large creeks, slippery rocks, climbing ladders, steep ravines/drop-offs, suspension bridge

GEAR SUGGESTIONS: Child carrier or child harness, hiking poles/walking sticks, waterproof hiking footwear, insect repellent, sunscreen/sun protection, snacks, water, and camera

Considering that most of the Indianapolis area is flat and doesn't have mountains, Turkey Run being only 1.5 to 2 hours away (depending on where you are located in the city) is a treasure.

It's a lush area with various canyons or "runs," which means there are various spots where water pools and kids can splash, look for frogs, check out little creeks, and climb up and down boulders. Make sure you are wearing water shoes or waterproof shoes if you are hiking in cooler months.

Depending on when you hike Turkey Run, it can be a perfect temperature for getting on trails, especially if you go in the late summer or early fall. There might be some rain, which can make parts of the trail slick if a lot of leaves have fallen, but it's nothing to be too concerned about. The park is open all year, but with the icy winters the area gets, a few trails are best avoided.

As for animals, expect to see deer, turkeys, beavers, turkey vultures, and woodpeckers. The 2,300-acre park has wonderful old growth of walnut and sycamore trees, along with ferns and moss aplenty. The abundance of water makes the landscape in this park lush.

Terrain on some trails is moderate to very rugged, and some parts of the trail are steep and have steep ravines and even require climbing ladders. This means some parents might be hesitant to take small kids to these more adventurous trails; but when

visiting the park, you will see tons of kids out there from babies and toddlers to school-aged kids. In the canyon areas that require climbing over boulders, smaller kids should be cautioned to walk slowly, or consider carrying them through these parts.

The hardest trails are some of the most photographed. One is the "Ladders" trail (part of Trail 3), which is recommended to take alternate routes if you have small children. But if you are adventurous and confident with your hiking skills, you might give it a go. "We did it and managed just fine by carrying the kids in carriers on our backs. You climb up and down wooden ladders throughout to get down to the canyon floor. For a new or inexperienced hiker, this is probably something to just take a look at and walk past/continue to Trail 5, which picks up right where "Ladders" starts, says Hike it Baby ambassador Bailey Ludlam.

Trails 1 and 2 are pretty toddler friendly. On a Hike it Baby hike earlier this year, Bailey reports that they had two preschoolers who did the entire hike on their own with no carriers. One spot—Box Canyon—required a little bit of scrambling but it was manageable for everybody. Nobody felt uneasy at any point with their kids hiking the whole thing.

Trail 4 is another toddler favorite. You walk on the canyon floor, so there's lots of room for toddlers to roam and plenty of places to splash. Toddlers will love the small and large boulders to climb and slide down (of course, whatever parents are comfortable with), and then there is a section that narrows—you can either walk through the water if wearing good boots or step up to the side.

Consider hiking to the punch bowl and then walk through the rocky hollow to do some tougher trails—loads of stairs and the Ladders. For toddlers, the first part to the punch bowl might be a great out and back hike that they can do on their own feet and get some exploring in.

The general overall consensus by Hike it Baby members is that this park is worth staying the whole day if you can. Pack a lunch, hike the trails, and take a break at Sugar Creek, which runs right through the park. The beauty of Turkey Run is that it offers multiple trail loops that intersect with one another and many are super accessible. Several trails cross creek beds. Depending on the time of the year, they could range from being dry to impassable.

Don't worry about parking at Turkey Run. The park has a few large lots: one near the Turkey Run Inn and another two lots near the park nature center.

WHY IT'S A FAVORITE

"Turkey Run State Park is a gem nestled in the rolling farmland of Indiana. Every trail has a new adventure around the bend. Each section of these trails offers a specific geological point of interest: the "Ice Box" on the No. 3 section of the trail, Falls Canyon & Boulder Canyon on the No. 9 section of the trail, and of course the "Ladders" section on the No. 5 section of the trail. Each area gives a sense of being somewhere other than where you are, almost like getting lost in time." —ABBY CZACHUR

INSIDER'S TIP

If you have a child who just isn't feeling like hiking, the park offers designated playgrounds. Start off there to warm them up, and then talk about how many geological features within the park are available to also climb on. That could provide a nice transition to getting your little one out there. Don't miss seeing the "Ladders" portion of Trail 3, even if you don't attempt it with children; it is definitely worth seeing.

EAGLE CREEK PARK, INDIANA, EDESSES TRAIL

ACTIVITIES: Hiking, biking, swimming, fishing, birding, playgrounds

LENGTH OF HIKE: 3 miles

OUT AND BACK OR LOOP: Loop

DIFFICULTY OF TERRAIN: Easy–moderate

ELEVATION GAIN: Varies

PARKING FEE/PASS: $5 county residents/ $6 out-of-county residents

TOILETS: Yes

CHANGING TABLE: Yes

NURSING BENCHES: Yes

DOGS ALLOWED: Yes

BIKES/HORSES/MOTORS ON TRAIL: No

CELL RECEPTION: Good

DRINKING WATER AVAILABLE: Yes

POTENTIAL CHILD OR BABY HAZARDS: Steep hills, uneven terrain, portion of trail surrounded by water, lake/reservoir

GEAR SUGGESTIONS: Good footwear, child carrier, hiking poles, insect repellent, sunscreen, snacks, water

While most of the adventures in this book are more rural and escape town, we decided to include this city adventure because Eagle Creek is the largest municipal park in the US, covering 3,900 acres of land and 1,400 acres of water within the Indianapolis city limits. While most cities have parks, few can boast that in the morning you might see a mother deer nursing her little one as you hike along one of the 6-mile trails and then kayak a little later. All in the middle of the city!

Locals report seeing not just deer, but all kinds of wildlife thriving in the park from large turtles and cranes to woodpeckers. You can even cast a line and pull in a fish in the early morning before heading off to work, making this park feel like you are on a great adventure, even if the interstate is just a stone's throw away. In a city of 1 million people, finding refuges like this are critical for raising little outdoor-loving children, which is why this spot is one we feel we should call out.

The park is filled with toddler-friendly trails, and there's a trail that runs along the reservoir so perfect for toddlers to throw rocks in if you have a kiddo you need to keep busy. There are also plenty of playgrounds you can head toward as a reward for that little hiker who keeps pushing on through the hike. And, of course, on a blustery day, the nature center does a story time and regularly offers community hikes.

Littles can definitely walk most portions of the Edesses Trail. The section that goes through the bird sanctuary is flat, has a lot of rocks that are perfect for throwing into the water, and is great for watching for birds. On parts of the trail that head up and down the ridge to and from the Ornithology Center, the terrain could be a bit more uneven, making it harder for little feet, but it's still doable. The trail near the bird sanctuary is more suited for little hikers to get down and explore along the gravel part. Start with some of the shorter loops like this one within the park if you want to get the full experience that Eagle Creek has to offer. What's great about this park is that as your kiddo gets stronger, you can work up to the longer, more challenging hikes. It's perfect for every little hiker in training.

In the summer there's a swimming beach located within the park that's perfect for cooling off after your hike. It might get crowded, but if you just jump in for a quick dip posthike, it's perfect. The park is open and accessible year-round, but consider checking it out in autumn, when the leaves and the reservoir offer a very peaceful landscape.

If you are a nursing mama or have an elderly family member who might need a rest, there are a few nice benches along the bird sanctuary portion of the trail, but they are in a more open area and not as secluded. There also is a picnic table on this portion of the trail that is a great place to stop for a snack. Also, the Edessess portion of the trail is mostly shaded and wooded, but as you head onto the portion of the Blue Trail where it crosses the bird sanctuary, this is fully exposed, so bring a hat.

One thing to be conscious of with this trail is the uneven terrain on the portions of the trek along the ridge. Also be cautious of roots sticking up and steep hillsides. A large portion of this trail is surrounded by water on both sides, so make sure if you have a runner, you are staying close by. In addition, due to the location of the trail near the water, be aware of mosquitoes and always be prepared for potential tick exposure.

WHY IT'S A FAVORITE

"Once inside the park, you can't hear the city much, which is awesome to have without going far. We hike it regularly, and I am always amazed at how big it is and how it feels like we keep finding new trails." —BAILEY LUDLAM

INSIDER'S TIP

Even though this trail is in the middle of the city, you should pack a lunch and make a day of it! There is so much to see and explore not only on the trails, but with the Ornithology Center and Earth Discovery Center as well.

JESTER PARK, IOWA,
HICKORY RIDGE TRAIL

ACTIVITIES: Hiking, birding, geocaching, camping

LENGTH OF HIKE: 1.5 miles

OUT AND BACK OR LOOP: Out and back

DIFFICULTY OF TERRAIN: Moderate

ELEVATION GAIN: Minimal

PARKING FEE/PASS: No

TOILETS: Yes

CHANGING TABLE: No

NURSING BENCHES: Yes

DOGS ALLOWED: Yes

BIKES/HORSES/MOTORS ON TRAIL: No

CELL RECEPTION: Yes

DRINKING WATER AVAILABLE: Yes

POTENTIAL CHILD OR BABY HAZARDS: Mosquitoes in the summer, ticks and poison oak if going off trail, but should be fine if staying on the trail

GEAR SUGGESTIONS: Carriers for little people. Water shoes to play in the creek at the turn-around point.

Located in the 2,000-acre expanse of Jester Park, this trail is one of the favorites in the area because it starts at the Natural Playscape, which is an awesome place for kids to play and get their wiggles out before getting serious about hiking. There's also a great water feature (bring swim gear and water shoes!), sand pit, wood blocks, and other perfect toddler things to explore throughout the park.

The hike is a short out and back if you turn around at the creek crossing. Stop here, pause, and explore, depending on the time of year. If you cross the creek, the trail continues. But with walking toddlers, this might be a good turnaround point, which makes the hike 1.5 miles total. There is some minimal elevation on this hike, but little walkers can do fine for most portions of it. This trail is all-terrain stroller-friendly, but be mindful that there are stairs at the beginning of the hike and loose gravel on another section.

To access the trailhead from the Natural Playscape, you have to cross the park road. It's not a busy road, but if you have kids who run ahead, just be aware of this. May and June are the best times to visit for the wildflowers and mild weather (no mosquitoes yet!), and September and October are best for cooler temps, fall colors, and less mosquitoes. If you get "bugged" easily, avoid this park in the summer months or have your spray handy at all times. At least you won't melt from the summer sun, because the hike is almost all shaded—perfect for hot-weather hiking.

While we want to get you on trail, it's hard not to mention the Natural Playscape be-cause it's so much fun for kids! There are also some benches there for nursing. There are a few hidden surprises along the trail that kids love to find—a teepee-like structure made out of sticks and a few other gems. The Discovery Pond just up the road from the Natural Playscape is also worth a stop for more exploration. Bring water nets and see what you can find—snails, frogs, fish, and bugs galore!

Speaking of wildlife, the Hickory Ridge Trail is also where the bison and elk exhibits are located. If the animals are nearby, take some time to watch them graze on the prairie grasses as they slowly amble through the landscape. But that's not all that you'll find here. Once a year, a huge migration of 3,000 to 8,000 American white pelicans stop off here in late August as they migrate for the winter.

There are no park rangers, but Polk County Conservation owns the park, and they do a ton of family-friendly activities throughout the year at this location. They are in the process of building a Nature Center there, too. There is an equestrian center at the park for year-round horseback riding, snowshoe rentals in the winter, and other fun seasonal activities.

WHY IT'S A FAVORITE

We love this park and this trail season round. I love that each season brings something different to explore and notice. In the spring, we love watching for the bison and elk babies as well as the monarch butterflies. In the summer, I love dipping my feet in the water feature at the playscape after hiking while my son collects and stacks rocks. I also love watching other kids explore and play with the different features in their own unique ways. Some kids like to take the wood blocks and haul them over to the water feature to see if they float or sink or if they can create a dam with them. In the fall, the colors here are beautiful, and it's fun to notice how different animals prepare for winter. We feel so lucky to have this park nearby!" —KATY SEVERE

INSIDER'S TIP

There is a back entrance to the park that brings you directly to the Playscape, so you can avoid the long, winding main road all through the park (which takes forever, but is beautiful!). At the main intersection of NW 120th Ave. and NW 128th St., you would normally turn right to get to the main entrance of the park. Instead, turn left and follow NW 128th St. all the way until it ends, then turn right to enter the park from the back entrance. The Playscape will be on your right after you turn the first corner.

MONUMENT ROCKS NATIONAL LANDMARK
KANSAS, **MONUMENT ROCKS**

ACTIVITIES: Exploring, historic site

LENGTH OF HIKE: 1 mile

OUT AND BACK OR LOOP: Loop

DIFFICULTY OF TERRAIN: Easy

ELEVATION GAIN: No

PARKING FEE/PASS: No

TOILETS: No

CHANGING TABLE: No

NURSING BENCHES: No

DOGS ALLOWED: Yes, on leash

BIKES/HORSES/MOTORS ON TRAIL: No

CELL RECEPTION: No

DRINKING WATER AVAILABLE: No

POTENTIAL CHILD OR BABY HAZARDS: Rattlesnakes

GEAR SUGGESTIONS: Sunblock, sun hat, water

Located on the western edge of Gove County is Monument Rocks, a series of large, heavily sculpted chalk monoliths that are sometimes referred to as the Chalk Pyramids.

Known as one of the eight wonders of Kansas, these awe-inspiring 70-foot-tall formations of Niobrara chalk seem to rise up out of nowhere. These formations came into existence about 80 million years ago, when Kansas was part of an inland sea.

Today, you can find layers of shells and other fossilized prehistoric life in this area thanks to the mucky clay layer that formed and then hardened, cementing everything alive in the thick layers. Probably the best-known fossil from these beds is the famous "fish-within-a-fish" on display at the Sternberg Museum in Hays. But there have also been reports of turtles, sharks, giant clams, swimming dinosaur-age reptiles like mosasaurus and plesiosaurs. Today the chalk beds routinely give up these fossils.

Look for the keyhole arch when you are out there. This is a popular photography spot. According to locals, this was man-made after someone started shooting at a thin part of the rocks, creating a hole, and then it was quickly eroded by weather.

In spite of the desolate-looking landscaping, there's actually a lot of life out here. Look for whitetailed and mule deer, many species of hawks, pronghorn antelopes, jackrabbits, coyotes, and raccoons. Also, be aware of rattlesnakes during the hotter part of the year.

Keep in mind that even though this is a national natural landmark, it is located on private land, so be conscientious of the fact that you are in someone's backyard. Also, don't expect facilities in this area because it is basically in the middle of a cow pasture 6 miles down a gravel road. It's good to have a car with high clearance to venture out to this one, but really any car can get here.

The following are not allowed—climbing, fossil hunting, camping, littering, or bonfires. Do not honk at cattle. Please take only pictures and leave only footprints. Also, clay can be very slick and thick on a rainy day so bring boots if heading out during rainy weather.

WHY IT'S A FAVORITE

"This is a nice little break for the whole family when you're making the long trek between Denver and Kansas City to get out and stretch your legs and get in a bit of history of the area. You get the whole area to yourselves, and the kids can run and get all their pent-up energy out and be as noisy as they want. Sunset is one of the best times to be there for picturesque photos." —VONG HAMILTON

INSIDER'S TIP

Cars with high clearance do better getting out here due to it being out on a gravel road. Probably not a great idea to head out here during rainy weather in a two-wheel-drive car.

ERNIE MILLER NATURE CENTER, KANSAS,
UPPER RIDGE TRAIL AND SOUTH TRAIL

ACTIVITIES: Hiking, birding, geocaching

LENGTH OF HIKES: 0.5–3 miles

OUT AND BACK OR LOOP: Loop

DIFFICULTY OF TERRAIN: Easy

ELEVATION GAIN: No

PARKING FEE/PASS: No

TOILETS: Yes

CHANGING TABLE: Yes

NURSING BENCHES: Yes

DOGS ALLOWED: No

BIKES/HORSES/MOTORS ON TRAIL: No

CELL RECEPTION: Yes

DRINKING WATER AVAILABLE: Yes

POTENTIAL CHILD OR BABY HAZARDS: Poison ivy, ticks

GEAR SUGGESTIONS: Bug spray, water shoes

Built in 1985, Ernie Miller Nature Center, named after a prominent local citizen and the very first nature center in the county, covers 116 acres and offers multiple hiking trails that cross through prairie grass, meadows, woods, and streams. The trails are varied with easy, shorter paved paths for strollers or wheelchairs, but there are also dirt trails into the woods for those wanting something a bit more rugged. You can hike shorter trails, such as the Upper and Lower Ridge Trails, along the creek; or if you have more time to explore, the South Trail is an excellent option with almost 2 miles of trails. The woods, prairie, and creek along a rocky ridge make for interesting changes of scenery.

There are two parking lots where you can park to start your adventure. The larger one is near the Nature Center and leads down a paved path past prairie grass. You can visit the Nature Center, which houses an exhibit gallery called "Our Changing Landscape" and has many hands-on activities for all ages, including a beaver lodge tunnel for kids to crawl into and a water table to splash in. You can also learn more about the diverse local animals that call Ernie Miller home and their habitats through live animal displays and a 500-gallon aquarium with native stream fish. You can also familiarize yourself with the grounds and trails with an interactive 3-D map of Ernie Miller, where you can see the various trails light up with the push of a button.

The smaller parking lot near the large shelter at the entrance to the park gives you more direct access to the South Trail if you want to bypass visiting the Visitor Center. If you choose to park at the Nature Center, before beginning your hike, it's also a good time to use the restrooms, change diapers, and fill up water bottles at the Nature Center, as there aren't any of these amenities available once you're on trail.

Upper Ridge Trail requires a bit of an uphill hike and takes you above the creek along a ridge for great views. At one end, you cross a larger creek over big rocks that might be unstable for tiny kiddos to maneuver or a mom with a carrier, so be careful to assess the potential hazard of slipping and falling if the rocks are slippery and water level is high. The creek's depth depends on the rain supply. The other end offers a safer option to cross the creek with a bridge that's very popular for photography or just to sit on the nearby rocks and take in the beautiful scenery.

The South Trail is the longest trail and covers a large area of the southern portion of the grounds. The trail is paved near the amphitheater and small parking lot, but the majority takes you into the woods on dirt trails. There are downed trees for climbing a few small creek crossings and, fortunately, the water is pretty shallow most of the time so it's very toddler friendly. Kids can walk all of the South Trail; however, there are lots of exposed roots and portions of the trail are rocky, so make sure new walkers are careful not to trip. Because of the stream crossings and rocky sections, good sturdy shoes are recommended.

Lots of wildlife can be seen on the grounds, such as chipmunks, squirrels, deer, and birds. In the Nature Center, there are rescued birds of prey (red-tailed hawks and native owls), as well as snakes and turtles on display and native fish in the aquarium. Raccoons, foxes, and possums also make their home at Ernie Miller. There are also lots of great trees on the grounds, such as oak, hickory, pawpaw, redbud, and locust.

WHY IT'S A FAVORITE

"We love going to Ernie Miller because it's on the outskirts of town, so we don't often run into too many people on the trail—meaning we sometimes get the whole place to ourselves to take our time and be noisy! Although not too technical, the South Trail is great for young hikers because it's flat and easy but has just enough short sections where the trail gets rooty and rocky to give kids a bit of a challenge. And with multiple small creek crossings, the kids like to get rewarded with mud and water play, and it helps break up the hike. We like to end at the amphitheater and recover after a hot hike and have a snack, followed by mini performances by the kids." —VONG HAMILTON

INSIDER'S TIP

For a bit of fun and a challenge, there's a preschool scavenger hunt that offers young visitors the chance to look for items both inside the Nature Center and outside. And once those things have been checked off the list, there is a great wildlife viewing room for moms, dads, or caregivers to relax in as the kids spot birds coming into the feeders.

RED RIVER GORGE, KENTUCKY,
ROCK BRIDGE TRAIL

ACTIVITIES: Hiking, rock climbing, camping

LENGTH OF HIKE: 1.5 miles

OUT AND BACK OR LOOP: Loop

DIFFICULTY OF TERRAIN: Moderate

ELEVATION GAIN: Starts at 1,144 feet and descends 887 feet (and will have to ascend 887 feet)

PARKING FEE/PASS: No

TOILETS: Yes

CHANGING TABLE: No

NURSING BENCHES: Yes

DOGS ALLOWED: Yes

BIKES/HORSES/MOTORS ON TRAIL: No

CELL RECEPTION: Spotty

DRINKING WATER AVAILABLE: No

POTENTIAL CHILD OR BABY HAZARDS: Cliffs, copperheads, rocky trail, exposed roots on trail, water hazards

GEAR SUGGESTIONS: Water gear, change of clothes for little ones if they play in the water, sunblock, bug spray (mosquitoes and ticks), water, and snacks; if baby/toddler-wearing, bring a pair of trekking poles.

Outside of Lexington, everyone tends to go to Red River Gorge. There are tons of hikes, anywhere from 0.5 mile to an overlook to the 323-mile Sheltowee Trace hike. But the most popular one is the Rock Bridge Trail, which is a 1.5-mile loop. It starts off with a steep descent down toward the river with stone stairs that have been carved into sandstone. At one time it was paved at the start, though you can hardly tell now with how broken and uneven it is. Mother Nature has started to take it back. This could be slow going with a toddler, so consider wearing through this part. It's a short hike, so there will be plenty of areas he can walk.

Next, follow Rockbridge Fork Creek about 0.5 to 0.6 mile until you come to Creation Falls on the right. Just past this and before the natural arch over the creek (why it's called Rock Bridge), there are water access points. It's normally shallow and still, and with the sandstone creek bed, it makes a great place to stop and enjoy the view, have a picnic, and splash in the creek. It's shallowest during the summer, so Hike it Baby groups often stop to have snacks and let the kids play in the water.

Farther along the trail around 0.6 mile, you will see the only Natural Bridge in Red River Gorge on the right. This natural arch is the only one in Red River Gorge that actually goes over water. Once past this, it's pretty much all uphill back to the parking lot, but it has pretty views and resting points for nursing moms or tired tots.

Don't miss Creation Falls or the Rock Bridge Natural Arch (you may see people crossing it—but please don't; it's not allowed). There is a small spur that allows for better viewing of Creation Falls. It does have a wall here, so you cannot get down (and harder for kids to fall). There are some beautiful views on the left on your hike back up and out.

Expect to see old-growth forest, Eastern hemlocks, ferns, rhododendrons, rock houses, and magnolias; and while you don't often see birds, you can hear them and the squirrels. "We especially like this hike out of all that are in the Red River Gorge because it's a shorter loop that has some spots that aren't near cliffs or edges and that toddlers can walk," says Keira Wickliffe Berger.

If you are a more advanced hiker and want to take this adventure a little further, consider continuing with this hike and add on Swift Camp Creek Trail with a view of Hell's Kitchen and a steep cliff drop-off (although it's easy to hike along if you are carrying) to Pooch Turtle Falls. Keep in mind that this area does require some scrambling, so caution is advised if carrying a little one. This will turn the hike into a 5-mile journey, so definitely bring food and water and expect the hike to take a good portion of the day. This one can also be turned into a backpacking overnight trip.

Keep in mind this is close to Lexington, so on weekends, especially in the afternoon, the park can get busy. This means parking is a little more challenging. Go during the week and it's normally never an issue. There is a parking lot with spaces, and if those are filled, there are spots along the side of the driving loop around the picnic area.

Want to spend the weekend in Red River Gorge? There are campgrounds nearby, and there is permit backcountry camping, but most of those campsites are not on this trail and are off of the Swift Camp Creek Trail. You might see signs of camping next to the trail in places (and even at the base of the waterfall), but these locations are not allowed, so please respect this and remember to Leave No Trace always.

WHY IT'S A FAVORITE

"This is truly one of our favorite hikes. It might be short, but it is mighty! It really is one of the Red River Gorge hikes that should not be missed, especially with children. We love this trail because it's a beautiful trail that has a bit of everything. It has the old-growth forest, a waterfall, and the only true bridge arch in all of Red River Gorge. On hot, summer days, the creek is wonderful for kids to splash around in and play."
—KEIRA WICKLIFFE BERGER

INSIDER'S TIP

Earlier mornings during the week are the best times to go to avoid the weekend warriors. You might have it mostly to yourself during those times. You want to take this trail counterclockwise by starting at the trailhead sign and ending on the opposite side of the parking lot by the bathrooms.

NATIONAL PARK JUNKIES
MELODY BUCK FORSYTH

Melody Buck Forsyth was a late bloomer to hiking, discovering her passion for it when she was nearly 40. A mother of three with a fourth child on the way, she said she was sadly about to write off hiking and adventuring when she found out the daughter she was expecting had Down's syndrome. She just didn't think it would be possible to go to remote places with a child with a disability.

"I remember thinking, 'Okay, we're not going to be able to do much anymore, especially not outside, so we better get it out of our system.'" So while pregnant, she went on a family trip to Zion and hiked the Narrows and Emerald Pools, among other hikes. It was there that they saw a family with a severely disabled child in a wheelchair dining in a restaurant. The family was clearly there adventuring with their kiddo, which made Melody realize if they could do it, so could her family.

Early on, getting out with new baby Ruby was a little challenging because of food issues. She needed her breast milk thickened with additional substances to prevent her from choking on the milk. As Melody got comfortable with the feeding challenges and getting around with Ruby, she began longing to get on trail with her little one. When Ruby turned 10 months old, the doctor gave them the okay to use a frame carrier, and there was no looking back. Melody immediately started hiking with Ruby.

Babies with Down's syndrome don't move as much in vetro, so mothers will often say they might not have felt as strong a connection with the baby inside of them as they had with other children prebirth. For Melody, this was the case, but she said once Ruby was born, she felt that connection. And then when she started carrying her on trail, the bond grew even stronger. "From the first time I put her on, I was hooked. I feel like when I carry her, it helps show her that I've got her no matter what. I'll always be there for her," explains Melody.

When Ruby was a bit over a year, Melody got this idea that it would be incredible if she and her husband could make a goal of taking Ruby (and their other three children) to every national park across the US and share their stories through Instagram. Not only could it help other families who had children with disabilities, but it could also help those with multiple children, so they could see that if the Forsyths could do it with four kids, anyone could do it.

By January 2018, they had shared pictures of more than 29 national parks and monuments around the country, as well as many state parks and reserves in Utah. They also had gained quite a following on their Instagram. "People will often message and thank me for showing them you can get out there in spite of limitations you might think you have, whether it's with a troop of kids or a child with a disability."

What are Melody's tips for getting out there if you have any medical issues to consider with your child? "Talk to your doctors. Let them know what you want to do. Explain what your goals are, and they will give you good advice. Most of the doctors want kids to do as much as they can. Then take baby steps. Set goals, and see what you can and can't do. Some children will have a longer tolerance for being in a pack. Try different carriers and packs. The biggest thing is starting them when they are little. They just get used to it, and being in a carrier is the norm. They don't complain after the first few times. The younger you start them the better."

FAVORITE HIKE:
My absolute favorite hike is Little Cottonwood Trail near Salt Lake City. There is a beautiful river that runs along the trail and has several bridges. It's right next to tall mountains and Ruby loves to run on the trail. It's also a great place to snowshoe in the winter!

ACADIA NATIONAL PARK, MAINE,
WONDERLAND TRAIL

ACTIVITIES: Hiking, birding

LENGTH OF HIKE: 1.4 miles

OUT AND BACK OR LOOP: Out and back

DIFFICULTY OF TERRAIN: Easy

ELEVATION GAIN: No

PARKING FEE/PASS: $25

TOILETS: No

CHANGING TABLE: No

NURSING BENCHES: No

DOGS ALLOWED: No

BIKES/HORSES/MOTORS ON TRAIL: No

CELL RECEPTION: No

DRINKING WATER AVAILABLE: No

POTENTIAL CHILD OR BABY HAZARDS: Ocean

GEAR SUGGESTIONS: Hiking poles, water gear for summer

Follow a wide and flat trail just over 0.5 mile through a pine forest to the wild Atlantic coast. Unlike many of the other more popular trails at Acadia National Park, which follow close to cliffs or feature rung ladders up cliffsides, toddlers will be safe here. This trail is easy enough that even the newest of walkers can walk most of it on their own. The coastline is perfect for exploring among the scattered pink granite rock chunks along the shore. If you time your hike right for low tide, you can even search for sea life in the tide pools.

One of the great things about this trail is that it may be short, but the foliage and ocean make you feel like you are wandering off on a distant peninsula where few have been before to listen and watch as the waves crash along the shore. Acadia National Park is incredibly popular in the fall, but this hike is a source of solitude as it's located on the quieter side of the park.

Despite the crowds elsewhere in the park, fall is still the best time for a visit. The bright red blueberry bushes, the canopy of stunning yellows and reds above you, and the carpet of colorful fallen leaves beneath your hiking boots make this short hike feel like you're walking into a storybook. Late July would also be a fun time, when the blueberries are ripe for the picking! This is also a great hike on a rainy day as you'll have it all to yourself and, unlike a lot of the other trails in Acadia, you won't have to worry about the ground being slippery when wet since it's so flat.

WHY IT'S A FAVORITE

"Acadia National Park will always hold a very special place in our family's hearts for several reasons. One of our fondest memories from our week spent exploring the area was our short hike on the Wonderland Trail. What an aptly named hike for this magical little trail that gives visitors the sensation of being in their own world. This was such a

great hike for our newly walking toddler to explore, and though the rain drizzled down on us, I have nothing but warm memories from this hike."
—BOBBY AND MAURA MARKO

INSIDER'S TIP

If you're looking to explore more after completing the Wonderland Trail, stop by Bass Harbor Head Lighthouse a little over 1 mile west of the trailhead. A scenic view of the lighthouse is just a few steps down a staircase from the lighthouse parking lot.

ACADIA NATIONAL PARK, MAINE,
JORDAN POND WESTSIDE TRAIL

ACTIVITIES: Hiking, trail running

LENGTH OF HIKE: 3.5 miles

OUT AND BACK OR LOOP: Loop

DIFFICULTY OF TERRAIN: Easy

ELEVATION GAIN: 115 feet

PARKING FEE/PASS: $25

TOILETS: Yes

CHANGING TABLE: No

NURSING BENCHES: Yes

DOGS ALLOWED: Yes

BIKES/HORSES/MOTORS ON TRAIL: No

CELL RECEPTION: No

DRINKING WATER AVAILABLE: Yes

POTENTIAL CHILD OR BABY HAZARDS: Wooden bridges that go over streams, bigger boulders along the pond shoreline, boardwalk over some wetlands

GEAR SUGGESTIONS: Baby carrier if needed

While our inclination as hikers is to always go for the full hike, sometimes starting with a modification and seeing how far you get is the best way to go with toddlers and babies. The Jordan Pond Loop is a good trail to consider this. While this is an easy 3.5-mile loop that follows the path around the shores of the 150-foot-deep Jordan Pond, Hike it Baby contributor Anna Fedorowycz suggested not to feel like you have to start with the full loop but to consider exploring the open area between the south side of the pond and Jordan Pond House that has paved trails. This area leads to different carriage roads, the nature trail, and the west and east side of the full Jordan Pond loop. Her reasoning behind suggesting this one is the ease of the trail and the fact that it's not too close to the pond, so it's easy to let little kids run free. There are boardwalks and bridges along this trail, but nothing that should concern a parent.

"This is a good hike for toddlers because there's room for them to run around in the open area along the south side of the pond as well as walk the start of the trails in this area. The Jordan Pond House isn't too far from the start of the different pond trails, so you can get some food before or after a hike, as well as go to the bathroom and do a diaper change before or after," says Anna.

She also liked that this hike would be easy for parents who are new to having a baby in a carrier or are managing two young kiddos because it's not a strenuous hike. For those who have double strollers, there is ample room to navigate this trail, and while there is some uphill, it's totally doable.

When you arrive at the pond split, if you take the right and travel along the east side, there's a compact surface. The left will take you over a boardwalk on a bog that is trickier to navigate. Cell service isn't great, so keep this in mind as you head out. Nursing moms may not find many benches along the way, but there are plenty of rocks in the area to sit on. And at the south area of the pond, there are a few Adirondack chairs.

Overall, there is a good amount of various easy hiking options in this area that aren't too strenuous on parents, and toddlers can start out on the hike. But if you go the distance, expect to carry little ones in areas that are close to the pond shoreline. Also note the boardwalk areas were created to keep people off of any ecosystem preservation that is occurring, so be aware of that if you have eager little hikers who like to explore off trail.

WHY IT'S A FAVORITE

"I loved this adventure because I felt my son really connected with his surroundings. He had a bunch of open space to run around in at the front of the Jordan Pond House, and he loved playing in the dirt and small rocks that made up the paved path of the trail. I definitely felt that his adventurous spirit came out not only during this hike but during all of our adventures in Acadia National Park!" —ANNA FEDOROWYCZ

INSIDER'S TIP

Park at the Jordan Pond North parking lot for this trail. This is located around 3.7 miles south of the Cadillac Mountain Summit Road turnoff. There is also parking in the smaller Jordan Pond House parking lot. Keep in mind both of these hikes (and much of the park) will be crowded in the summer, so plan accordingly. You might opt to leave your car at the Hulls Cove Visitor Center and take the Island Explorer Bus.

WARD RESERVATION, MASSACHUSETTS, YELLOW LOOP AND BLUE TRAIL

ACTIVITIES: Hiking, biking, snowshoeing, birding

LENGTH OF HIKE(S): 1-mile, 2-mile, and 3-mile loops

OUT AND BACK OR LOOP: Loop

DIFFICULTY OF TERRAIN: Easy–moderate

ELEVATION GAIN: 420 feet

PARKING FEE/PASS: $5 for nonmembers

TOILETS: Yes

CHANGING TABLE: Unknown

NURSING BENCHES: Yes

DOGS ALLOWED: Yes, on leash

BIKES/HORSES/MOTORS ON TRAIL: Bikes allowed

CELL RECEPTION: Yes

DRINKING WATER AVAILABLE: No

POTENTIAL CHILD OR BABY HAZARDS: Mosquitoes and ticks

GEAR SUGGESTIONS: Insect repellent

Ward Reservation may be a small parcel of land with just 729 acres to explore 20 miles to the north of Boston, but it has been well developed and offers Bostonians a quick getaway into the hills. There are 13 miles of trails with well-marked beginner to intermediate paths to follow.

Starting from the main parking area on Prospect Road, follow the Yellow Loop trail toward the bog and then to the top of Holt Hill to enjoy the incredible view from the Solstice Stones. This is an excellent beginner trail for new hikers, and nursing moms will be happy to find benches to stop and rest on as they hike. Solstice Stones is a large group of granite stones that were installed by the Ward family, who owned the property, to mark the sunrise and sunset on the longest and shortest days of the year. The land is private but was donated to the Trustees of Reservations as a memorial for Nicholas Holt in 1940.

Look for wildflowers in the spring and early summer on this reserve. Pyrola, hepatica, starflower, lady's slipper, bright purple violets, and lush green ferns thrive in the area. Also look for bluebirds, butterflies, and herons.

If you are successful with the easy Yellow Loop, consider moving on to the Blue Trail to Elephant Rock. Keep an eye out for two different spots where you come out of the woods in a large clearing. You can move quickly through this area if you choose, but consider stopping and having a picnic or taking a rest here.

Journey on and hike to Holt Hill for about a 420-foot elevation, which is the highest point in Essex County. If you're a history buff, you might know about this hill because on June 17, 1775, the townspeople climbed to the top to watch the burning of Charlestown after the Battle of Bunker Hill during the Revolutionary War.

"I loved that we could be in the middle of the woods for a few hours and still see the city of Boston in some places," says Hike it Baby ambassador Melanie Lekaj. Melanie hiked this trail with five kids aged 1 to 5 years old and said all of the kids were able to walk most of the trail (other than the 1-year-old, who wasn't walking yet). "We carried one of the 3-year-olds for the last mile, but all of the kids really seemed to enjoy the entire hike. There were tons of places to stop and play, explore, and climb."

Expect mosquitoes on this hike because it's near a swampy bog, and deer ticks are common in the area. Also if you are off trail, keep an eye out for poison ivy. Trails are wide and even and flatten out at the top of the hill, making it perfect for little walkers.

WHY IT'S A FAVORITE

"This is an interesting hike that keeps changing. There are so many different things to see and climb. There are giant rocks and bridges and beautiful views. I saw a Scottish thistle the size of a baseball near Elephant Rock!" —MELANIE LEKAJ

INSIDER'S TIP

If you're there in the summer, it's just a short ride to Big Dipper Ice Cream in North Reading, MA. It's a great local way to end a wonderful hike!

BLUE RIDGE MOUNTAIN RANGE, MARYLAND, **SUNRISE TRAIL TO SUMMIT**

ACTIVITIES: Hiking

LENGTH OF HIKE: 4.5 miles

OUT AND BACK OR LOOP: Loop, by combining trails

DIFFICULTY OF TERRAIN: Moderate

ELEVATION GAIN: 382 feet

PARKING FEE/PASS: No

TOILETS: Yes

CHANGING TABLE: No

NURSING BENCHES: No

DOGS ALLOWED: Yes

BIKES/HORSES/MOTORS ON TRAIL: No

CELL RECEPTION: Yes

DRINKING WATER AVAILABLE: No

POTENTIAL CHILD OR BABY HAZARDS: The Sunrise Trail is steep, so you should carry little ones or hold their hands on the way up if they are climbing with you. It's very rocky in parts, but fun for excited little climbers.

GEAR SUGGESTIONS: Baby carrier, water

Located on Sugarloaf Mountain in Maryland, this mountain has a series of looping trails that are well marked, easy to navigate, and has a short climb if you want to reach the peak. It's totally doable with families. "We hiked it when the kids were younger and then went back with tween and teens. The older kids loved all the rocks to climb on, and our toddler loved chasing his older siblings all over, jumping in the Onya

Baby soft carrier as needed when his little legs got tired," said Angela Malson, whose family of seven lives in a veggie-fueled RV and hikes around the U.S. Follow them at ecowomb.com..

The ascent to the summit is difficult enough to make it exciting; and when you reach the top, the views are amazing. There are plenty of fun rocks to climb on or hide under, and at the top of the mountain, the land opens up and there is plenty of space to find your own spot to take in the views or have a snack or picnic lunch. The descent includes an awesome set of stairs around some cool giant rocks that are well known as a hot spot for local rock climbers. As you continue to make your way down the mountain, the trail flattens out and widens and is great for little runners who want to roam and explore. Even as you round the base of the mountain and get back to the parking lot, there is a great viewing spot that overlooks the east side of the mountain and across the valley with some more fun rocks to explore. Take a break here at the picnic table and toilets.

Expect to see a few whitetailed deer on and around the mountain. Other wildlife includes flying squirrels, red foxes, Eastern cottontails, and raccoons. Overhead, look for forest birds like the great horned owl, pileated woodpecker, wild turkey, and red-shouldered hawk. During the spring and fall, many migratory species of songbirds can be heard singing in the trees. Be aware that this is the habitat of the timber rattlesnake and the copperhead, so make sure your little ones are aware of this as they climb around rocks.

This is a great family hike for all ages. It's a little more adventurous for those who are avid hikers and want a bit of a challenge, but you could also utilize the other trails if the one straight to the summit is too steep. "This area has such a great combination of trails to meet the needs of all family members, and since our kids are such climbers, they love the climb to the summit. Yes, even the toddler," said Angela.

WHY IT'S A FAVORITE

"Sugarloaf Mountain holds special memories for us as a family. It was the first mountain we hiked together when our older boys (now teens) were little. It was also the first mountain I hiked as a mama with a baby in a sling and a toddler in tow. I remember looking at the trail and thinking, "Just go for it!" And, after I made it up that first steep part to the summit, I jumped for joy. I was so pumped I did it with my babies! I was then hooked on hiking for life! Sugarloaf Mountain will always hold special family memories as it was

the mountain that first got us hooked on hiking!" —ANGELA MALSON

INSIDER'S TIP

Park in the East View parking area so you can get great views right away. It's a fun picnic spot, with toilets if you need them, and rocks to climb on while you get set for the trail. Then, you can take the Sunrise Trail to get right to the summit (0.25 mile) and get a great workout right from the start. Once you reach the top, you can spread out (to the right there are a few big rocks that you can climb up, under, and around, which is loads of fun for the kids) and take in the amazing views! And then, by combining trails and taking the loop trail back around the mountain, you have a more relaxing descent through the forest. There are loads of trails, but this by far is our favorite combination.

SWALLOW FALLS STATE PARK, MARYLAND, **CANYON LOOP TRAIL**

ACTIVITIES: Hiking, swimming, water play

LENGTH OF HIKE: 1.5 miles

OUT AND BACK OR LOOP: Loop

DIFFICULTY OF TERRAIN: Easy

ELEVATION GAIN: 354 feet

PARKING FEE/PASS: $9

TOILETS: Yes

CHANGING TABLE: No

NURSING BENCHES: Yes

DOGS ALLOWED: No

BIKES/HORSES/MOTORS ON TRAIL: No

CELL RECEPTION: Spotty

DRINKING WATER AVAILABLE: No

POTENTIAL CHILD OR BABY HAZARDS:
Rocky, exposed roots, waterfalls/rapids, ticks

GEAR SUGGESTIONS: Poles could be helpful for the rocky trail but definitely not necessary

One of the most beautiful spots to view waterfalls in Maryland, this is a great place to cool off in the summer, when the nearby cities get hot and the kids need to play. There are rocks to climb, water to splash in, and scenic views of cascading waterfalls. The trail follows along the Youghiogheny River and has four scenic waterfalls to offer. The largest is the 53-foot Muddy Creek Falls.

Wander through tall hemlocks where you might see deer, squirrels, chipmunks, birds, wild rhododendron, and mountain laurel. If you keep your eyes open, you might spot fossils as you meander down the trail. There are also black bears in western Maryland, but Jessica says no one in her family has seen one in person in the 60+ years they've been visiting. Still, it's best to make sure you look for them (this is a great opportunity to sing "We're Going on a Bear Hunt" to keep your kids moving forward!). There are park rangers, but little to no organized events, so expect to explore this park on your own. There are many opportunities to wander down to the water and cool down.

One interesting thing you might notice is a field of trees with tops that have snapped off. This is the result of Superstorm Sandy in the fall of 2013, which toppled and broke the tops off many trees. Efforts are underway to restore the scenic beauty of the area, but natural regeneration is being allowed in much of the area, which means it still has a bit of a beat-up appearance.

Another thing to note is that there is no cell service in the park. This is nice for the family because it's rare to have that time when you can just focus on your kids without the outside world interrupting. Also, the park offers an all-access trail to Muddy Creek Falls, which means children with walkers or wheelchairs and elderly can participate in the hike.

Once you're finished with your hike, there is an ice cream truck right at the parking lot! Their hours vary, but ice cream after a day in the woods is always welcome.

The nearby Deep Creek Lake has tons of family events, activities, places to stay, etc., but this area is much more touristy, which is why we are encouraging you to spend your time at Swallow Falls.

If you want to make a weekend adventure of this, consider staying at New Germany State Park, about a half hour away. The closest major city to this park is Morgantown, WV, about an hour away, but there are lots of smaller cities within that distance worth visiting. Cumberland, MD, is a favorite within an hour for the many historic spots to visit, including the C&O Canal National Historic Park, the Great Allegheny Passage Trail, and the Western Maryland Scenic Railroad.

WHY IT'S A FAVORITE

"The mountains of Garrett County, MD, have been a favorite getaway spot for our family for four generations. We go to get away from the hustle of everyday life and to gain a bit of adventure and a lot of peace and quiet. Swallow Falls and its Canyon Loop Trail has three waterfalls to view and has so many hiking options that it seems to grow with our family. We've had years where we stuck to the handicapped-accessible boardwalk for a waterfall view when we had an out-of-control toddler, but we've also had years we

could climb out on the rocks for some swimming in the rapids. We've stepped right at the edge of the top of the Muddy Creek Waterfall, the highest in the state of Maryland, and we've spent hours just inspecting the tree bark in the forest. The scenery is beautiful, but the park has done a wonderful job ensuring the trail is accessible and safe for all while maintaining a 'backwoods' experience." —JESSICA HUMAN

INSIDER'S TIP
Traveling with a four-legged friend? No dogs are allowed inside the park, but for a dog-friendly version or a different view of the river, park at the small gravel parking lot before the one-lane bridge (GPS 39.494283, -79.416224). This trail is just outside the park, so dogs are allowed.

THE ADVENTUROUS FAMILY

BOBBY AND MAURA MARKO

When their son Jack had his first-ever tantrum on a super-popular trail in Squamish, British Columbia, Bobby and Maura Marko stood there totally shell-shocked and unsure of what to do as their son let out ear-piercing shrieks and screams.

"We had no clue what to do, and people were beginning to stare. Looking back now as a mother to two emotional children, it's funny how embarrassed I was," says Maura. Like most parents discover, tantrums on the trail are a common occurrence and one of the big changes even the most outdoorsy parents can't prevent as their little ones age up.

Maura continues, "When our kids are at their worst, when tantrums and tears are being thrown at me almost nonstop, we go outside. Both of our children thrive when in the outdoors. It is there that they can truly be themselves. Scream as loud as they want, climb, run, jump, observe, explore, do whatever it is they need to do to find their calm."

The outdoors has been a big part of Bobby and Maura's lives since meeting at a Boy Scout camp in Wisconsin where they worked. From their early days together, every vacation they took included an outdoor element, whether that be day hiking in the French Alps or backpacking the 120-mile Kerry Way in Ireland. When their son, Jack, was born, they knew they wanted to continue an adventurous lifestyle. They took Jack on his first hike at 2 weeks old; and when Rowan joined the family 2 years later, she beat out her brother by hiking on Mom and Dad when she was just 11 days old.

Maura first joined Hike it Baby in Seattle for a hike, then moved to Minnesota a month later and formed a branch there. One of the things that Maura has found so powerful about her community is how open people are able to be with one another on trail. "I spoke for the first time about a devastating miscarriage while on a Hike it Baby hike. I took unsteady and scared steps out after that loss when I was newly pregnant with Rowan on a Hike it Baby hike," she says. "My community has deeply impacted me as I've struggled with postpartum depression and anxiety. I know the power of the outdoors and the strength that comes from the community around you."

To encourage outdoors for their family even more, they took it one step further in 2017 by embarking on a 3-week journey through the remote Boundary Waters Canoe Area Wilderness (BWCA). First, they biked in and then went paddling, followed by a week of camping and day hiking along the picturesque Gunflint Trail. They documented their trip and have shared it with both the Hike it Baby community and on a Facebook group they started called Backpacking with Babies.

"It is our hope that our children will grow up thinking that hiking, camping, canoeing, and backpacking are normal family vacations," explains Maura. "Backpacking is an extremely difficult endeavor with young babies and toddlers along. Failure is a very natural part of the experience."

Maura continues, "We were planning a 6-day, 65-mile trek through some of the wildest terrain in the state of Minnesota. It was by far the loftiest goal we had ever set as a family. We made it approximately 2.5 miles in before turning around and heading back to the car. We car camped and day hiked instead and had an amazing time doing so!"

FAVORITE TRAIL:
Many have the perception that Minnesota is a flat, frozen wasteland of 'You Betcha' but it is, in fact, an incredibly scenic state with breathtaking scenery. Our favorite is an almost 8 mile trail called Bean and Bear Lakes Loop along the Superior Hiking Trail that offers incredible vistas over an undulating landscape that are some of our state's finest

10 ESSENTIALS FOR
BACKPACKING WITH BABIES

1. **READING MATERIAL.** Just because you're in the backcountry doesn't mean kiddos won't want a story before bed or some form of camp entertainment should inclement weather hit and you find yourself trapped in a tiny tent with a tiny tyrant. I like to bring along kids magazines like Rick Jr. or Highlights as a great, disposable form of reading material and entertainment.

2. **FOOD.** How many trips have we had go terribly awry because we didn't bring enough snacks or forgot the formula at home? Seriously, the importance of food and snacks on a trip cannot be emphasized enough. Make sure to pack extra formula, as additional and/or larger bottles should be offered to prevent dehydration. If you have a nursing mother along in your crew, bringing additional snacks along for her is equally important, as her body is working some serious overtime.

3. **WATER FILTRATION.** Simply bringing along a lot of water isn't going to cut it when exploring the backcountry. Having the appropriate water filtration system along is vitally important for survival. We love our Platypus Gravity Works Filter.

4. **PACK TOWEL.** Bringing along a small pack towel is a smart idea should you run low on wipes and need an alternative means of taking care of a soiled baby. Should a massive blowout occur that requires a quick bath in a nearby water source, a way to get your babe dry and warm quickly will be vital.

5. **CHILDREN'S BENADRYL.** I'm always nervous that my kids will encounter something they turn out to be allergic to when in the backcountry. This hasn't ever happened, but I did ask my doctor for the appropriate dos-

ages of liquid Benadryl for each child should something come up when we are far from medical assistance.

6. **FIRST-AID TRAINING.** When heading into the backcountry, it's always smart to have additional first-aid training. The importance of this seems astronomically higher when venturing with young children and babies. They tend to be clumsier and are more prone to small-scale injuries. The National Outdoor Leadership School (NOLS) offers a wonderful Wilderness First Aid course that greatly helped me, as a parent, feel more comfortable in emergency-type situations when out in the woods with my babies.

7. **LAYERS.** No matter the forecast, it is incredibly important to be prepared for any weather event. Pack warm layers and raingear for every member of a crew.

8. **DIAPERS.** I would hate to have a trip cut short because we ran out of diapers. In the weeks leading up to a trek, keep a running tally of the number of diapers used in a day. Average that number, then add one bonus diaper per day. This has worked out perfectly for us when planning treks.

9. **EMERGENCY BEACON.** If you envision a trip with your kids that takes you into very remote locations, it may be a good idea to invest in or rent an emergency beacon. Not only can this help to ease your own concerns about safety, it can also assist in calming nervous family members. We used a Garmin InReach during a recent trek into the deep wilderness and were able to text daily with grandparents to assure them that we were all safe.

10. **SPECIAL TREATS.** Having a secret, favorite incentive to get your kids that last little way on a trail can mean the difference between a fun last few miles or complete, whiney misery. We like Dum Dums or Smarties for warmer weather as they won't melt but have also found the Nutella snack packs, M&Ms, and s'mores can all keep tiny legs moving and motivated.

Maura Marko is a badass mom of two who has carried up to 50 pounds of gear (and baby!) while backpacking. Here are her top tips on what to carry. Want to follow the Markos further on their adventures? Check out their blog (www.wefoundadventure.com) and join their Facebook group (www.facebook.com/groups/backpackingwithbabiesandkids/).

HIKING SAFETY
DURING HUNTING SEASON

Fall is my absolute favorite time of year to be out on the trails here in Michigan; the bugs are gone, the air is crisp and cool, and who can forget the beautiful fall foliage? But as the last leaves are falling, another group of people may start frequenting some of your favorite hiking spots—sportsmen! Hunting is a very popular outdoor activity here in Michigan. In fact, in northern lower Michigan and the Upper Peninsula, many schools will close for "Opening Day," and, yes, my family does actually own a hunting cabin "Up North." Whether you agree with hunting or not, we share the same spaces with sportsmen, and it's important to stay aware and safe during the weeks of hunting season.

Here some tips to keep you and your family safe on the trails during this time of year:

1. **KNOW WHEN HUNTING SEASON IS.** Your state agency (www.wheretohunt.org) will have details regarding dates for deer season, as well as waterfowl and other small game. There are also different seasons for bow hunting and firearms. Additionally, a few states don't allow hunting on Sundays, which may be another option for safe hiking.

2. **KNOW IF HUNTING IS ALLOWED IN THE PARK YOU INTEND TO HIKE IN.** If you are hiking in an area that allows hunting, please be sure to indicate this in your hike description. This gives families the ability to decide if this hike is for them and to dress accordingly.

3. **BE AWARE OF SIGNAGE.** Some states don't allow hunting near trails, while there are no rules in other states. Occasionally, hiking trails will also be closed to nonhunters during the season. Signs will indicate what you need to know!

4. **WEAR BRIGHTLY COLORED CLOTHING.** Orange and red are good colors because they will stand out. White, black, brown, and other earth tones are obvious no-no's.

5. **DON'T FORGET YOUR FURBABIES!** Put a brightly colored vest or sweater on Fido. It's not just a fashion statement—dogs can easily be mistaken for a woodland critter.

6. **STAY ON THE TRAILS.** Sportsmen tend to stray away from heavily used trails. This is not the time to go geocaching or bushwhacking, because hunters will be looking for movement in more wooded areas.

7. **MAKE NOISE.** Hike it Baby is a super-safe group to hike with during hunting season for obvious reasons. Children chattering and babies babbling will probably scare the deer—and hunters—off.

8. **AVOID HIKING AT DAWN AND DUSK.** These are prime hunting times because it is when deer are most active. It is also more dangerous because hunters may have a more difficult time making out colors and shapes due to the lack of light.

9. **HEAD FOR HIGH COUNTRY.** There are places that are great for hiking but not so great for hunters. You won't find many animals at high altitudes, but there are plenty of beautiful views!

10. **CHOOSE A HIKE IN A NATIONAL PARK OR CITY PARK.** The majority of these types of parks do not allow hunting at all and are, obviously, the safest options.

Each state has its own rules and regulations for hunting. Even if you are not a hunter, using hunting websites can be extremely helpful in finding out where the hunters will be and at which seasons! The US Forest Service also has some helpful tips on how to hunt and hike safely during the hunting season. Hunters and hikers can coexist as long as we take the proper precautions. A little extra planning will help ensure a safe day for everyone out on the trails!

Annie Fortunato lives in Ypsilanti, Michigan, with her husband, Mike, their two children, and two furbabies. She is a former environmental educator and currently the Hike it Baby Ann Arbor branch ambassador.

TAHQUAMENON FALLS STATE PARK, MICHIGAN, **LOWER FALLS TRAIL**

ACTIVITIES: Hiking, snowshoeing

LENGTH OF HIKE: 1 mile

OUT AND BACK OR LOOP: Out and back

DIFFICULTY OF TERRAIN: Easy–moderate, paved

ELEVATION GAIN: Minimal

PARKING FEE/PASS: $11 Michigan parks fee /$9 daily for nonresidents

TOILETS: Yes

CHANGING TABLE: No

NURSING BENCHES: Yes

DOGS ALLOWED: Yes, leashed. Dogs may not be left unattended.

BIKES/HORSES/MOTORS ON TRAIL: No

CELL RECEPTION: Spotty

DRINKING WATER AVAILABLE: Yes

POTENTIAL CHILD OR BABY HAZARDS: Mosquitoes, black flies, horseflies

GEAR SUGGESTIONS: Snowshoes in the winter

What toddler doesn't love a good waterfall? Located in the middle of 50,000 acres, there are two falls to view in this park. Upper Falls is more talked about as it's one of the largest falls east of the Mississippi. Originally home to the Chippewa Indians, who camped, farmed, fished, and trapped along its banks, this park has 25 miles of trails for visitors to explore.

We chose the Lower Falls to mention here (although both Lower and Upper are easy to visit) because of the ease of the hike for little legs. Lower Tahquamenon Falls is located 4 miles east of the Upper Falls along M-123. There's a paved walkway and a 0.5-mile walk through a thick forest, which ends up at a viewing platform. You'll appreciate the mist from the falls on a warm summer day; and if you keep walking, you'll find access to the river so you can splash a bit.

When you are there, you might hear people refer to the falls as "Root Beer Falls" because of the brown color and frothy appearance. The brown, interestingly, is not from minerals in the water or pounding of mud at the bottom, but from tannin leached from the cedars, spruces, and hemlocks in the swamps drained by the river.

Mosquitoes are very present on this trail much of the year (not in the dead of winter, of course), so you will want to keep yourself thoroughly coated with bug spray. If camping, consider getting a bug lamp of sorts, like a Thermacell, to ward bugs off your campsite. It's also good to have a net tent over the kitchen and eating areas. Spring is the least buggy time if you want to get the sunnier weather.

There is a boardwalk surrounding the falls, which is fairly safe, but make sure to keep an eye on your little walkers. The trail from Hemlock to Lower Falls isn't overtly technical, but there are some small drops, so watch little ones around this area. Hiking boots are suggested on this trail as well, since there is some uneven ground, but it is doable in runners. As for sun, the hike is very wooded, so there's not a ton of exposure.

Keep your eyes open for the moose that live in the park, the occasional black bears, coyotes, otters, deer, foxes, porcupines, beavers, and minks to name a few of the animals living in the park. Birds are aplenty with bald eagles high above, spruce grouse, sharp-tailed grouse, pileated woodpeckers, and a variety of waterfowl and songbirds.

WHY IT'S A FAVORITE

"This was a great hike to take from our campground to the Lower Falls area. This was the perfect little adventure as the terrain wasn't perfect but decent for little walkers and we had a fun destination to visit the falls. The Lower Falls itself was spectacular, and we had fun walking along the boardwalk to view the two sections."
—JESSICA FEATHERSTONE

INSIDER'S TIP

Visit this spot in winter, and you can borrow a free pair of snowshoes or take part in a guided afternoon snowshoe hike. There is a 1-mile lantern-lit snowshoe trail and cross-country ski trails to enjoy in the winter. Viewing a waterfall in the winter is a whole different experience from the summer splash. Warm up by the bonfire, and complete your visit with a trip to the Tahquamenon Brewery and Pub, which is open all winter.

SLEEPING BEAR SAND DUNES, MICHIGAN, **DUNE CLIMB**

ACTIVITIES: Hiking, sandboarding, swimming, kayaking, beachcombing

LENGTH OF HIKES: 260 feet to the top

OUT AND BACK OR LOOP: Out and back

DIFFICULTY OF TERRAIN: Moderate

ELEVATION GAIN: 110 feet

PARKING FEE/PASS: $15 for a week

TOILETS: Yes

CHANGING TABLE: Yes

NURSING BENCHES: Yes, picnic area

DOGS ALLOWED: No

BIKES/HORSES/MOTORS ON TRAIL: No

CELL RECEPTION: Yes

DRINKING WATER AVAILABLE: Yes

POTENTIAL CHILD OR BABY HAZARDS: Sand can get hot.

GEAR SUGGESTIONS: Lots of water, sun hats, sunscreen

Sleeping Bear Sand Dune National Lakeshore is a unique place in the great state of Michigan. Where else can you find 400-foot sand dunes that descend to a sparkling freshwater lake? Nowhere! These are the largest freshwater sand dunes in the world. There are also many opportunities for outdoor activities, from hiking and camping to kayaking and canoeing. Take a bike ride on the Sleeping Bear Heritage Trail, which goes right past the Dune Climb and is a perfect biking path through the park. Or if you have a baby and don't mind carrying some distance, you can add to your day by hiking the 3.5 miles to Lake Michigan, where there are sugar white sand beaches that are spectacular.

No need to head all that way to the beach if you just feel like taking a little climb. The view at the top of the Dune Climb cannot be beat, with Glen Lake on one side and Lake Michigan on the other. It should be on every little kid's bucket list to climb the 450-foot dune and run down! This is especially fun for older kids (ages 4 and up).

Interested in the wildlife of this area? You might see a bald eagle scanning the grounds for chipmunks and little sparrow-like birds called plovers flying about. Also roaming this park are white-tailed deer, red foxes, porcupines, gray and fox squirrels, bats, and raccoons as well. There's a visitor center located at the base of the Dune Climb with information and special activities as well, so stop in if you want more info.

Not sure when to visit? Each time of year is special in its own way. Hike it Baby Ann Arbor Branch ambassador Annie Maxine enjoys going in early October to see the changing colors of the leaves. "It makes the landscape pop! But going in summer is fun because you can take advantage of the area beaches," Annie says.

Keep in mind that this is a very popular tourist destination in Michigan. The parking lot is nearly always packed on a summer weekend. The sand can also get very hot. There is not much shade, so be sure to put on sunscreen and consider carrying an umbrella if you are fair skinned. The heat will reflect up from the sand as well, so sunglasses are strongly suggested, even for babies.

WHY IT'S A FAVORITE

"The sand is fun for the children to play in! It feels like you are in a giant sandbox, so definitely bring sand toys and toy trucks for extra fun for the littles. If they aren't interested in hiking, you can just head into the sand and play for hours." —ANNIE MAXINE

INSIDER'S TIP

Make a weekend of it and camp at DH Day Campground nearby. It's a no-reservation campground with a beautiful and not-so-busy beach. Also drive along M-22 and enjoy the rolling landscape of the wineries while your little one naps in the back! This is also prime cherry area, so be sure to stop and pick cherries as you pass the farms.

SUPERIOR NATIONAL FOREST, MINNESOTA, **OBERG MOUNTAIN LOOP**

ACTIVITIES: Hiking, birding

LENGTH OF HIKE: 2.3 miles

OUT AND BACK OR LOOP: Loop

DIFFICULTY OF TERRAIN: Moderate

ELEVATION GAIN: 230 feet

PARKING FEE/PASS: No

TOILETS: Yes

CHANGING TABLE: No

NURSING BENCHES: Yes

DOGS ALLOWED: Yes

BIKES/HORSES/MOTORS ON TRAIL: No

CELL RECEPTION: No

DRINKING WATER AVAILABLE: No

POTENTIAL CHILD OR BABY HAZARDS: Roots and rocks, cliffs, steep drop-offs, ticks

GEAR SUGGESTIONS: Bug spray, hiking ploes

The Oberg Mountain Loop is one of the best day hike sections of the 310-mile-long Superior Hiking Trail. This trail begins from the trailhead with a short 0.5-mile hike where you climb about 200 feet along a couple of switchbacks. Mud can be a common concern along this trail so, thankfully, boardwalks have been put into place in an attempt to keep hikers' boots a little less muddy.

At the top of the climb is a bench for you to rest or nurse if needed, but from there on out, it's an easy 1.3-mile loop around the summit of Oberg Mountain. The trail features a series of eight overlooks, but it feels like you are seeing infinitely more as this hike provides almost constant breathtaking, sweeping views of one of the most scenic spots in the state of Minnesota. Highlights include Lake Superior, views across the rolling hills of Superior National Forest, and Oberg Lake nestled in the forest below you.

Be cautious with young children on this hike as there is some steeper/more cliff-like terrain. You will want to keep small children close or in a carrier during those sections, but there is plenty of room to stay safely away from danger along the trail.

Fall is definitely the best time to visit this trail despite the crowds. In late September, watch the Minnesota DNR's Fall Foliage map on their website to time your visit for peak color. You can't go wrong with a summer visit either as the bold green of the trees contrasts strongly against the pure blue of Lake Superior as you watch from above Oberg Mountain. In the winter, bring your snowshoes and you're guaranteed solitude.

WHY IT'S A FAVORITE

"After we moved back to Minnesota with our 7-month-old son, we knew we wanted to introduce him to the beauty of Minnesota's North Shore. Oberg Mountain was the perfect place for him, as we were able to capture almost all of the elements that make this area so spectacular in a single, short hike perfect for a morning or afternoon. The only thing that's missing is a waterfall!"
—BOBBY AND MAURA MARKO

INSIDER'S TIP

If you're looking for more hiking in the same area, a second day hike option begins from the same trailhead. From the west end of the parking lot, you can hike the 3.2-mile LeVeaux Loop, which is also along the Superior Hiking Trail.

RICHARD T. ANDERSON CONSERVATORY, MINNESOTA, **RICHARD T. ANDERSON TRAIL**

ACTIVITIES: Hiking, birding

LENGTH OF HIKE: 1.2 miles

OUT AND BACK OR LOOP: Loop

DIFFICULTY OF TERRAIN: Easy

ELEVATION GAIN: 100 feet

PARKING FEE/PASS: No

TOILETS: Yes

CHANGING TABLE: No

NURSING BENCHES: Yes

DOGS ALLOWED: Yes

BIKES/HORSES/MOTORS ON TRAIL: No

CELL RECEPTION: Yes

DRINKING WATER AVAILABLE: Yes

POTENTIAL CHILD OR BABY HAZARDS: Roots and rocks

GEAR SUGGESTIONS: Bug spray, water

Finding somewhere close to Minneapolis where you can feel like you're away from it all can be difficult. Richard T. Anderson Conservatory, a hidden gem only 20 minutes from Minneapolis, grants you the feeling of being in the wilderness without spending hours in the car. The trails wander up and around hills, along prairie-laden ridges, through a big woods forest, and into sedge meadows, providing an amazing amount of diversity in a short hike.

This area's protection was truly a community effort. It was saved from development by a bond referendum of local citizens in 1994 and named after a leader of preservation of parks in the city of Eden Prairie. As you share this place with your family, it's nice to remember the impact each of us has on protecting the wild places in our communities.

The 1.2-mile Overlook Trail takes you through some of the best parts of this park while keeping the distance little-leg friendly. Toddlers will love climbing up the initial hill to another hill overlooking the trees with views across the Minnesota River and Minnesota Valley National Wildlife Refuge. The hill is just steep enough and full of sandy big steps and tree roots to keep kids engaged while not being overly exhausting. The hills throughout the trail are also small enough that they aren't too hard if you're pregnant or new to hiking. Plus, there is usually a bench or picnic table to be found at the top of each hill to provide a great spot for snacks or to feed a baby. Scattered throughout the park are several small creek crossings that provide great splashing opportunities.

As you follow the trail, keep a lookout for seven interpretive signs that describe the ecosystems you're wandering through. This way you can describe to your kids the plants and animals around you without having to be an expert botanist or birder. Be on the lookout for cedar waxwings, nighthawks, and if you're really lucky, a great horned owl.

Like a lot of hikes in Minnesota, fall is the best time of year to visit for the bright reds and oranges of the sugar maples. The cooler temps also mean the mosquitoes are nowhere to be found! On those hot and humid summer days, it's best to pick somewhere else to hike as the mosquitoes are known to be overwhelming. In the winter, bring Yaktrax or Microspikes to help with traction; the trail can become ice covered. Springtime is mud time, and the hills can be tricky, so it's best to let the trail dry out a bit.

WHY IT'S A FAVORITE

"This is our family's go-to hike when we want to hit the trails quickly and we're short on time. It's rarely crowded, and the interconnected trail system gives our toddler son the opportunity to feel in control as we let him pick which way he wants to go at each trail intersection. We know eventually the trails will lead us back to our car no matter which direction he chooses!" —BOBBY MARKO

INSIDER'S TIP

Be on the lookout for the natural spring flowing year-round near the parking lot for a geology lesson. It's one of two natural springs maintained and tested regularly by the city for water quality. If you have time after your hike, check out the nearby small town of Chaska, MN. Highlights include getting a milkshake at Tommy's Malt Shop and playing at the amazing beach, playground, and splash pad at City Square Park.

SUPERIOR NATIONAL FOREST, MINNESOTA, **BOUNDARY WATERS CANOE AREA WILDERNESS**

ACTIVITIES: Hiking, paddling, birding

LENGTH OF HIKE: 7 miles (or a smaller 3-mile out and back trail)

OUT AND BACK OR LOOP: Out and back

DIFFICULTY OF TERRAIN: Moderate

ELEVATION GAIN: Minimal

PARKING FEE/PASS: Only for overnight use; $16/adult permit fee, $8.50/child

TOILETS: No

CHANGING TABLE: No

NURSING BENCHES: No

DOGS ALLOWED: Yes

BIKES/HORSES/MOTORS ON TRAIL: No

CELL RECEPTION: No

DRINKING WATER AVAILABLE: No

POTENTIAL CHILD OR BABY HAZARDS: Ticks, poison ivy, stinging nettles, water, roots and rocks

GEAR SUGGESTIONS: Bug spray, water shoes

I f you are a fan of water and lakes, the Boundary Waters Canoe Area Wilderness (BWCA) contains over 1 million acres of area to explore. With about 1,175 lakes that vary in size from 10 acres to 10,000 acres and streams aplenty, this unique landscape offers visitors the opportunity to paddle great distances easily. This fact makes it one of the most visited wilderness areas in the US and for good reason! Canoeing is a great way to get outside or camp as a family because you can bring more equipment with you to keep everyone comfortable. For example, you can use special cooler portage packs to bring fresh, refrigerated food along for meals.

The Markos are big fans of alternative travel, which is why they wanted to share this adventure with Hike it Baby families. This avid outdoor-loving family of four who has thoroughly explored Minnesota even did a 3-week bike, hike, and canoe trip in 2017 in this area. They have two favorite trails in the BWCA that they suggest for families: Eagle Mountain and Magnetic Rock.

Eagle Mountain is a 7-mile out and back hike that takes you to the highest point in Minnesota. Ironically, there are no views from the summit as it's hidden in the forest, says Bobby. "But just before the summit, you are rewarded with a gorgeous overlook of the lakes of the Boundary Waters."

What makes the BWCA unique is that families can canoe in, go distances even with young children, set up camp, and then venture on shorter, more little-legs-friendly outings. Unlike backpacking, canoeing allows you to be a little more luxurious with what you bring because you don't necessarily have to haul much on your back if you find a good camp close to water. This makes adventures much easier when a family has a toddler or two.

Magnetic Rock is located near the end of the historic Gunflint Trail (which is a road not a trail). Magnetic Rock is a 1.5-mile out and back hike to a 30-foot monolith glacial erratic sticking straight out of the ground! Bring your compass to test out how magnetic it is. Your kids will love climbing all over the rock, and if you bring magnets, the kids can hold them to the rock and watch them stick.

June through September is the best time to visit and provides the best weather. The Marko family prefers July and August for warmer temps and fewer bugs, but the bugs will always be there. Look out for ticks, mosquitoes, and biting gnats. Also note that there are cliffs in the area.

For wildlife, expect to see the whole food chain in action from black bears and maybe gray wolves, to red foxes, lynx, minks, and deer. In the water, there are otters, frogs, beavers, and fish like lake trout, walleye, Northern pike, small-mouth bass, perch, and crappie. Overhead, look for bald eagles, loons, and peregrine falcons in the day and bats at night. If you're lucky, you may spot a moose.

Interested in a little history about how such a large expanse of land and water could become a park? There is evidence of man being in the area since as early as 500 B.C., first with the Sioux then the Ojibwe tribes. Europeans arrived around the late 1600s, bringing in the fur trade. But the area still remained fairly undeveloped until the late 1800s, when mining and then logging arrived. In 1902, Minnesota's forest commissioner, Christopher C. Andrews, managed to get 500,000 acres of the area set aside and protected from logging, which eventually became the Superior National Forest.

WHY IT'S A FAVORITE

"When we moved to Minnesota from Washington State, we longed for a wilderness experience like we had found in the Cascades. We found our answer in the BWCA. It's a great place for families, too, as you can make your trips as easy or as hard as you want based on how deep into the wilderness you want to go. The BWCA isn't just for canoeing, either. There are plenty of hiking opportunities as well." —BOBBY MARKO

INSIDER'S TIP

If you want to try canoeing, there's no need to buy new gear. There are a lot of outfitters in the area that can provide you with everything you need. They can even plan your entire trip (including food!). The Markos love Sawbill Outfitters and Sawtooth Outfitters. Also, don't miss Northern Expressions for great ice cream in Ely.

ELEPHANT ROCKS STATE PARK, MISSOURI, **BRAILLE TRAIL**

ACTIVITIES: Hiking, rock climbing, bouldering, fishing

LENGTH OF HIKE: 1 mile

OUT AND BACK OR LOOP: Loop

DIFFICULTY OF TERRAIN: Easy

ELEVATION GAIN: No

PARKING FEE/PASS: No

TOILETS: Yes

CHANGING TABLE: No

NURSING BENCHES: Yes

DOGS ALLOWED: Yes

BIKES/HORSES/MOTORS ON TRAIL: No

CELL RECEPTION: Yes

DRINKING WATER AVAILABLE: No

POTENTIAL CHILD OR BABY HAZARDS: Ticks, rock exploration risks

GEAR SUGGESTIONS: Water, bouldering equipment, climbing equipment during climbing season (must check in with ranger's office prior to climbing with equipment)

The Braille Trail was built in 1981 as an interpretive trail for the blind and is one of around 100 trails in the country established for families with visual disabilities. When you visit, you can see why this would be an amazing tactile experience for someone who can't see, because the coarse granite boulders are easy to walk along and guide you through the trail.

The park was named Elephant Rocks because of the 1.5 million-year-old massive round granite boulders that definitely resemble elephants. The largest has been aptly named Dumbo Rock and weighs in at 680 tons. This trail will give your little one a wonderful opportunity to try scaling rocks and hilarious photo moments with the "look how strong I am! I'm lifting this boulder" image possibility.

There's a quarry pond that was mined in the late 1800s that's a great place to stop and check out birds. This is also a popular climbing spot, so in the summer when things are in full swing, it's fun because the kids can watch climbers as they easily negotiate their way up the rocks.

Feel free to visit any time as this is a year-round park. It might be a bit slippery in winter, so keep this in mind.

Why Hike it Baby mom Jamie Sperry loves this location is because there are tons of "secret" areas for kids to explore, from the tunnels and rock formations to an old quarry trail engine house ruin on the nearby Engine House Ruin Trail (1.5 miles) that you can also visit in the same day.

The only hazards to be aware of in this park are ticks and the quarry wall into the pond. Otherwise, this is a great park to let the little ones run wild. Most of the trail is shady, and there are great places to stop and rest for a new nursing mom. There are also 30 picnic spots, so plan to bring lunch and make a day of it.

WHY IT'S A FAVORITE

"Expansive area of granite boulders located next to an old quarry offering hiking, rock exploration, bouldering, rock climbing, and fishing opportunities. Elephant Rocks State Park is a great getaway from St. Louis or perfect to tack onto a weekend/weeklong getaway in southeast Missouri. It's an easy hike to the top of the granite boulders for a fantastic view of the St. Francois Mountains. Let the kids lead and see what "secret" boulder-enclosed areas they find!" —JAMIE SPERRY

INSIDER'S TIP

Make sure to stop at the quarry and look for snakes, lizards, turtles, frogs, and tadpoles. It's busy here in the summer, so don't expect to be alone on this adventure, but consider early morning and late afternoon if you would like to avoid the crowds.

PRAIRIE STATE PARK, MISSOURI, **GAYFEATHER TRAIL**

ACTIVITIES: Hiking, animal viewing

LENGTH OF HIKE: 1.5 miles

OUT AND BACK OR LOOP: Out and back

DIFFICULTY OF TERRAIN: Easy

ELEVATION GAIN: 45 feet

PARKING FEE/PASS: No

TOILETS: Yes

CHANGING TABLE: No

NURSING BENCHES: Yes

DOGS ALLOWED: No

BIKES/HORSES/MOTORS ON TRAIL: No

CELL RECEPTION: Spotty

DRINKING WATER AVAILABLE: Yes

POTENTIAL CHILD OR BABY HAZARDS: Ticks, herd animals

GEAR SUGGESTIONS: Water

This adventure is just under 2 hours from Kansas City, making it a perfect day excursion. Stop in the park center to ask the rangers what trail to catch the best glimpse of the bison (and grab an awesome free bison sticker!). Bring your binoculars and watch out for the bison patties on trail!

Explore the beauty and tranquility of the last remaining tallgrass, a species of prairie grass that was cut down by settlers farming in the 1800s. The grass has been replanted in this park, and it offers the best example of tallgrass in Missouri; however, this is still only 1 percent of what it used to be in the state. Some things to be aware of as you venture through are ticks, herd animals, and note that some trails go through electric livestock fencing. You can almost be guaranteed to see bison, elk, and coyotes.

There are a number of easy trails in this park to enjoy from the Gayfeather, which is 1.5 miles to the Coyote Trail, where you just might come across a den of baby coyotes sleeping. We thought we would mention the Gayfeather Trail as a great starting point, but consider checking with the rangers upon arrival for the trail with the best bison viewing.

Call ahead to make sure the herds are out and roaming. Spring and fall are personal favorites for Jamie Sperry, who says this is also when you get the gorgeous weather. Prairie State Park hosts a monthly bison hike if you want a ranger's lead the first time you go. Check out their calendar for child-centered activities as well. The park rangers will know the best trails to venture on to see the herds, so make sure to stop and ask. This will also get you free park stickers.

WHY IT'S A FAVORITE

"Is there anything better than getting 300 feet away from your child's favorite animal on a quiet trail in a beautiful prairie?" —JAMIE SPERRY

INSIDER'S TIP

If you have a good little walker, consider doing the Coyote Trail (3.2 miles) over the Gayfeather, and get a good walk through the park. There are a number of easy trails in this park, but the biggest thrill for your little one will be bison viewing.

GLACIER NATIONAL PARK, MONTANA,
MCDONALD CREEK TRAIL

ACTIVITIES: Hiking, splashing, animal viewing, fishing

LENGTH OF HIKE: 5 miles

OUT AND BACK OR LOOP: Out and back

DIFFICULTY OF TERRAIN: Easy

ELEVATION GAIN: 282 feet

PARKING FEE/PASS: Park entrance fee

TOILETS: Yes

CHANGING TABLE: No

NURSING BENCHES: No

DOGS ALLOWED: No

BIKES/HORSES/MOTORS ON TRAIL: Horseback riding

CELL RECEPTION: Spotty

DRINKING WATER AVAILABLE: No

POTENTIAL CHILD OR BABY HAZARDS: Bears

GEAR SUGGESTIONS: Hiking poles, bear spray

Glacier is absolutely beautiful with scenic mountain moments around every bend. The sheer size of the mountains and vast array of trails, creeks, and alpine lakes make it seem like a lot to cover, but if you select your trails wisely, you can cover a lot of ground with baby in tow.

The Malson family's favorites in the park included: McDonald Creek, Avalanche Lake, Rocky Point, and St. Mary/Virginia Falls. They also suggested Hidden Lake at Logan's

Pass, where you can see wildlife, wildflowers, melting snow patches, and you can walk through an alpine meadow.

"We saw Columbian ground squirrels, a marmot, and mountains up close. We also saw bighorn sheep along the Going-to-the-Sun Road," reports mama-bear Angela Malson.

Glacier National Park and the surrounding area have been home to humans for as far back as 10,000 years. In more recent history, the region was home to the Blackfeet, Bit-terroot Salish, Upper Pend D'Orielle, and Kootenai tribes, who used the plentiful land-scape for hunting, fishing, ceremonies, and gathering plants.

The landscape feels sacred, thanks to mountains jutting up toward the sky and big animals roaming freely in spite of the area's popularity on the national park circuit. The Blackfeet call this land "Backbone of the World" and the "shining mountains," which is not surprising considering the park is over a million acres and has around 150 peaks over 8,000 feet tall.

No matter where you go in Glacier, you can't go wrong for capturing beautiful scenic mountain moments wherever you look, but you may find that this park can feel limited for little ones because it's so vast. If you pick your trails wisely, you'll still experience all the vastness Glacier has to offer without feeling limited with new little walkers.

The Malsons suggest that you plan your trails ahead of time if you want to make sure your little walkers can enjoy the journey. One easy trail they really enjoy is McDonald Creek. With many spots along the way to stop and nurse, change a diaper, or for adven-turous toddlers and kids to climb rocks and trees, this trail is a winner for the Eco-Womb family. "We love that it has so many waterfalls and rushing waters for the baby to sleep to. And if you go all the way to the end of the trail, you move inland away from the creek and through a beautifully secluded and peaceful forest," says Angela.

There are several waterfalls along the way and overlooks to view the creek as it winds through the mountains. The bridge is a gathering spot, as there are several big rocks to hang out on and have a picnic, as well as a giant fallen tree that the kids will enjoy climb-ing on. The less crowded spots are just past the bridge as the trail continues up along the creek. A bit farther and you can even access a small beach-like area that is nice and secluded, a perfect place for lunch, swimming, and skipping rocks.

"You can see horses along the way, too," says Angela. This trail also intersects a horse trail, so that is another fun thing for little ones to look out for. Keep your eyes open for fish in the creek and chipmunks along the trail. Other wildlife you can expect to see regularly are deer, hawks, and signs of beavers and bears. "We swear we even heard a bear while in the forest part of the trail, grunting and tree snapping," says Angela.

Most of the trail is level along the creek with lots of fun things to look at and explore, trees to climb, rocks to skip, and benches for resting. As for the crowds? Parking is at

the trailhead, down by the north part of the lake. There is plenty of parking whether late July or early August. There is also parking by the bridge in the middle of the trail, so that may get full as the bridge is also a viewpoint for people who don't hike the trail. Consider parking at the trailhead and hiking the whole trail for the best experience. You can also walk down to the north part of the lake from the trailhead and actually walk out toward the lake, which is fun for the kids.

WHY IT'S A FAVORITE

"I loved McDonald Creek best because there were so many waterfalls, and the trail winds along the creek at the upper end of Lake McDonald. All of the running water helped get Baby Izzy to sleep. We also found a great rock to change him at the viewpoint. We hiked that one twice and walked along the lake, too. Great views of the surrounding mountains. It was beautiful!" —ANGELA MALSON

INSIDER'S TIP

To avoid the crowds, definitely go past the bridge where the trail narrows. It goes through a beautiful forest and has more secluded spots to access the creek.

GALLATIN NATIONAL FOREST, MONTANA,
PINE CREEK FALLS

ACTIVITIES: Hiking, waterfalls, fishing, camping

LENGTH OF HIKE: 2.5 miles

OUT AND BACK OR LOOP: Out and back

DIFFICULTY OF TERRAIN: Moderate

ELEVATION GAIN: 460 feet at waterfall

PARKING FEE/PASS: No

TOILETS: Yes

CHANGING TABLE: No

NURSING BENCHES: No

DOGS ALLOWED: Yes

BIKES/HORSES/MOTORS ON TRAIL: No

CELL RECEPTION: No

DRINKING WATER AVAILABLE: No

POTENTIAL CHILD OR BABY HAZARDS: Giardia reported in the water, unsafe to drink.

GEAR SUGGESTIONS: Drinking water

A beautiful mountain hike just south of Livingston, Pine Creek Falls is a family favorite because there are beautiful views of all that the Absaroka-Beartooth Wilderness has to offer. The second highest mountain in Montana, Black Mountain at 10,941 feet can be seen off in the distance, adding to the "big" feeling this trail gives you.

Expect a little bit of climbing but nothing a 4-year-old can't do. It's dog friendly and fairly well trafficked most of the day. If you plan to hike alone first thing in the morning in the summer, consider bear spray.

The trail extends a lot farther to a popular but very hard hike called Pine Creek Lake, if you want to go beyond the 2.5 miles. The waterfall and narrow footbridge to cross the creek below the falls are fun for little ones to experience. Stop to play in the pool of water, and play with the small rocks that have been swept down by the falls.

Be sure to bring your own drinking water, as giardia, the microscopic parasite that causes diarrhea and requires antibiotics to cure, is ever present in this area. Also there are bears and other large animals, so making noise can alert animals to your presence and encourage them to move on before you arrive on the trail.

Remember this trail is near Yellowstone National Park, which makes it a popular destination for those visiting the park, so expect to see a lot of people on the trail in the warmer months. This is a trail you can snowshoe and hike in the winter as well, so if you are looking for more solitude, consider hiking it then. You can also hike out on various side trails from this main trail to get a little more mileage in.

Want to make it an overnighter? Check out the 25 single camping sites at Pine Creek Campground. They are first-come, first-served, plus there is a reservation group site. There is water at the campground, and the campground is handicapped accessible.

WHY IT'S A FAVORITE

"This is a favorite hike for our family, both just as a day trip and also when we camp at Pine Creek Falls Campground. While it does get crowded in the middle of the summer, it's nice in the spring and fall, too. The trail is a bit rocky and has some elevation gain, but in general, it is really kid friendly. It's shaded well in the summer, and the views of the falls are pretty at the end. The trail is also dog friendly." —AMELIA MAYER

INSIDER'S TIP

The road to the trailhead is located a short drive through the camping area. There are several parking areas (which become full on a busy summer day) and the trailhead is clearly marked.

LATE BLOOMERS
ALANA AND CURT DIMMICK

Alana Dimmick and her husband, Curt, have the trails deep in their blood. Both were park rangers when they met one summer at Old Faithful in Yellowstone National Park (he was law enforcement and she was interpretation). Since then, they have both been rangers, and their kids have grown up living in Yellowstone, the Everglades, and Great Basin National Parks. Curt was also a ranger in Big Bend, Grand Canyon, Coronado National Memorial, Great Smoky Mountains, and Crater Lake and is now at Mount Rainier National Park in Washington. Alana says, "We've had national parks in our backyard, literally, their entire lives."

Surprisingly, neither of the Dimmicks discovered their passion for trails until they were adults. But when they found it—and each other—there was true love, and these beautiful iconic places are the only homes their children have known since birth.

Curt is currently the chief park ranger at Mount Rainier, and Alana leads regular hikes for her branch in Eatonville, WA. She explains when you live and work in national parks that are often remote, hiking obviously becomes an automatic favorite thing to do on days off for her family. Shortly after they moved to the area for Curt's job, Alana found Hike it Baby, which helped her and the kids find a community that shared their passion for the trails. "I love that Hike it Baby has the power to make newcomers to an area feel more welcome."

As "late bloomers" to hiking, the Dimmicks have been intentional about exposing their children to getting out on trail as early as possible. "I had to recover from C-sections each time I had a child, so I didn't hike with any of my three until they were about 2 months old," she says. "I took it easy even then, but those first hikes always felt amazing. It was like I was getting part of myself back after those first all-consuming months with a new baby."

Currently, the Dimmicks hike at least once a week near their home at the base of Mount Rainier (and during Hike it Baby 30 months, they try to get out even more). What they are most excited about is how much their children know about the natural world at such young ages (at the time of this book, all three of their kids were under 9 years old).

"They appreciate beauty, get excited about wildlife and natural wonders, and can educate anyone on park rules and why they exist. They have told us they want to be park rangers or live in certain national parks when they grow up. I also love how comfortable they are outdoors, whether hiking or camping. There's no fear of the dark, of insects, of the woods, or getting wet or dirty! I think it makes them more adventurous."

FAVORITE TRAIL(S): CRATER LAKE NATIONAL PARK, OREGON
The Dimmick family's all-time favorite hiking trails are in Crater Lake National Park, and if they have to pick just two, they suggest Annie Creek Trail and the Castle Crest Wildflower Garden.

10 WAYS TO TURN YOUR TODDLER
INTO A TRAIL STEWARD

WHAT PARENT DOESN'T WANT THEIR LITTLE ONE to turn into an amazing trail steward who protects all of the beautiful parks and trails around us? It all starts with teaching them from an early age. Here are 10 tips that Hike it Baby families use to help little ones learn about their role in land protection. You can also learn more about trail respect or consider taking a course through Leave No Trace (www.lnt.org).

1. Take kids hiking as early as you can! (If they grow up loving nature, they will become adults who love and protect it.)

2. Model the behavior yourself, and keep it simple for their new little learning minds.

3. Introduce them to "Trail Heroes," such as park rangers, trail association volunteers, people practicing Leave No Trace and their work on the trail.

4. Read books that feature positive examples of respectful trail behavior, our national parks, and historic "trail heroes." Some great reads are S is for S'mores or Curious George Goes Camping. Look for familiar kids' characters interacting with nature positively.

5. Encourage them to be mindful on the trail (encourage them to stop and use their senses like listening for birds and frogs and footsteps on rocky paths so that they are aware of how other people and animals are using the trail).

6. Give them age-appropriate "jobs" and encourage teamwork while preparing for adventures on the trail. They can clear paths of branches that have fallen, take a picture of a damaged bridge to alert the park, and pick up a can someone carelessly left on trail.

7. Help children identify nature around them at home, on the street, and on trails. You don't have to be deep in a forest to offer reminders that nature is all around. On a windy day with leaves and branches hitting the house, talk about wind and then show your child a fallen branch from the storm the next day to remind them of how nature is always present.

8. Take indoor activities outdoors as often as possible. If your child likes to read, have them find a spot outside to read! If they like to sing, have them sing to your garden. It will help the plants grow. Even trucks and teddy bears can play in the forest. Maybe

have a bin of "forest toys" your kiddo can pick from so you don't have to worry about a toy taking a mud bath.

9. Include your children in your outdoor activity planning. Kids love maps. Show them maps early on. Draw maps of your local parks and trails, and have your children help talk about stumps they stop at and creeks they cross. Draw a spider you once saw on that trail or a slug that crossed your path.

10. When your child does the wrong thing (like littering or stomping on bugs), calmly and gently discuss it with them. Let them know that Mommy or Daddy gets sad when the flowers get smashed because that means they will stop growing and not be there for the next friend to enjoy. The goal is to educate, not punish, as your child gets more in touch with nature.

BOTTLE FEEDING ON TRAIL
ALWAYS BE PREPARED

For the Gawron family, there was no question that their newborn daughter was going to be a bottle baby. Carrie was a med student when they got pregnant, which meant she was in the thick of her program when their child was born. She went back to work when Olive was 10 weeks old, leaving Joe as the full-time stay-at-home daddy.

Joe, an active outdoorsman, knew that he would want to take Olive on adventures, so he needed to perfect the art of bottle feeding from early on. "Everything I did caused me to carry a lot of weight, but it was worth it," says Joe.

For shorter hikes, he would carry a thermos of hot water (he liked the wide-mouthed soup-style containers that could keep water warm for 10 hours). To heat milk, he would drop frozen or fresh milk pouches into the container for less than a minute and then pour into a bottle.

On longer hikes or hot days, he would bring two bottles so he didn't have to worry about rinsing out rancid milk residue or curds. He also suggested adding the milk to his bag frozen regardless of the distance he was hiking because it could be on him for 3 to 4 hours without him worrying about it spoiling. "Early on, I always planned where I would stop and get comfortable and set up to nurse. I wasn't rushing to get somewhere and then having a screaming baby. It's always better to have a fed, content baby on a hike."

Why not fill the bottle before you head out and pack it? Joe explains that if you're carrying breast milk, it will slosh on a hike and "churn" too much, thickening like butter, especially with small amounts. This is why bags are the preferred carrying system over bottles. Think about storing the bags in small amounts, just a few ounces, so it's easy to add one bag to a bottle and use it all up before cracking into another.

For overnight or really long walks away from home (same with flying solo on airplanes), use packit freezable lunch bags over small bags. This can carry 5 or 6 feedings' worth of frozen milk, and it will keep for a day or so if packed in a small portable cooler or ice pouch.

If you are hiking in the hot summer, you will want to start with frozen milk bags; and if you will be using the milk soon, you can thaw them out quickly in a pocket. Or purchase a small envelope-sized freezer bag. These are easy to find online and cost is minimal. They will help keep fresh milk cool until you are ready to use and warm up. In the hot summer, you can put the milk up against your skin to warm it up and melt it as you hike. If it's not too cold in the winter, you can do the same for a preliminary warming.

Getting out there with a bottle is totally doable and will give you a lot more freedom to hit the trails. Whether breast milk or formula in the bottle, keeping the milk fresh, bottles clean, and baby fed is key to a happier hike.

Joe Gawron has been a part of Hike it Baby since 2014. He served a term on the Board of Directors and has helped encourage more Dads to solo hike and camp with their young children and babies.

HIKING FROM TODDLER-DOM
TO KID-LANDIA

THE FIRST TIME I STEPPED ONTO THE TRAIL with Mason, I was terrified. I was scared of bugs, sun exposure, and smothering my newborn in an awkwardly foreign carrier. I thought I'd be so tired that I would faint or that Mason would cry the whole way, and I'd panic and not know how to quiet him.

Well, we've both survived babyhood and toddler-dom, and Mason is now 4 years old. Technically, he's no longer a toddler, but he's definitely still my baby! What I have learned over the years from Mason and from watching friends with kids is that every age and stage comes with challenges, especially when you are heading out into the unknown. The best way to manage getting on trails with kids is just to commit and then do it. Once you're out there, you'll be glad you made the effort.

With that in mind, here are the top 10 things I have learned that have helped me transition with Mason from baby to toddler to kid:

1. **EXPECT THE UNEXPECTED AND DON'T PANIC.** You might forget critical things like wipes and then, of course, have a poopy blowout. It's okay because there was a time when baby wipes didn't exist. Find a bathroom and clean up with paper towels, or find that balled-up T-shirt in your trunk and you are set.

2. **TODDLERS LOVE TO SIT DOWN JUST AS YOU GET GOING.** It never fails. Go with it. Be ready to shift your big plans and find a really cool slug or spider and make that your new focus. The harder you try to push your kid forward, the more likely he will resist.

3. **DON'T BE AFRAID TO ASK FOR HELP.** Need a carrier strap buckled or unbuckled? Stop a stranger on the trail. Most people are more than happy to stop and help a parent with a kid.

4. **WHEN A TANTRUM STARTS, BE READY FOR IT.** I carry secret weapons like suckers or other bribery tools that I only pull out in extreme emergencies. Try to work through the tantrum, and if it's clearly not going to stop and you are trying to move forward, it just might be lollipop time.

5. **IF YOU DON'T LIKE A KID'S BEHAVIOR, CHANGE TACTICS.** Think about your normal reaction (maybe a raised voice or a threat to go home) and try something new. Start singing a song that your little one likes and see if that breaks the pattern.

6. **DON'T HAVE YOUR HEART SET ON ONE SPECIFIC TRAIL.** Think of options so if a meltdown is coming, you can cut it short and try something easier. I know it's not fair, but remember that you are going to be telling your child that life isn't fair for the next 15 years, so suck it up yourself this time.

7. **GO WITH OTHERS WHEN YOU CAN.** Kids keep entertained and on trail. Even if you are not a group hiker normally, look for at least one friend to go with or a nature hike that a park is putting on. A park ranger can really keep a 4-year-old occupied and interested on trail.

8. **BRING LUNCH FOR THE END OF THE HIKE.** Even if you have plans to go to lunch or make it home, travel with an extra lunch. There's nothing worse than a hangry toddler and a hike that just went on longer than you expected.

9. **LOOK FOR TRAILS WITH INTERESTING FEATURES LIKE A BRIDGE OR AN OLD, ABANDONED, RUN-DOWN CABIN.** Turn this place into a magical story about a troll under a bridge or a witch's castle. This will help little kids remember the trail and have a destination that is more tangible than just the end of a trail or a loop that takes them back to a parking lot.

10. **REMIND YOURSELF IT'S ABOUT THE JOURNEY, NOT THE DESTINATION IF YOU ARE FRUSTRATED.** Be prepared for one of those days when you will literally make it a block past the parking lot and then that's it. Take the time to learn more about the trail, read signs, look around at what other features are on the trail. Get better with your smartphone camera, and shoot pictures of your shoes. Don't spend all of your time on your phone, but those slow-as-molasses hikes are part of it all. Remember that there will be a time when your kids won't want to hang out with you at all, so cherish these moments with your little ones.

PLATTE RIVER STATE PARK, NEBRASKA, WATERFALL TRAIL

ACTIVITIES: Hiking, paddling, fishing, camping

LENGTH OF HIKE: 5.1 miles

OUT AND BACK OR LOOP: Loop

DIFFICULTY OF TERRAIN: Moderate

ELEVATION GAIN: 200 feet

PARKING FEE/PASS: Yes

TOILETS: Yes

CHANGING TABLE: No

NURSING BENCHES: Yes

DOGS ALLOWED: Yes

BIKES/HORSES/MOTORS ON TRAIL: Bikes and horses

CELL RECEPTION: Spotty

DRINKING WATER AVAILABLE: Summer only

POTENTIAL CHILD OR BABY HAZARDS: Trails are moderately difficult in some places

GEAR SUGGESTIONS: Towels or wet wipes if walking in the waterfall, baby carrier, water, bug spray, not ideal for strollers

Just 20 minutes from Omaha or Lincoln, this hidden gem of a park is a mere 519 forested acres, but packs it all in from archery and skeet shooting ranges, to paddleboats, a lookout tower, trails for the adventurous, and camping if you just don't feel like going home at the end of the day.

While locals report the trails aren't very well marked, you might want to consider lightweight pants and bug spray to battle nettles and mosquitoes if you plan to adventure deep. If you stay on the main trail to the mini waterfall, you should be able to find it easily enough; however, there are a lot of offshoots to be aware of that may lead you astray. Most of the trails are relatively easy and can be hiked by toddlers with the occasional steep spot. And since the park isn't too large, you should be able to keep fairly on course. For wildlife, don't expect too much beyond birds and bunnies.

This park came about through a merge between a Girl Scout camp and two other properties to become a state park. Remnants of the camp's past are still here in the 21 vintage cabins that are now rented out to the general public. The park has numerous amenities beyond cabins, such as teepees to rent and paddleboats. For $8 per half hour, you should have ample time to paddle around and explore.

Is your kiddo a climber? There are not one but two lookout towers for kids to check out. Climb 85 feet in the air and get to the top of the Lincoln Journal Tour and take in the panoramic view of the Platte River. Don't worry; they are completely child safe and have metal fencing that requires serious Spiderman skills to scale.

In 2016, the state dedicated part of a $34 million recreation budget to this park, so expect to see new elements added to the area, including more mountain bike trails, a climbing wall, a zip line, and better access for canoes and kayaks.

Also keep in mind if you get through this park and want to hike a bit more, just 7 miles down the road is Eugene T. Mahoney State Park and Schramm Park State Recreation Area for more toddler-friendly, easy hikes.

WHY IT'S A FAVORITE

"I loved this park! A lot of our 'trails' here are paved walkways through smaller parks—very urban trails. They're great for strollers and beginners, but getting out in dirt and nature is really what I love and want to share with my boys. My husband is a lifelong Boy Scout, and he loved it as well. It was beautiful scenery, easy enough for my 3-year-old to traverse, but still had enough tricky spots like large rocks and steep hills to keep it interesting." —CHRISTINE STEWART

INSIDER'S TIP

Do your kiddos love trains? Well then, you are in luck because a train track runs alongside the riverbank and is still in use. "Being that close to a 'real' train was maybe the highlight of our littles' adventure in the woods," says Christina Stewart.

FONTENELLE FOREST, NEBRASKA,
FONTENELLE FOREST TRAILS

ACTIVITIES: Hiking, nature play area, wildlife rescue

LENGTH OF HIKE: 2.3 miles

OUT AND BACK OR LOOP: Loop

DIFFICULTY OF TERRAIN: Easy

ELEVATION GAIN: 308 feet

PARKING FEE/PASS: Membership or day rate to enter

TOILETS: Yes

CHANGING TABLE: Yes

NURSING BENCHES: Yes

DOGS ALLOWED: No

BIKES/HORSES/MOTORS ON TRAIL: No

CELL RECEPTION: Good

DRINKING WATER AVAILABLE: Yes

GEAR SUGGESTIONS: Strollers (on the boardwalk), baby carrier on trails, bug spray, sunscreen, water bottle, snacks

With 2,000 acres of land and 26 miles of trails, Fontenelle Forest is an excellent choice for families with little ones if you are in the Omaha area. Starting at the Nature Center, you can do an easy walk on the Fontenelle Forest Trail for a leisurely couple of miles. If you want to go for a harder hike, you can venture off onto other trails, but we suggest this one loop if you want your little one to walk it all.

At the Nature Center, you'll find a message board in the main building with all the insects and birds spotted on the trail. There are also informational boards along the boardwalk trail explaining more about the wildlife in the area. Expect to see deer, rabbits, and squirrels. There's also a children's play area outdoors and one indoors in the lower level of the Nature Center main building.

This is an easy hike to do at a child-led pace, but you can also bring a stroller on trail. There are benches all along the boardwalk portion that are great for breaks and nursing. If you venture farther to the forest trails, plan to carry kids.

Nature is plentiful in this area. There are wild turkeys, bald eagles, deer, turtles, and raccoons to name some of the wildlife. Fontenelle Forest is also home to a raptor recovery program that takes in 400 to 500 birds a year from around Nebraska and Iowa. The Raptor Woodland Refuge is open daily from 8 a.m. to 5 p.m. Look for a fun suspension bridge for kids to climb around on here.

WHY IT'S A FAVORITE

"Fontenelle Forest is one of our favorite hiking destinations. Depending on what level of difficulty we are up to that day, we can walk a couple miles around the boardwalk with the stroller or we can go "off road" on the miles of trails that wind through the woods. At the beginning of the trail, there is an outdoor children's play area, which, among other things, includes a water feature, several tree houses, a digging area, and wooden xylophones. Should the weather not cooperate, there is an indoor play area in the lower level of the main building. Fontenelle is also a raptor rescue, and they have a dedicated area where you can learn about the birds." —JESSICA KADAVY

INSIDER'S TIP

The best time of year is early spring or late fall, but there is good shade cover on the trails, so it can be hiked year-round. If you are visiting on a rainy day, the boardwalk can be slick, so walk slowly.

RED ROCK NATIONAL CONSERVATION AREA, NEVADA, **LOST CREEK CANYON**

ACTIVITIES: Hiking, petroglyphs

LENGTH OF HIKE: 0.75 mile

OUT AND BACK OR LOOP: Loop

DIFFICULTY OF TERRAIN: Easy

ELEVATION GAIN: 165 feet

PARKING FEE/PASS: $7/car

TOILETS: Yes

CHANGING TABLE: No

NURSING BENCHES: No

DOGS ALLOWED: Yes

BIKES/HORSES/MOTORS ON TRAIL: No

CELL RECEPTION: No

DRINKING WATER AVAILABLE: No

POTENTIAL CHILD OR BABY HAZARDS:
Uneven terrain, heat, sun

GEAR SUGGESTIONS: Water, sunscreen, hat

Warning: This hike can be very crowded, especially in the hotter part of the year. The reason is the shade, a major commodity in this area in the summer months. It's also an easy hike for the whole family, which means little walkers are included. Add in the pool at the base of the waterfall, which can easily be overrun with people. It's still a nice addition and a hike that's a win for all. At the edge of the waterfall, try to sit to the left or up above the pool for a little quiet zone away from everyone.

"We like to go in the spring. The waterfall is running heavier, and we found frogs in the pool!" says Jennifer Calvaresi. She says spring means you are generally by yourself and the pool is frozen. Part of the trail hosts signs with information about the trail and the area.

Another reason this is a popular trail, especially for kids, is that there's a self-guided interpretive trail with a brochure showing where the nine interpretive signs are for a little lesson on the terrain and trail. Good for all ages, this trail explains the desert and all of the features that can be found in the hot, dry landscape from ancient petroglyphs, to animals hiding beneath rocks and underground, to a hidden seasonal waterfall (December through April) that can be found in the canyon.

Look for prickly pear cacti as you meander down the trail, and keep an eye out for another trail off this one called Willow Springs Loop. This trail runs along the base of a rock wall and will add another mile on the trail, taking you by more petroglyphs. Interested in how petroglyphs are so permanent? According to signs in this park, the paints were made by mixing powdered minerals, clay, or charcoal with plant juice, saliva, or egg whites.

Trail maps are only available at the Visitor Center not at the trailhead. Also, get your potty break in here. There is a vault toilet in the parking area, however, there's no water. Much of the hike is exposed and away from shade, so bring hats and sunscreen.

The main road in the park is a big one-way loop, so if you see something interesting, pull off and take a look. Parking areas at the popular trailheads, especially ones near the entrance, fill up quickly in the peak season.

WHY IT'S A FAVORITE

"My kids love this hike! It is short enough for the baby to walk a little or have me carry him. They know this trail well since we go so often, and I feel comfortable with them running ahead a bit. It is a little hot during the summer, but the canyon provides nice shade and a slightly cooler temperature. This is a good spring hike to find frogs in the desert." —JENNIFER CALVARESI

INSIDER'S TIP

This trail is easy to navigate but not well marked, so pay attention as you wander around. There are offshoot trails. If the hike starts to climb, then you are off trail. There are some cliffy, ledge hikes in the area so be aware if you start adventuring beyond this trail. Bring lots of water!

FRANCONIA NOTCH STATE PARK, NEW HAMPSHIRE, **FLUME GORGE**

ACTIVITIES: Hiking, kayaking, swimming

LENGTH OF HIKE: 1.8 miles

OUT AND BACK OR LOOP: Lollipop

DIFFICULTY OF TERRAIN: Moderate

ELEVATION GAIN: 515 feet

PARKING FEE/PASS: Adults 13+: $16; ages 6–12: $13; under 5: free

TOILETS: Yes

CHANGING TABLE: No

NURSING BENCHES: No

DOGS ALLOWED: No

BIKES/HORSES/MOTORS ON TRAIL: No

CELL RECEPTION: Yes

DRINKING WATER AVAILABLE: Yes

POTENTIAL CHILD OR BABY HAZARDS: Wooden boardwalk has openings young children could fall through

GEAR SUGGESTIONS: Backpack with snacks, camera

Located at the bottom of Liberty Mountain, Flume Gorge has a fun historical story. It was discovered in 1808 by 93-year-old "Aunt" Jess Guernsey while fishing. Apparently her family didn't believe her discovery and took some convincing before they went to explore this mythical waterfall-filled fall canyon. These days it's hardly a secret and actually has a cost associated with hiking it, but those who visit will tell you it's totally worth the fee. The area is meticulously maintained with boardwalks through-out the hike, allowing visitors to get up close and personal with the waterfalls.

While the walkways make this an easy "hike," there are stairs, which means you can expect there will be some carrying. But the Earley family said they loved how the stairs took them deeper and deeper into the chasm and that it was worth the carrying. You'll love this hike because of the spectacular waterfalls along with gorgeous granite rock formations shooting up 70 to 90 feet that can be seen throughout the area.

As you head out, one of the things you will see right away is a giant glacial boulder that's great for a photo op. Apparently this boulder was once suspended overhead in the gorge and wedged between rocks, but in a huge flood in 1883, it was swept away and came to rest in its current spot. Don't worry; like most "don't miss this" things in Flume Gorge, this is clearly marked.

Another fun thing kids will love to run through is the bright, barn red Flume Covered Bridge. From this point, the Flume Path also goes past Boulder Cabin and Table Rock, an area of granite that was worn smooth by the river.

We highly recommend this hike for new mothers because of the shorter distance and great benches for relaxing and nursing by the Visitor Center. Best time to visit is May through October, with peak times obviously being in the middle of the summer. Note that you could end up in a long line to purchase tickets, too, so be ready to entertain your little one.

Also, this is a seasonal hike, so make sure you check online before visiting to see if it's open during the tail ends of the season. You can turn this into an overnight by grabbing a campsite at nearby Franconia State Park.

WHY IT'S A FAVORITE

"We loved that walking on the board-walk allowed us to walk over water-falls and also inspect the flowers, mosses, and ferns that grew on the rocks." —DAPHNE EARLEY

INSIDER'S TIP

Make sure to catch the 20-minute film showcasing Franconia Notch State Park in the Visitor Center. Also, if you're a photographer, plan on bringing a tripod to get some amaz-ing long exposures of the waterfall.

CHEESEQUAKE STATE PARK, NEW JERSEY, **GREEN LOOP**

ACTIVITIES: Hiking, swimming, sledding

LENGTH OF HIKE: 3.2 miles

OUT AND BACK OR LOOP: Loop

DIFFICULTY OF TERRAIN: Moderate

ELEVATION GAIN: 315 feet

PARKING FEE/PASS: Park fee/car Memorial Day–Labor Day

TOILETS: Seasonal near campsites, available in the Interpretive Center, a little way along the trail, 7 days a week in the summer and Wed–Sun during the off-season.

CHANGING TABLE: No

NURSING BENCHES: Yes

DOGS ALLOWED: Yes, on leash

BIKES/HORSES/MOTORS ON TRAIL: No. *There is a small section of the trail toward the end where vehicles can pass through.

CELL RECEPTION: Yes

DRINKING WATER AVAILABLE: Yes

POTENTIAL CHILD OR BABY HAZARDS: Stairs, water

GEAR SUGGESTIONS: Carrier, water, bug spray

Cheesequake State Park offers something for everyone. With six different trail options, the local Hike it Baby ambassadors say they have been able to offer everything from adult-paced carrier hikes to toddler-led hikes in this park, making it a perfect well-rounded park, no matter your ability level or experience on trails.

For example, if you are still not comfortable with a carrier, there is an option to do a stroller hike, which allows families who are new to hiking with a baby to get out there on a trail hike.

Opened in 1940, this 1,200-acre parcel of land boasts all kinds of activities from freshwater and saltwater marshes and a tidal estuary. The park sits on the edge of the Lower New York Bay, and Cheesequake Creek runs through it, making it a great location for fishing, boating, paddling, and swimming; and, of course, there are miles of trails. In the winter, you can come back for sledding as well.

The different trail options that are Hike it Baby–friendly range from 1.5 to 3.5 miles, and all work well for toddlers. There's also one trail designated for mountain biking, so no need to worry about toddlers who run ahead getting in the way of a biker.

If you have a toddler who is not quite ready to hike or is just having a rough day, start off in the Nature Center just off the Green/Red/Blue Trail. The center offers live displays of animals that can be found throughout the park, murals of the park's ecosystems, and exhibits depicting the park's local history. There are also several bird houses located outside the Nature Center.

Our suggested trail to start with in the park is the Green Trail, which is typically hiked at an adult pace, so there is not much meandering, but older toddlers with some hiking experience can easily hike the whole thing. Newer walkers will be up and down.

Look for exposed root systems on the sandy parts of the trails, and expect to find several fallen trees next to the trail (leftovers from Hurricane Sandy) that seem perfectly placed for climbing and practicing the balance beam.

This trail also has several flights of stairs, and there are a couple areas where you have to navigate roots, but according to Ali Chandra, they have a core group of moms with infants under 6 months old who hike this trail every week without a problem.

"This trail is great to stop and play. There are multiple decision points where the different colored trails intersect, and these make natural stopping points," says Ali.

One of the other trails they hike often in this park is the Yellow Trail. It's a short, easy one that Ali says they often tack on as a toddler-paced hike at the end of a longer adult-paced hike if the kids have been carried for too long.

Bugs? Ticks? Poison ivy? Jersey has it all, so be aware of any off-trail adventuring. The one good thing about this trail is it's a really shaded trail, so sun exposure isn't an issue. And for footwear, hiking boots are probably best, but if you have sturdy hiking sandals, you should be fine.

The best time to hike this trail is in the fall. The crowds have subsided and the colors are incredible. This trail goes through a mix of hardwood (Atlantic white cedar) and pine forest, and both salt- and freshwater marshes. Make sure to bring a camera to capture the wide array of golden glowing colors and all of the animals.

There are 53 tent and trailer sites open April 1 through October 31. NJ residents pay less! There are also six group sites open May 1 through October 31 that can accommodate up to 25 campers each. No showers in group campsites. No pets in any campsites.

WHY IT'S A FAVORITE

"This trail has something for everyone. Boardwalks wind through marshy areas, the trees form tunnels over the path, and there are lots of exposed root systems and fallen trees alongside the trail for little ones to explore. This trail takes you past a pond with a little birdwatching blind and up and down several flights of stairs. Our kid leaders never get bored because the terrain is constantly changing and they're always excited to see what's next." —ALI CHANDRA

INSIDER'S TIP

There is a bench at the beginning of the main trailhead and another bench where the Red/Green Trail splits; however, several of our new mamas have found fallen trees and old tree stumps to sit on along the trails.

PYRAMID MOUNTAIN NATURAL HISTORIC AREA, NEW JERSEY,
PYRAMID MOUNTAIN TO TRIPOD ROCK

ACTIVITIES: Hiking

LENGTH OF HIKE: 3 miles

OUT AND BACK OR LOOP: Either

DIFFICULTY OF TERRAIN: Moderate

ELEVATION GAIN: 900+ feet

PARKING FEE/PASS: No

TOILETS: Yes, porta-potties at trailhead

CHANGING TABLE: No

NURSING BENCHES: Yes

DOGS ALLOWED: Yes

BIKES/HORSES/MOTORS ON TRAIL: No

CELL RECEPTION: Spotty

DRINKING WATER AVAILABLE: No

POTENTIAL CHILD OR BABY HAZARDS: Steep in some places

GEAR SUGGESTIONS: Baby carriers, bug spray, good hiking shoes

This is a fun trail with the reward of seeing an interesting natural sculpture as well as two scenic overlooks. The Morris County Parks Commission describes Tripod Rock as "a 160-ton boulder balanced on three smaller boulders deposited by the Wisconsin Glacier over 18,000 years ago." The trail is rocky and uneven, but lots of fun for experienced hikers. There's a cute toddler trail at the trailhead if you have a toddler who will be carried on the main hike, but who needs to stretch her legs before jumping into the carrier!

This is not a good trail for your first hike, but this is a great trail for families with all ages, especially after you pass the first mile and the trail becomes relatively level. But don't let this scare you off. Just plan to carry a bit for sections of the trail if you have a new little hiker.

Expect to see deer, squirrels, chipmunks, maybe a black bear, coyotes, snakes (some are venomous, but most are not), foxes, turtles, and frogs. These are all standard animals on New Jersey trails. As for birds, look for red-bellied woodpeckers, black-capped chickadees, scarlet tanagers, and yellow warblers.

Tripod Rock is the main attraction and why you'll want to visit this trail. Lucy's Overlook is another reason with a great view and a climb to about 934 feet, which will allow you to see a very distant Manhattan skyline and four mountain ranges on a clear day. This is an easy park to navigate if you are visiting for the first time. Trails are well marked, and there's a Nature Center to help direct you if you want additional guidance. The Nature Center is open Wednesday through Sunday, 10 a.m. to 4:30 p.m.

WHY IT'S A FAVORITE

"My favorite spot on the trail is Tripod Rock. It's a big, open area with lots of boulders, basically a natural playground! The toddlers toddle all around and the bigger kids climb the rocks. Everyone tries to climb on top of Tripod Rock, but no one comes close! It's a great spot for a picnic or just a stop to play." —MELANIE LEKAJ

INSIDER'S TIP

There is a large parking lot, but it does get crowded on the weekends, so plan to visit early in the morning if it's a nice day. If you're hungry, the Pompton Queen Diner is one of the best diners in NJ, and that's really saying something as diner-eating is a quintessentially Jersey experience. It's located at 710 NJ-23, Pompton Plains, NJ 07444. It's about a 15-minute drive from the parking lot but worth every second.

SANTA FE NATIONAL FOREST, NEW MEXICO, **JEMEZ FALLS**

ACTIVITIES: Hiking, camping, water play

LENGTH OF HIKE: 0.7 mile

OUT AND BACK OR LOOP: Out and back

DIFFICULTY OF TERRAIN: Easy

ELEVATION GAIN: 147 feet

PARKING FEE/PASS: No

TOILETS: Yes

CHANGING TABLE: No

NURSING BENCHES: Yes

DOGS ALLOWED: Yes, on leash

BIKES/HORSES/MOTORS ON TRAIL: No

CELL RECEPTION: Yes

DRINKING WATER AVAILABLE: No

POTENTIAL CHILD OR BABY HAZARDS: No

GEAR SUGGESTIONS: Trekking poles—it gets steep and rocky at the end of the trail

Located in the Santa Fe National Forest, this less than a mile out and back hike starts at 7,800 feet and is great for the whole family, including four-legged family members on leash. The reward for the short hike that is perfect for new walkers is a 70-foot waterfall at the end. There is some exposed rock along the trail, but the majority of the hike is completely toddler doable. The end of the trail near the waterfall is where you can expect the little bit of negotiating that needs to happen, so by that point in the hike, you should feel pretty comfortable with the trail.

We love this hike for our community because it's great terrain for a new walker with a lot of space on the dirt trail to move around and plenty of rocks to climb and play on. Parking is also easy, and the picnic area is nice, a major plus if you are going to make a whole day of it. If you are feeling up for the extra adventure, there's also an option to take a longer 4-mile hike to McCauley Spring (also a campground).

When you are hiking, pay attention to the trail, as there are a number of spurs that branch off and the signage isn't great. Also be aware that this is the desert so there are scorpions and centipedes. Rattlesnakes are less likely to be seen because of the traffic on trail, but they are present.

Visit this spot from March to October, and bring water shoes to take a dip in the shallow pond at the top of the falls. This is a hike that definitely can be done in hiking sandals, and you can expect your feet to get wet. What's also nice about this trail is that even in the hot middle of summer, tall pine trees offer ongoing shade throughout the hike and there is a scenic overlook at the end.

WHY IT'S A FAVORITE

"The highlight of this hike is the amazing view of Jemez Falls. It's shady and cool in the summer. It's popular with families and pets. My son loved saying hi to all the dogs we saw on the trail." —CARRIE KASER

INSIDER'S TIP

If you have time to check out the hot springs, it's worth the visit. While reports vary on how "hot" they actually are, it's always nice to visit a natural hot springs, especially in the summer.

WHITE SANDS NATIONAL MONUMENT, NEW MEXICO, **INTERDUNE BOARDWALK**

ACTIVITIES: Hiking, sandboarding (sledding), camping

LENGTH OF HIKE: 0.4 mile

OUT AND BACK OR LOOP: Out and back

DIFFICULTY OF TERRAIN: Easy

ELEVATION GAIN: No

PARKING FEE/PASS: $3/person

TOILETS: Yes

CHANGING TABLE: No

NURSING BENCHES: Yes

DOGS ALLOWED: Yes

BIKES/HORSES/MOTORS ON TRAIL: No

CELL RECEPTION: Yes

DRINKING WATER AVAILABLE: No

POTENTIAL CHILD OR BABY HAZARDS: Dehydration from heat

GEAR SUGGESTIONS: Hats, sunscreen, water, sunglasses

White Sands is a place where you can sit and contemplate life or you can forget about it completely as you wander through the otherworldly white sand landscape. Vast sand mountains that seem to go on forever make White Sands National Monument appear as if it is a place out of a dream. With 275 acres, this is the largest gypsum dune field in the world, which makes it truly worthy of being on your national monument "bucket list."

You can spend hours exploring the dunes or just bring a bucket, shovel, and some toy dump trucks and let your toddler sit in the sand because what little kid doesn't find happiness in a giant never-ending sandbox? For bigger kids (and parents), there's nothing more fun than rolling down sand dunes. The Visitor Center rents out round plastic saucer-like sleds ($16 with $5 back when you return) that you can use to slide down the dunes. To get speed, you will need to climb the steeper hills, so this may not be as easy with a toddler in tow.

What kind of wildlife can you expect in this area? Look for lizards, beetles, rattlesnakes, and roadrunners roaming through the area. Also, keep an eye out for crickets, mice, and moths that, like many of the critters and crawlers in this area, have turned lighter shades to mimic the white sands and hide from predators. Wander along the boardwalk for the easy new-walker option, which will provide stability. Then head out onto the trail through the sand and consider hiking barefoot to feel the surprisingly cool gypsum sand under your feet. Remember, when walking in the sand, it takes double the exertion, so little walkers might get tired fast; be prepared to carry them. Bring a lot of extra water because it's drier than you think. And don't forget sunglasses, even for babies, as the sun reflects from the white sand up into your eyes.

Like much of New Mexico, it can be hot and exposed midsummer, so midday will be hot. Consider visiting in late September when the higher elevation (over 4,000 feet) and later season means a cooler climate. Mid- to late afternoon, the heat subsides and the sand actually gets quite cool to the touch. Another reason for a later hike: The sunsets are spectacular!

Want to try backcountry camping? You can do it here but will need to hike at least a mile to get to the permitted primitive camping. Overnighters are probably better suited for families with older kids or those experienced at camping with babies because there are no facilities or shelter in the open desert. But if you do choose to venture out, you will most likely be alone—a rarity at many national parks and monuments.

WHY IT'S A FAVORITE

"My toddler loved climbing the sand dunes, which she called "mountains," and was so proud she could climb them on her own. Sometimes, if you're lucky, you will see rain in the distance, since you can see so far out in the horizon, and you will see some magnificent rainbows with sunset. It's spectacular!" —DAPHNE EARLEY

INSIDER'S TIP

Hit up the local Walmart on the way in and purchase a plastic sled saucer to slide the hills if you don't want to rent one on site.

SANDIA NATIONAL PARK, NEW MEXICO,
TECOLOTE TRAIL

ACTIVITIES: Hiking

LENGTH OF HIKE: 2 miles

OUT AND BACK OR LOOP: Out and back

DIFFICULTY OF TERRAIN: Easy–moderate

ELEVATION GAIN: 321 feet

PARKING FEE/PASS: No

TOILETS: Yes

CHANGING TABLE: No

NURSING BENCHES: No

DOGS ALLOWED: Yes

BIKES/HORSES/MOTORS ON TRAIL: No

CELL RECEPTION: Good

DRINKING WATER AVAILABLE: No

POTENTIAL CHILD OR BABY HAZARDS: A couple of steep switchbacks

GEAR SUGGESTIONS: Water, sunscreen, a good camera with lenses to capture the views

This surprising little hike up the east side of the Sandia Mountains is only 30 minutes from Albuquerque but offers spectacular views overlooking the vast valley to the west upon reaching the summit. Our trail pick for this area is called the Tecolote Trail, which translates to "owl" in Spanish, but we're not quite sure what the reasoning for the naming of this trail is.

"Our 14-month-old would have had a blast walking on this trail, but it would've taken us more time than we had to get up and down in a timely, efficient manner so we chose to carry," says Glenna from Hike it Baby Albuquerque. Also, there are some steep switchbacks going into the hike that you wouldn't necessarily trust wobbly balance on. But once you reach the top, there's plenty of flat space to explore.

This is a pretty, bare-bones, straight-forward hike. There is no nature center or nursing benches, and the outhouses aren't open year-round, but the simplicity of it adds to the intrigue as well as keeps the crowds away. Look for a little cave at the beginning of the hike. Then you'll come to a few steep switchbacks on the ascent and descent. Watch out for cacti that you will want to keep your little ones away from. But other than that, we think you'll enjoy this little journey through the coniferous pine trees to the viewpoint.

As you head up, you'll stay fairly covered thanks to tall trees surrounding the trail. But once you reach the top, the hike is exposed with shorter trees and shrubs, so be prepared with sunscreen. The best time of year for this hike is in October, when the weather is perfect. You can feel a bit of the crispness of the higher elevation, but the sun warms the hike perfectly, so you won't break a sweat.

What you'll enjoy about this hike is the pretty drive and that it's far enough out of town to really feel like you're in some backcountry. Yet the trail itself is very manageable and well groomed. Also because it's far enough off the highway and the parking lot isn't well marked, you'll never find yourself jockeying for a space, unlike some of the more popular hikes closer to town. Look for a sign signaling the hike start just past the outhouse.

WHY IT'S A FAVORITE

"This hike is perfect for a quick adventure! Not too long but far enough from town and enough of a climb to really feel like an explorer. Great views at the top will give little hikers a wonderful sense of accomplishment. The trail is well groomed, which helps little feet stay on it." —GLENNA BULLOCK

INSIDER'S TIP

Don't miss all the beautiful perspectives that the summit has to offer of the Sandia National Park along with the sweeping views of the valley. Go slow and really check everything out.

ADIRONDACK FOREST PRESERVE, NEW YORK, **SHELVING ROCK FALLS**

ACTIVITIES: Hiking, camping, fishing, boating (on Lake George)

LENGTH OF HIKE: 1 mile

OUT AND BACK OR LOOP: Out and back

DIFFICULTY OF TERRAIN: Easy

ELEVATION GAIN: A couple hundred feet

PARKING FEE/PASS: No

TOILETS: No

CHANGING TABLE: No

NURSING BENCHES: No

DOGS ALLOWED: Yes

BIKES/HORSES/MOTORS ON TRAIL: No

CELL RECEPTION: No

DRINKING WATER AVAILABLE: No

POTENTIAL CHILD OR BABY HAZARDS: Waterfall

GEAR SUGGESTIONS: Carrier, hiking poles (optional), water, sunscreen, snacks/lunch, fishing equipment if you want to extend your hike to reach Lake George

Located on the east side of Lake George, this trail has a fantastic waterfall and a wide, open path that can fit five people across due to its being an old carriage road. This makes it an obvious Hike it Baby pick for your family. Little ones will love the amount of water spilling from the falls, as well as the fact that they can splash around at the base of the falls (depending on the time of year and how shallow it is) or wade in the shallow water that is next to the trail leading up to the falls.

In the hot, muggy New York summer, a watery hike is a sure win for all. While we are suggesting one of the easier trails in this region, there are a ton of mountain hikes throughout with beautiful views of Lake George and that leave from the same dirt road. It just depends on how far you want to hike.

What Natalie Kendrach likes about this hike is that her 2-year-old can walk the whole thing, and there are numerous places to stop and play along the way, stretching what may seem like a short hike into a few hours of toddle waddle play.

There are no benches or picnic tables, but you can sit on the rocks at the base of the falls to have lunch or continue down toward Lake George and eat at the water's edge.

The trail to the top of the falls is extremely easy, but getting to the base of the falls is a little more challenging. It will be especially so if you are front carrying, so keep that in mind. A toddler can do it with help, but you'll want free hands. "I've led this as a Hike it Baby hike with seven families and have also done it pregnant while wearing a toddler on my back. You just need to go slowly and be careful because it is a tad steep. Hiking poles might help," says Natalie. The end result is amazing and totally worth the small down/uphill detour.

After checking out the falls, you can either continue along the trail (back at the top of the falls) or head back. If you turn back after the falls, it will be a 1-mile round trip. If it is a nice day, Natalie says they let the kiddos play in the water alongside the trail on the way back to the cars to make the adventure longer. If you are feeling extra adventurous and the terrain is feeling good for you, consider hiking Shelving Rock Mountain for another 3.4 miles.

Keep your eyes open around the lake for loons and beavers. In the sky, you might spot a bald eagle, or high in a tree napping, an Adirondack owl. Throughout this area there are bigger animals like moose, black bears, and coyotes, but chances are on a day venture around Shelving Rock Falls, you won't spot any. If you make a camping trip out of it and head deeper in to one of the 12 primitive camping sites, you might see one of these larger animals.

As for hazards that would be immediate on this hike, ticks are common in New York, so bring protection and do a tick check at the end of the day. Fortunately, poison ivy and other creepy crawlies don't seem to be present in this area. Also be aware of ice in the winter. You can definitely hike this with microspikes on the flat part of the trail. If you aren't wearing a child, you can get to the base of the falls in the winter as well.

It can get a tad crowded during the summer with folks trying to escape the city. Expect the parking lot to fill up. There is no cell reception in this area so it's important to map this hike if you are going. According to Natalie, the trailhead is located off a dirt road that provides access to Shelving Rock Falls, Buck Mountain, and Sleeping Beauty.

The parking lot for Shelving Rock Falls is the farthest one and can be found with the following GPS coordinates on Google Maps (43.553012, -73.5966742). You will take the dirt road for what feels like forever. The parking lot will be located immediately after a one-lane bridge. On the bridge, there is a very small sign that says "Shelving Rock Falls."

WHY IT'S A FAVORITE

"Shelving Rock Falls is one of our most favorite hikes near Lake George, NY. The view of the falls is gorgeous, and it's fun to swim at the base in the summer. This is one of the places we always take family or friends when they come to visit. We also like to extend the hike and go all the way down to Lake George to sit by the water for lunch or to fish." —NATALIE KENDRACH

INSIDER'S TIP

There are a handful of first come, first serve primitive campsites down a 4 mile dirt road toward Shelving Rock Falls. You can stay up to 3 days for free without a permit and longer with a free permit. This area is open year round with the exception of closing briefly in mud season.

BLACK CREEK PRESERVE, NEW YORK,
BLACK CREEK PRESERVE TRAIL

ACTIVITIES: Hiking, fishing

LENGTH OF HIKE: 2 miles

OUT AND BACK OR LOOP: Loop

DIFFICULTY OF TERRAIN: Easy

ELEVATION GAIN: 440 feet

PARKING FEE/PASS: No

TOILETS: No

CHANGING TABLE: No

NURSING BENCHES: No

DOGS ALLOWED: Yes

BIKES/HORSES/MOTORS ON TRAIL: Yes

CELL RECEPTION: Yes

DRINKING WATER AVAILABLE: No

POTENTIAL CHILD OR BABY HAZARDS:
Ticks, bugs in the spring after lots of rain

GEAR SUGGESTIONS: Bug spray, water

Fantastic Hudson River views, an easy trail for toddlers, and pockets of silence are just a few of the reasons the 130-acre Black Creek Preserve is so popular for Hike it Baby members. While 2 miles may seem like a short hike, there's a lot of terrain variety as well as shady spots to hang out in and make the hike seem longer. Look for old stone walls, a reminder that this was once a farming area for early settlers, now overgrown as the park takes the land back. This area was protected and developed in

1992 to create a space that would allow urban dwellers to experience the shore of the Hudson River in a more natural state.

To hike this trail, look for a kiosk at the end of the parking area, and follow signs from there to the yellow-blazed Black Creek Trail and hike along the creek. Soon after you start hiking, the trail will cross a 120-foot suspension bridge that most kids love. Across the creek, expect some switchbacks, and then eventually the path will flatten out. You'll pass vernal pools, seasonal breeding grounds where frogs lay their eggs, so make sure to point that out to your little ones.

What makes this a pleasant hike is the combination of hiking through hemlock forests and open spaces, with a bubbling, gurgling creek running throughout. Head down to the water and you'll enjoy large bluestone slate rocks that are easy to climb around.

A few things to watch out for are ticks in the warm season and the fact that this trail can get buggy in the spring after lots of rain. Also, thick muddy trails are to be expected in shoulder seasons, so wear good hiking shoes. The hike ends at the Hudson River, and there are small rock beaches that you can climb down to, but doing this will require supervision for children. At high tide, there are no rock beaches.

WHY IT'S A FAVORITE

"This trail is really interesting, only 2 miles, and covers a variety of terrain. The trail starts with a bridge that crosses Black Creek, which kids love and gets them excited. The trail covers rocky terrain, passes marshes, crosses a couple old stone walls, and meanders through sections of thick forest. The trail ends (before looping back) at the Hudson River. The views of the river are beautiful. Find a stone beach to skip rocks and eat a snack before starting the loop back." —ANN PETERS

INSIDER'S TIP

Summer and fall are the best times to visit. Dry summer weather means fewer bugs, and full-leaved trees mean shaded trails. In the winter, steep sections can be dangerous due to ice, so this is a better trail for families in less "weathery" months. At the end of the hike, dip your toes into Black Creek where there are often people fishing.

MOSES LAKE, NEW YORK,
GREEN TRAIL

ACTIVITIES: Hiking, birding

LENGTH OF HIKE: 2 miles

OUT AND BACK OR LOOP: Out and back

DIFFICULTY OF TERRAIN: Moderate

ELEVATION GAIN: 200 feet

PARKING FEE/PASS: No

TOILETS: No

CHANGING TABLE: No

NURSING BENCHES: No

DOGS ALLOWED: Yes

BIKES/HORSES/MOTORS ON TRAIL: No

CELL RECEPTION: Yes

DRINKING WATER AVAILABLE: No

POTENTIAL CHILD OR BABY HAZARDS:
Uneven terrain, can be muddy, ticks

GEAR SUGGESTIONS: Water

The Green Trail is the Hike it Baby Staten Island pick because it is a friendly hike leading to Moses' Mountain, with many interesting spots that are toddler height. This is part of the Greenbelt Trail system, which boasts six greenbelts to travel on and explore with terrain that will work for all abilities and access needs. Whether you're on a bike, in a wheelchair, tandem-wearing kids, or leading a new walker down the trail, there's something for everyone here. Four of the greenbelt trails are walking only.

What we love about this trail are huge, hollowed-out oak trees to poke your head in, board walkways to venture across muddy spots, and a few streams with short bridges that are fun for watching stream life float by and for jumping off the end onto the trail. Thanks to Staten Island's temperate climate, there are also trees like persimmon and sweet gum that one would expect only in the South.

In the spring and summer months, there are vernal pools, which are breeding grounds where you can see tadpoles and salamanders grow. The stumps and roots of trees are great places to observe a multitude of crawly things, such as beetles, centipedes, a few varieties of ants, worms, etc. A variety of birds also call the green belt home. Expect to see chipmunks, gray and black squirrels, and the occasional deer.

As you climb the gentle mountain, there are many excellent nature stopping points along the way. Once you reach the top of Moses' Mountain, you can see all the way to New Jersey on a clear day. There are large rocks suitable for sitting, feeding, or changing a diaper.

The only slight hazard you might find is one spot on the trail that crosses Manor Road. It is well signed, and rumble strips and a pedestrian crossing have been put in. There shouldn't be any issue crossing, but it's worth noting. Every so often you might see a dog or bike on the trail, so just be aware if your little one is running ahead. Of course, like most of the East Coast, ticks are a concern when it's over 50 degrees.

WHY IT'S A FAVORITE
"This hike is enjoyed by hikers of many ages. The first and last lengths are manageable for little legs with a great many things to look at, plants and critters alike. The climb has a wide trail, which makes it easier to manage with kids, and the view at the top is gorgeous!" —SHANNON RINELLI

INSIDER'S TIP
Staten Island and most likely these walking areas were home to famed naturalist Henry David Thoreau in the summer of 1843. He lived here with his friend, Ralph Waldo Emerson, tutoring his three children. Apparently he spent every morning walking through the area, exploring the landscape, and recording things such as the "17-year locust," a hatching of cicadas that happens en masse every 13 to 17 years.

MASHOMACK PRESERVE, NEW YORK,
MASHOMACK PRESERVE YELLOW TRAIL

ACTIVITIES: Hiking

LENGTH OF HIKE: 3 miles

OUT AND BACK OR LOOP: Loop

DIFFICULTY OF TERRAIN: Easy to moderate

ELEVATION GAIN: No

PARKING FEE/PASS: Only accessible by ferry ($1 walk-on/$17 round-trip vehicle)

TOILETS: Yes

CHANGING TABLE: No

NURSING BENCHES: Yes

DOGS ALLOWED: No

BIKES/HORSES/MOTORS ON TRAIL: No

CELL RECEPTION: Spotty

DRINKING WATER AVAILABLE: No

POTENTIAL CHILD OR BABY HAZARDS: Nearby water, ticks

GEAR SUGGESTIONS: Tick repellent

Looking for a hike that offers a variety of different landscapes? From the classic "forest" hike to overlooking a beach, crossing over boardwalks through a marsh, and roaming through big, open fields of cotton, this is the place. Hike it Baby's Lindsay Sousa says her favorite time to visit is in the fall, when the air is crisp and all the colors of nature are popping around you.

What makes this hike a winner is that there are no steep inclines, so it's perfect for young walkers. But there is some distance at 3 miles, so you might do a little carrying or use a jogging stroller. If you feel like you need more distance, you can add other intersecting trails like the Red Trail for 1.5 more miles.

Kids love this preserve because it's set up for little ones. Part of the Red Trail boasts a Kid Scavenger Hunt. Check out the Welcome Center for more info before you head out to the trails. Also, the Nature Conservatory hosts multiple kid events throughout the year.

The reason your toddler will love this 2,100-acre preserve is that it's a breeding and protection habitat for osprey. Established in 1980 to shelter these beautiful birds, the area now has one of the densest populations of these birds on the East Coast. There are also 12 miles of coastline hugging the preserve's edge, which is a mix of tidal creeks, woodlands, and fields and brings in many other birds and marine life to the area to make this natural space a complex and rich environment.

Another fun highlight is to look for an old cemetery on the preserve where you will find the graves of the original European descended settlers. Shelter Island was originally inhabited by the Manhansets, who were part of the widespread Algonquin culture. The area was deeded to a sugar merchant from Barbados by the "chief" of the area in 1653.

Fall is the best time to go on this hike because all the leaves on the trees are changing and vibrant with color. Ticks are low at this time, and the cool air makes it feel like you could keep hiking forever. Go on a weekday if you can, and you will have the place all to yourself.

WHY IT'S A FAVORITE

"This hike has some of the best views Long Island has to offer. Each section of the preserve has its own unique look to it, making it very exciting to keep moving along and discovering each new section." —LINDSAY SOUSA

INSIDER'S TIP

You will need to ride a ferry to get here, so be prepared to wait in line if it's a busy weekend. The ferry holds around 12 cars.

TACONIC STATE PARK, NEW YORK,
SUNSET ROCK TRAIL

ACTIVITIES: Hiking, birding, boulder scrambling

LENGTH OF HIKES: 1.5 miles

OUT AND BACK OR LOOP: Out and back

DIFFICULTY OF TERRAIN: Moderate

ELEVATION GAIN: 150 feet

PARKING FEE/PASS: $7/vehicle

TOILETS: No

CHANGING TABLE: No

NURSING BENCHES: Yes

DOGS ALLOWED: Yes

BIKES/HORSES/MOTORS ON TRAIL: No

CELL RECEPTION: Spotty

DRINKING WATER AVAILABLE: No

POTENTIAL CHILD OR BABY HAZARDS: Ticks, rocky ground and short ledges, scant poison ivy, rattlesnakes

GEAR SUGGESTIONS: Hiking poles, sunscreen, bug spray

The Sunset Rock Trail at Taconic State Park is a favorite of Hike it Baby Columbia County. It's located in the southeast corner of the county, where the Taconics meet the Berkshires and the Hudson Valley. The trail is named for the highlight of the trek: a rocky ledge in a small clearing, looking out over a 180-degree vista of the rolling Hudson Valley and Catskill Mountains. There are two ways to get there: a 3- or 5-mile loop for older kids and fit parents looking for a workout while carrying, and a brief, 1-mile there-and-back trail perfect for toddlers, new walkers, and adults who are up for something mellower. The air is fresh, the lichens and ferns grow like crazy, there are hobbit-like corridors through mountain laurel and scrub oak and pine, wildflowers in spring and summer, and of course, Sunset Rock itself is great for picnicking and scrambling!

To make the hike to Sunset Rock into a 3-plus-mile trail with substantial elevation gain, park at the entrance to Taconic State Park off Route 344 in Copake Falls, and check out the map by the HQ office. This is recommended for fit adults carrying smaller kiddos.

Maybe the best thing about the Sunset Rock Trail is that it's nearby so many other gorgeous trails that straddle the Taconic range. Bash Bish Falls (can be done with a rugged stroller), Guilder Pond Loop, and the Appalachian Trail to the Mount Everett Summit (recommended for carry/preschool for the first, toddler/carry/rugged stroller up to big views for the second); and the entire South Taconic Trail connects the Copake Falls portion of the park to the southern Rudd Pond portion just outside Millerton. Finally, the Harlem Valley Rail Trail runs along the park at the base of the mountains and offers a wonderful, safe riding experience for families through woods and farmland (and cross-country skiing in winter).

Taconic State Park has a nice playground and a shallow, freshwater splash pool in the summertime. If you like exploring back-mountain roads and the kids need a nap, drive through the mountains into Massachusetts, and make your way to Great Barrington for sightseeing in the Berkshires, restaurants, ice cream, and many other outdoor pursuits. If staying closer to the trail, Cross Roads Food Shop in Hillsdale is the family-friendly local food place to go for breakfast and lunch. Hillsdale is on the way to Hudson, New York, and the rest of the Hudson Valley/Capital Region, with plenty of sightseeing and natural areas to explore.

One thing to consider when hiking here: Disease-carrying ticks are always a risk in the area. Dress appropriately,

check and brush clothes with a lint-roller posthike, and check again during bath and before bedtime. Also, rattlesnakes live here, but rarely pose a threat. Just be aware. Lastly, Sunset Rock rests on a ledge outcrop. There is no big drop-off, but plenty of small ledges that older children will find fun, but that are dangerous for babies and wobbly toddlers.

WHY IT'S A FAVORITE

"The Sunset Rock Trail at Taconic State Park, Copake Falls, is one of our favorite trails in Columbia County. There is a gentle climb, then a long, flat, wooded corridor, followed by

hobbit tunnels through the mountain laurel and pine. At the summit is the Sunset Rock, great for very low-key bouldering, exploring, and picnicking. This is a peaceful place to come—it is quiet and feels far away but is pretty easy for anyone with a car to get to."
—JILL JAKIMETZ

INSIDER'S TIP

Best time of year to visit: anytime! If it's cloudy and there's no view, the trail is still worth it. Every season has its beauty: Spring wildflowers, summer blooms and greenery, fall leaf colors, and winter all have their own quiet beauty. Remember that it is always colder and windier up at the top of the Sunset Rock Trail. Bring two extra layers of clothing appropriate for a mild climb in the day's worst forecast.

Judgers Gonna Judge

Here's a pic of the first really gnarly hike I ever did with Hike it Baby in October 2013. It was a stormy day, and all of these mamas were hiking together in a total downpour that turned into a hailstorm with babies ranging from 2 months to 1 year old. I am in the center, and Mason was 3 months old. There were 11 women. I remember thinking no one is going to show up for this hike, yet all of these women showed up. We had a blast hiking in the rain. Afterward, I realized it was one of the best hikes I've ever done, and I was hooked. It helps having a supportive community around you to encourage you to get out there.

I've received plenty of negative comments about getting outside, not to mention going out in bad weather, with a baby. Chances are, if you get out there on days people might not expect you to be out there, you might experience sideways looks and comments. The best advice I can offer: Ignore them. If you are reading this book, you are doing it right!

Currently we are living in a country that's battling obesity, ADD, ADHD, and a whole myriad of health and behavior issues. Being outside in nature is not the problem; it's part of a complicated puzzle that's the solution. With each step, you are taking initiative in helping your family minimize these topics that are plastered across the news daily.

So the next time you are out with your little one walking or hiking and you get one of those comments or looks, simply smile and say, "Lovely day, isn't it?" and keep on walking. Then head home and look up the next Hike it Baby or other outdoor event, or put a big camping adventure your family can take on the calendar so you can find your people. We all understand your need to get outside, and we're here to support one another in our experience to raise amazing outdoor-loving children.

DADDY TIME ON TRAIL
RYAN IDRYO

Ryan and his husband are avid hikers and campers and have been adventuring with their son, Ansel, since he was just 4 months old. Like most new parents, they didn't know how their adventures would change once a child came into their lives, but they quickly saw that things could continue on, it might just be a little slower.

"Our son was born 8 weeks early and, at 3 pounds, 13 ounces, he didn't meet the minimum threshold for any of these carriers for several months. We were a little nervous to get out with him being a preemie," says Ryan. "Certainly there were ways to wear the Moby wrap with a tiny baby, but it wasn't worth any risk. Babywearing was on hold for many months," says Ryan of their early days with their son.

When their son was just shy of 4 months, they decided he was strong enough. Feeling a little stir crazy from staying inside with him for so many months, they decided to go big and head for one of their favorite places on the planet to visit: Yosemite.

"We only hiked about a mile to Mirror Lake and mainly did things off the side of the road, but we still had such a great time that we decided we needed to visit the park at least three times a year in different seasons," says Ryan. Prior to that, they had only visited the park during the craziness of summer. Seeing the leaves falling in November, they experienced a different Yosemite than they had ever known.

That first trip helped remind them how important nature was to them, and they also decided then and there that they were going to commit to getting out hiking more with Ansel and to set a goal of doing a backpacking trip every Father's Day. The next June, when Ansel was just 10 months old, they did their first backpacking trip! This boosted their outdoor confidence. Being avid outdoorsmen, they knew what they needed for themselves but had to figure out what they needed for Ansel. "He was only crawling, so we knew he wouldn't wander away. We were more worried about sleeping at night. Luckily, he really loved it and loved crawling around on the rocks, and exploring everything made him really happy."

Ryan says the best part about exploring nature with a child for him is watching the joy of continual discovery. Every stick is exciting; one is a sword, while another is a motorcycle. And of course their little guy can sit by a stream for an hour and throw rocks and be content.

"We had to scale back some of our adventures. Even now we haven't gotten back up to the mileage we would get on a backpack trip because if we are carrying him, that's a lot more pounds. And if we're not carrying him, we go pretty slowly. We just do smaller adventures, and they are still fun. If you work at it, you can make anything an adventure," says Ryan.

The hardest thing about hiking with a toddler in Ryan's opinion is not carrying the weight or the going slow, it's the food. For their family, it started with having to thaw frozen breast milk on the go when Ansel was a baby, then figuring out what their picky eater would consume on trail. "At home you can find something else if your toddler doesn't like what you give him, but on the trail you have to make sure he's going to eat. You would think he would eventually eat when he gets hungry, but nope, that doesn't work. Ansel will clamp his mouth shut and spit things out. This is where you have to become a Zen parent and just relax and let it pass and not freak out."

FAVORITE HIKE: YANT FLATS, DIXIE NATIONAL FOREST, UT
"The trip we did to southern Utah was amazing. We discovered a little known trail, and Ansel liked this hike best. He did 6.5 miles that day, walking the frozen sand dunes! There were rocks and flat slabs of rocks he could stack and pools of water to throw rocks into. It just felt like such a surreal landscape, and you can spend a whole day there."

HOW TO HIKE
USING A FRAME CARRIER

IF YOU FIND YOURSELF STARTING TO HIKE MORE and feel you need more space to carry items than your soft-structure carrier allows, it might be time to consider a frame carrier. We found, with Mason, that a frame carrier took some getting used to and may not be comfortable right away for everyone.

Frame carriers are a great option for many reasons. We like that they give us some physical distance from Mason on a hot or a cold day so we can really insulate him or not perspire on him. Also, it's easy to place a sleeping baby in a frame carrier and they will sleep on, allowing you to go to the bathroom or have a picnic midway through a hike without disturbing your baby. They are great for wind, rain, and sun protection when they include a shade and with the additional weather protection options that are available.

The tricky part with frame carriers is they take some getting used to; the weight distribution and the adjustments are really important. Here are some things to think about if you are graduating to a frame carrier.

START SMALL. Start with small hikes in local parks so your baby can get used to the different carrier and not being close to your body. Remember, if you are carrying them in a frame carrier, they will get colder more easily, so add extra layers. Don't forget, you're exercising, but they aren't. Account for that.

ADJUST AT HOME. Make sure to do all of your adjustments in the warmth of your home so you aren't adjusting on trail or as you are hiking. There are heaps of adjustments to help make frame packs comfortable. Older models can be uncomfortable because the technology was not as good several years ago as it is now. Make sure you really try before you buy, and don't just get it because it's free or cost $10. A good frame pack will make a difference for both your back and a little one's comfort.

BRING A BACKUP. Mason was a small baby, and we had him in a frame carrier around 7 months old. Bigger babies can go in such a carrier around 6 months old, but we wouldn't suggest using one much earlier. We always carried the soft carrier or a lightweight sling on every hike as well, so we could switch him back and forth if we were on a long hike and he wasn't having it.

PREPARE FOR RAIN. Do not skimp and skip the rain cover. We have owned both a Deuter and an Osprey, and the rain cover was the best investment we made for those packs.

We just got the midrange pack instead of the high-range, and we got the rain cover. We used it a lot for wind, rain, and sun protection.

WORK UP THE MILES. If you are new to carrying with a frame carrier, make sure you really take it easy and work your way up in mileage. You might feel sore spots on your shoulders and hips when you first hike. This adjusts over time if you keep using the carrier. The packs take a little getting used to. If you have ever backpacked with a load, you know there will be some tender spots immediately following hiking.

TAKE ONLY WHAT YOU NEED. Don't load the carrier with a million things (it's tempting with all of that space). Pare your supplies, like diapers, wipes, and creams, to only what you need. At the same time, make sure to bring ample water, food, and extra layers for you and baby.

CARRY A MIRROR. If you are nervous about not being able to see your little one, get a mirror and clip it on so you can look behind you. This is also a fun toy when you are hiking and might halt a crying baby!

LET BABY OUT. Remember to take your baby out of the frame carrier every so often if on a long hike. He/she needs to move around a bit, especially if it's a long, cold hike. Every 20 to 30 minutes, stop and do a quick check of baby's hands, too! Add extra baby socks under gloves to help keep hands warm.

HELPFUL EXTRAS
FOR BABIES AND TODDLERS

IT'S EASY TO GET CAUGHT UP IN PACKING EVERYTHING but the kitchen sink. While I do advocate a "less is more" approach, I do believe in preparedness and safety—you should always have the Top 10 Trail Essentials (see page 267). But if you can squeeze in a few extra items, it can be worth it to make your journey that much more successful and fun.

Got Baby?

BINKY AND PACIFIER CLIP/HOLDER. Never lose a pacifier down a steep hill again! 'Nuff said.

FAST KIDDO SNACKS. Squeeze packs, yogurt bites, animal crackers, Goldfish. Of course, you know this. Hangry babies are no fun. But here's another thing to think about: How easy is it for a little one to hold it and eat while on trail on your back and with movement? Think about snacks that can be held in a hand and are less likely to be choke hazards if you are moving, like fruit leather, cheese sticks, and baby crackers (they melt in the mouth).

SMALL WATER-RESISTANT BLANKET. These days, there are incredible materials that are water-resistant and that can fold down to the size of a large pack of gum. Look for either of these brands: Monkey Mats or Matador Mini Pocket Blanket. Having something to throw down for an impromptu picnic or deal with a serious blowout is nice when on trail, especially if there is rain, mud, or slush on the ground.

WINDOW SHADE. Do you have a baby who gets sick while riding or cries a lot in the car? If he or she is facing backward as you drive to a hike and there is some distance, it could be carsickness. Consider getting a shade and pulling it down to prevent baby from seeing out the window at the fast-moving world rolling by.

Got Toddler?

FULL-BODY RAIN SUIT. While these may not be as critical everywhere as they are in Oregon, in the Hike it Baby community, we find people hike with these thin rain shells even in Texas. The beauty is that you can zip a kid in, let them roll around in a muddy

puddle, hose them down, and then pull them out of the suit, and they will be relatively dry. These are different from snowsuits in that there is no liner. Add layers underneath, and they can double as a snowsuit.

SOFT-STRUCTURED CARRIER. I leave one in my car at all times. It's too easy to get to a trail with a toddler and just realize it's not going to happen without a carrier. Some days are like that. Embrace it. You can find a carrier that will work for children as old as 5 or 6 if necessary (See carrier piece on page 234). Pockets and hoods are nice when you have a baby, but you can adjust with other things as a kiddo ages (add a fanny pack to your front if you are wearing a child on your back). Look for a carrier made with nylon for breathability on the trail and to withstand mud, rain, and vomit!

EXTRA SHOES AND SOCKS. It's easy to lose a shoe, especially if you are carrying a kiddo on your back and they like to kick their shoes off. If you are hiking far, definitely consider an extra pair because it's easy to end up with wet feet if there is any weather at all.

TRAIL TOYS. Once his binky was gone, Mason often liked to carry something on trail. This hasn't changed. Now it's more often sticks and pinecones; but for a long time, it was a little toy car, a key chain with a globe, a plastic shovel, or some kind of widget to distract him if he was having a hard time on trail. We also discovered Chums mirrors, a little retractable mirror that is useful when you are back carrying to see your little one. It can also distract her if she needs something to shift a tantrum or ease boredom. Small bottles of bubbles, notebooks, a pencil, or small things that can easily be pulled out can help ease trail troubles.

REUSABLE WATER BOTTLES. Mason never liked bottles, so we started with a Camelbak children's bottle when he was just a year old. He got used to sucking water from the little plastic nub, and, while he chewed it off a few times, he eventually got the hang of it. Later it was easier to give him water from our hydration systems on our backs. We always had kid-sized water bottles (smaller and easier to hold) around Mason from early on.

TRAVEL POTTY. Once you start potty training, a portable toilet is key. My son refuses to go in porta-potties and outhouses. Public bathrooms are a mixed bag. He is less shy about peeing on a tree, but this is probably not the best thing to get into the habit of doing. This is why the travel potty with bags goes everywhere. It collapses to nothing and can be whipped out on a street corner or stuffed in a backpack. You can also just travel with the potty bags, which are often easy to seal and include a pad to mitigate strong smells temporarily.

PISGAH NATIONAL FOREST, NORTH CAROLINA, **MAX PATCH TRAIL**

ACTIVITIES: Hiking

LENGTH OF HIKE: 0.75 mile

OUT AND BACK OR LOOP: Out and back

DIFFICULTY OF TERRAIN: Moderate

ELEVATION GAIN: 288 Feet

PARKING FEE/PASS: No

TOILETS: No

CHANGING TABLE: No

NURSING BENCHES: No

DOGS ALLOWED: Yes

BIKES/HORSES/MOTORS ON TRAIL: No

CELL RECEPTION: Spotty

DRINKING WATER AVAILABLE: No

POTENTIAL CHILD OR BABY HAZARDS: Ticks and other small annoying bugs. There's tall grass at the top as well, which could be a nuisance for kids younger than 2.

GEAR SUGGESTIONS: Sunscreen

Looking for amazing views, wildflowers blooming in early summer, and blackberries bursting from the bushes as the summer progresses. Located in the 500,000 acres of Pisgah National Forest, Max Patch is a short but steep hike to a bald mountaintop.

The trail is full of blackberry bushes, which will keep many a toddler happy and smiling as long as they are being fed the sweet juicy fruit. The top has a mix of tall grass and wildflowers in the summer with lots of spots for setting up a picnic blanket or a tent. This "bald" field came to be when it was cleared as pastureland in the 1800s. Today, this trail is no longer a field for farmers but is part of a 350-acre piece of open land with perfect views of Mount Mitchell and the Great Smoky Mountains.

Summer and fall are the best seasons to hike. Summer for wildflower viewing and wild blackberries, and fall is also spectacular for the foliage stretched out as far as the eye can see across the rolling hills below. You may spot a black bear, but it's unlikely. Expect to see more of the general forest animals like birds, deer, and the occasional fox.

If you are headed to Max Patch, make sure you have a good map in hand. GPS most likely won't work as you head out the long, bumpy road (people will often mention this road in reviews). Expect the trip to take over an hour from Asheville, and longer if your kids aren't loving the dirt road.

While the hike is fairly doable for all ages, there are some hazards with steeper portions, like loose footing, so consider carrying your little one when you hit that point. Also, it's a bald mountaintop, so there's no protection from sun, wind, and rain. Lightning is also a big factor, so be aware of summer storms creeping up. If you hike 10 minutes down and hit the Appalachian Trail, you'll be covered by a forest canopy and more shielded from the elements.

WHY IT'S A FAVORITE

"From the summit, you have a 360-degree view of the Blue Ridge Mountains, with one of the most beautiful sunsets and sunrises we've seen. There's a second trail that loops around the mountain, and you can also hike a section of the Appalachian Trail, so there are many other adventures you can go on with your kids. There are blackberry bushes all over the mountain, which kept my kids happily hiking. We saw lots of wildflowers and butterflies as well." —DIEGO DOS SANTOS

INSIDER'S TIP

Camping is prohibited at the summit, but down the trail there are many backpacking sites along the AT just to the northeast of the Max Patch hike. There are also great picnic spots that might be worth dipping into after you've climbed the summit and your toddler needs a nap in the shade. To find the campsites and picnic areas below, you will come to a fork where you turn left on the AT instead of climbing up the Max Patch summit to the right.

PISGAH NATIONAL FOREST, NORTH CAROLINA, **CAT GAP LOOP TO JOHN ROCK TRAIL**

ACTIVITIES: Birding, swimming, paddling, climbing, biking, fishing

LENGTH OF HIKE: 4.4 miles

OUT AND BACK OR LOOP: Loop

DIFFICULTY OF TERRAIN: Moderate

ELEVATION GAIN: 859 feet

PARKING FEE/PASS: No

TOILETS: Yes

CHANGING TABLE: No

NURSING BENCHES: No

DOGS ALLOWED: Yes

BIKES/HORSES/MOTORS ON TRAIL: No

CELL RECEPTION: Spotty

DRINKING WATER AVAILABLE: Yes

POTENTIAL CHILD OR BABY HAZARDS: Can be slick when wet and steep.

GEAR SUGGESTIONS: Shoes good for uphill terrain and that can get wet

There are many reasons Cat Gap Loop is a family favorite. Depending on what path you choose, you are in for a few different adventures. There are stunning mountain views, three waterfalls, camping sites, and areas to splash in the creek. If you decide to climb up to John Rock, you have an amazing view of Looking Glass Rock as well as the surrounding mountains.

This will be about 4 miles out and back. Once on top, sit and have a snack and watch hawks fly overhead while you take in the view. There's a pretty decent climb up to this point as well, so this is the best spot to take a breather. The view from John Rock is beautiful year-round, so there is no best time. But if you want to see mountain laurel and rhododendron blooms, then spring and early summer are good times. If colorful leaves are your thing, the coverage is an amazing fiery orange and red in the fall.

On the opposite side of the loop, you are closer to upper and lower Cedar Rock Falls. Those are about a mile in. Take Butter Gap, a side trail, and you can also get to Grogan Falls from this trail, which is a small but beautiful cascading waterfall.

"The first part of the trail follows along a creek, and you can hear the water rushing over the rocks from the trail. It's a great hike because it has so much to offer, yet it can be done in a few hours," says Chelsea Behforouz.

Depending on how much rain there has been, a lot of water crosses the trail in streams, and little tiny waterfalls can even be found right along the sides of the trail in places. Wildlife is plentiful, from hawks to snakes to centipedes. The forest floor is thickly covered with ferns and moss. Also look out for "rhododendron tunnels," where the rhododendron trees cover the trail and you feel as if you are in a tunnel.

This trail offers comfortable amenities for families, with comfortable benches for nursing and a great covered area in case your hike gets rained out; but these are at the beginning of the hike, not on the trail. There are a lot of secret things for kids to find, like tunnels in trees; and at the entrance of the park, there's ice cream, which you can use as a posthike bribe to get your 3-year-old down the rest of the trail.

As with any hike, there are a few hazards to be aware of. John Rock can be slippery, so we don't suggest toddlers roam free here. Also, be aware that the creek can have slippery rocks and the water is cold, cold, cold no matter what time of year. Keep kids out of overgrown foliage (adhere to Leave No Trace, of course) because there is lots of poison ivy in this area.

WHY IT'S A FAVORITE

"We have taken our little one on this trail since he was in my belly. He is now almost 3. He usually starts out on foot for the first 0.75 mile and then ends up in the carrier for the rest of the way. There are many areas where you have access to creeks as well as waterfalls with swimming holes, so be prepared to get wet!" —CHELSEA BEHFOROUZ

INSIDER'S TIP

Dolly's Dairy Bar sits right at the entrance to the Pisgah National Forest and has great ice cream with a big porch with rocking chairs to sit in while you enjoy your ice cream. A great way to finish off your hike!

THEODORE ROOSEVELT NATIONAL PARK, NORTH DAKOTA, **BUCK HILL TRAIL AND RIDGELINE TRAIL**

ACTIVITIES: Hiking, wildlife viewing

LENGTH OF HIKE: Main trail: 0.4-mile round trip; going past the end of the main trail: 0.75+ mile

OUT AND BACK OR LOOP: Out and back

DIFFICULTY OF TERRAIN: Easy

ELEVATION GAIN: 65 feet

PARKING FEE/PASS: Park entrance fee

TOILETS: No

CHANGING TABLE: No

NURSING BENCHES: No

DOGS ALLOWED: No

BIKES/HORSES/MOTORS ON TRAIL: No

CELL RECEPTION: No

DRINKING WATER AVAILABLE: Yes

POTENTIAL CHILD OR BABY HAZARDS: One drop-off spot to one side at the top of the hill

GEAR SUGGESTIONS: Water, sunblock

From grasshoppers leaping through the grasses to wild prairie flowers to expansive vistas, the 70,000-acre Theodore Roosevelt National Park is a perfect landscape for toddlers learning to walk or a new mom just getting back her hiking legs. Why we especially like Buck Hill Trail, a short, fast climb to 2,855 feet and the highest accessible point in the park, is because it's a climb that even a 2-year-old can do, according to Jennifer Bradwin.

At the top of the hill, look for a grouping of boulders that kids will love climbing on. "My son could have stayed on that rock pile forever and been happy," says Jennifer. "He also loved the grasshoppers in the sage grass and running down the hillside beyond the end of the main trail."

The view to the north from the boulders at the top of the hill is out across the badlands. The main trail stops at the top of the hill, but an obvious dirt trail continues beyond the boulders, meandering up and down the rolling hill crests. This trail goes on, but for little legs, continue to about the second crest for great views and then consider turning around.

As for wildlife, expect grasshoppers, mountain bluebirds, and bison throughout the park. You also might catch a glimpse of pronghorns, elk, bighorn sheep, coyotes and feral horses. And of course, as is common in the Dakotas, North and South, there are lots of prairie dog towns throughout the area.

Water is available in the park, as are benches, but not at this trail, so plan accordingly, especially in hot months as there is absolutely no shelter from the sun. There are plenty of bench-height rocks at the top to sit on if you need to nurse or take a snack break. Benches and picnic tables are also provided in other areas of the park.

The heat and exposure also meant bugs were not a problem at the time of year Jennifer visited, but she said tick checks should be performed. "It's not a super-high tick area, but if you wander off the main trail, the grasses are good tick habitat." Also be aware of rattlesnakes and prickly pear cactus if you do wander off trail.

Spring and fall are the best times to visit. The park stays open year-round, but the roads may close for snow and ice in winter. The summer gets rather hot and dry on the high plains.

Visit on a sunny weekend, and you may see one or two other families on the trail. The park, as a whole, is very quiet with few visitors as compared to what you normally expect in a national park. The parking lot at the trailhead is not very large, but with so few visitors, it doesn't need to be bigger.

If you want to adventure farther in this park, here are a few suggestions: the Boicourt Trail (hold onto the kiddos because this is a ridge with dizzying vistas), the Ridgeline Nature Trail, and the Wind Canyon Trail.

WHY IT'S A FAVORITE

"We loved visiting Theodore Roosevelt National Park! Bison, prairie dogs, and views were plentiful while people were scarce. The skies were big and visibility seemed endless. There are four great, toddler-length trails along the 36-mile scenic loop drive in the south unit, so you can easily sample different areas in one day. Because they are short

and most are hazard-free, they are perfect for toddlers to wander and are easy enough for new moms. Our favorite of the bunch was Buck Hill. My toddler could have stayed on top of the hill, chasing grasshoppers and climbing up and down the boulders, over and over, forever." —JENNIFER BRADWIN

INSIDER'S TIP

If you have the time, make the hour-long drive west to Makoshika State Park in eastern Montana, where you can hike through desolate badlands to dinosaur bones. Also consider camping in the Cottonwood Campground, and you will get a very up-close and personal visit from bison who often roam through.

HOCKING HILLS STATE PARK, OHIO,
ASH CAVE GORGE TRAIL

ACTIVITIES: Hiking, cave, waterfall

LENGTH OF HIKE: 0.25 mile

OUT AND BACK OR LOOP: Out and back

DIFFICULTY OF TERRAIN: Easy

ELEVATION GAIN: No

PARKING FEE/PASS: No

TOILETS: Yes

CHANGING TABLE: No

NURSING BENCHES: Yes

DOGS ALLOWED: Yes

BIKES/HORSES/MOTORS ON TRAIL: No

CELL RECEPTION: Spotty

DRINKING WATER AVAILABLE: Yes

POTENTIAL CHILD OR BABY HAZARDS:
Steep ledges, cliff, ticks

GEAR SUGGESTIONS: Swimsuit

Ash Cave Gorge Trail is just one of a few great hikes in this area that Hike it Baby ambassadors recommend if you ever find yourself in Hocking Hills State Park. The main trail to the 90-foot waterfall is a wide-open, toddler-friendly trail with no tight squeezes. It starts out by leading hikers on an asphalt trail that is easily accessible by wheelchairs and strollers and goes through a beautiful gorge lined with stately hemlocks. In just a quick 0.25 mile, the 700-foot-wide, 100-foot-deep cave is in front of you. Created by water erosion in the sandstone, Ash Cave is the largest recess cave in Ohio.

History on the cave's name was that a huge pile of ashes was found by early settlers in the cave shelter. The source of the ashes is still a mystery, but found within the ashes were arrowheads, animal bones, bits of corn cob, flint, and bits of pottery, so the best guess is this was an area Native American tribes used as a shelter when migrating through the region. Later this was used by settlers as a shelter for church services while working on more permanent buildings.

It's easy to see how the combination of the towering hemlocks, a cascading waterfall, and a wide recess cave make Ash Cave one of Hocking Hills State Park's most popular hiking trails. If you go in the spring, expect to see wildflowers blooming along the trail. Large flowered trillium, Dutchman's breeches, trout lily, jack-in-the-pulpit, and jewel-weed are just some of the flowery finds.

Once you reach the cave, the entire space under it is sand. Depending on your adventure level, viewing the cave from above or within are both options for different perspectives of this giant cave! If you go in the winter, columns of ice form, which can be spectacular to see.

A few slight dangers to be aware of: The Rim Trail has steep ledges, and you are able to walk right up to the edge of the cliff with no railing. Also, the parking lot for Ash Cave is on the other side of the road from the trailhead, so pay attention to your little ones there. And of course, ticks can be a problem in the Midwest any time of year, so make sure to do a tick check posthike.

Annie suggests going in April because the waterfalls will be flowing, and go early in the morning to avoid the crowds. There is a picnic area across the street, so bring a lunch. Consider bringing your bathing suit and sand toys, even though you won't be at the beach. The little ones will love splashing in the waterfall and playing in the sand if it's warm.

Plan to spend a weekend in this park and hike some of the other trails like Old Man's Cave. Or if you are feeling incredibly ambitious, you can hike Grandma Gatewood's Trail, a 6-mile tribute to the woman who is considered to be one of the first inspirations for "light packing" hiking. Grandma Gatewood used to thru-hike with just a wool blanket, a raincoat, and a shower curtain for coverage if weather came in. Hike between Ash Cave and Old Man's Cave, but plan on carrying your little one through sections of it. This is a totally doable hike, and you can actually do 10 miles from Ash Cave to Old Man's Cave if you want to leave a shuttle car at one end. Also, if you are staying overnight, there are both campgrounds and cabins in the area. Cell reception is limited.

WHY IT'S A FAVORITE

"Ash Cave is one of the largest recess caves and is completely handicap accessible, with a paved trail that makes up an out and back. However, you can also make it a bigger adventure by taking the Rim Trail, with spectacular views of the cliff below. There may also be an opportunity for children to splash in a waterfall." —ANNIE FORTUNATO

INSIDER'S TIP

If you want to be more ambitious, Hike it Baby ambassador Suzy Forshey suggests doing the Grandma Gatewood Trail. She says: "It's long but really flat the whole way. There are a few small inclines/descents, but it's very walkable for someone (like me) who is used to shorter 2- to 3-mile hikes. The great thing about it is that it easily connects to four of the major tourist sites in the park (Ash Cave and Old Man Cave at either end and Cedar Falls and Whispering Cave in the middle). Each attraction is only 2 to 3 miles from the previous, so you can just do a smaller loop back to your start. It's a pretty good option if you'll be there for a long weekend."

SUGARCREEK METROPARK, OHIO,
OSAGE ORANGE TRAIL

ACTIVITIES: Hiking, picnicking

LENGTH OF HIKE: 1.3 miles

OUT AND BACK OR LOOP: Loop

DIFFICULTY OF TERRAIN: No

ELEVATION GAIN: Unsure

PARKING FEE/PASS: No

TOILETS: Yes

CHANGING TABLE: No

NURSING BENCHES: Yes

DOGS ALLOWED: Yes

BIKES/HORSES/MOTORS ON TRAIL: No

CELL RECEPTION: Yes

DRINKING WATER AVAILABLE: Yes

POTENTIAL CHILD OR BABY HAZARDS: Poison ivy, nettle, roots

GEAR SUGGESTIONS: Big-wheel stroller, bug spray

The Osage Orange Trail is one of Hike it Baby Dayton's favorites because the terrain is easy enough for toddlers and strollers to hike side by side. Older kids and parents will enjoy the beautiful old-woods scenery and the history that goes with it, which includes some of Ohio's oldest oak trees—the Three Sisters—and a beautiful archway of Osage orange trees that used to line an old farm lane. Younger kids will love the enormous mud puddles in the rainy months and the fact that they are allowed to run wild without concern of any drop-offs or bikes on trail.

The start of this trail has a great nature play area where the kids can build a log structure, balance along fallen trees, and imagine a life in the woods. Remind your little ones that they can play as long as they want if they hike hard.

One of the highlights to look out for on this hike is the wildflower prairie before the main loop starts. This is a great spot to birdwatch while enjoying the bench swing. Also, feeding moms can take a pit stop here on their hike and feed a hungry one.

Another notable stop is the Three Sisters, three large oak trees over 550 years old standing magnificently not even a mile into the hike. In 2008, one died and fell, but two are still standing. It's fun to take a picture of them with your child standing next to them to get a feel for how tall they are.

Also make sure to check out the Osage orange archway tunnel of trees, which is amazing in every season. Osage orange is a hardwood tree introduced to Ohio in the 1800s and used for making fences and bows and arrows. These trees offer excellent shading on the trail during the summer thanks to the tunnel they form and the leaves overhead, and they make a white wonderland arch in the snow. These trees are a beautiful, if a bit eerie, site if you catch them when the fog rolls in.

Winter is great on this hike, as the stillness of the woods and the lack of leaves have a stark beauty. During the fall, the wildlife is easy to spot here as squirrels tussle through the falling leaves. The summer heat and humidity can be hard for little hikers, but early morning or evening hikes are great times to get out there. Bugs during late summer can be a nuisance, though.

Look for beautiful birds in this park. Owls hide in the trees high above in the woods and woodpeckers are plentiful. Elizabeth Mingus-Elam has one fond memory of a woodpecker in this park. "I remember seeing my husband get down to our 3-year-old's level, point up to the treetops, where our little girl could just make out the red speck of color of the downy woodpecker tapping the side of the tree. She was so amazed to find that the source of the sound was such a little bird, and the smiles she and her dad shared will always stick with me."

Squirrels and deer are also easy to spot wandering through the bushes. The Sugarcreek runs along the north edge of this Metropark, and although the Osage Orange Trail does not go along it, other trails do and it's a great spot to let some of the bigger kids play.

WHY IT'S A FAVORITE

"The best part about this trail is the history. My husband is a history buff, and we love that we can explore this trail and learn about its history along the way. It's easy to get to and many paths to explore, which keeps the trail fresh every time we go." —ELIZABETH MINGUS-ELAM

INSIDER'S TIP

Sugarcreek is part of the FiveRivers Metroparks system, and they have amazing naturalists who do many free events throughout the year. Check their website before you plan your visit to the area: www.metroparks.org/places-to-go/sugarcreek/.

HOLIDAY HIKES FOR FREE!

While we all love to support our parks, it's always nice to get in a freebie. Did you know that most state and federal parks have a few free days throughout the year? Make sure to look for these in your local newspapers and check the National Park Service website (https://www.nps.gov/) throughout the year. Look for local versions of these in your city and state, too, for additional days.

- Jan. 15—Martin Luther King Jr. Day
- April 21—First day of National Park Week
- Sept. 22—National Public Lands Day
- Nov. 11—Veterans' Day

CHARON'S GARDEN WILDERNESS, OKLAHOMA, **ELK MOUNTAIN TRAIL**

ACTIVITIES: Hiking, wildlife refuge

LENGTH OF HIKE: 2.2 miles

OUT AND BACK OR LOOP: Out and back

DIFFICULTY OF TERRAIN: Moderate

ELEVATION GAIN: 570 feet

PARKING FEE/PASS: No

TOILETS: Yes

CHANGING TABLE: No

NURSING BENCHES: No

DOGS ALLOWED: Yes, on leash

BIKES/HORSES/MOTORS ON TRAIL: No

CELL RECEPTION: Spotty

DRINKING WATER AVAILABLE: Yes

POTENTIAL CHILD OR BABY HAZARDS: Rocks, steep boulders, river

GEAR SUGGESTIONS: Carrier for younger children, hiking or trail shoes, sunscreen

If you like steps and a good workout, this is a hike you'll want to do if you are in the Oklahoma City area. Located almost 2 hours to the southwest in the western corner of the Wichita Mountains Wildlife Refuge, this hike is one where the Oklahoma views really show themselves off, especially if you hike in the morning before the heat starts. There's little shade, so consider hiking in cooler parts of the day and not in the middle of summer. Avoid this hike if it's over 90 degrees!

For a little history on Elk Mountain, it's located in the 59,000-acre Wichita Mountains Wildlife Refuge, which was established in 1901 and is the oldest refuge managed by the US Fish and Wildlife Service. Located within the park, you'll find a number of animals that were once wiped out in this area but now have been reintroduced, like bison, river otters, prairie dogs, and burrowing owls. Also grazing the prairies around this hike are Rocky Mountain elk and white-tailed deer, as well as Texas longhorn cattle.

This hike is located in the Charons Garden Wilderness area of the refuge and starts out from the parking lot by crossing over a deep river with a steep bank, so no water play in this one, unfortunately. Continue to the trailhead, and as you walk, you'll notice how much your kids will love climbing the rocks throughout the hike. Little legs can hike a good amount, thanks to well-manicured stairs, but as you get to the summit, consider holding hands.

Once on top of the summit, there are about 40 acres to explore, and you can spend a good hour or two roaming around taking in the views. Maybe have a picnic?

For new parents, there are no benches for feeding, but the boulders should suffice for snack breaks. The summit is pretty exposed, so it can get windy. Hiking boots would be ideal for the crushed rock/dirt surface and to climb up rocks, but any trail-type shoe will suffice.

Best time of year to visit this trailhead? The spring or fall is the nicest, as the summer can get hot with sun exposure. Despite its rocky nature, the trail is well maintained, and at the time she hiked it, Jennifer Campbell said even her 2-year-old enjoyed hiking it and was climbing over the rocks without a problem. Look out for the intense prickly pear cacti in this area, especially if you have dogs. One hiker reported picking thorns out of her dog's coat for an hour after the hike.

WHY IT'S A FAVORITE

"There are great opportunities for views most of the way. You just have to stop and turn around on your way up to the summit, otherwise you can see it on the way back down. We were there on an incredibly foggy day, so I would imagine there is quite a bit of sun exposure without fog, so be ready for that. There are only a few areas that are wooded. The rest are shrubs and rock landscape." —JENNIFER CAMPBELL

INSIDER'S TIP

Best time of year to visit this hike is in the spring, when the landscape comes alive with wildflowers like the bright yellow balsamroot and blue and purple spiderwort. In the fall, the upper part of the trail comes alive with scrub oak changing colors before dropping leaves. This is a perfect stop if you are traveling anywhere near I-40 or I-44, so take the time to visit and you won't be disappointed.

CARL G. WASHBURNE STATE PARK, OREGON, HECETA HEAD TO HOBBIT TRAIL

ACTIVITIES: Hiking, tide pools, historic landmark

LENGTH OF HIKE: 1 or 4.4 miles

OUT AND BACK OR LOOP: Out and back

DIFFICULTY OF TERRAIN: Moderate

ELEVATION GAIN: 400 feet

PARKING FEE/PASS: $5 or state park pass

TOILETS: Yes

CHANGING TABLE: No

NURSING BENCHES: Yes

DOGS ALLOWED: Yes

BIKES/HORSES/MOTORS ON TRAIL: No

CELL RECEPTION: Spotty

DRINKING WATER AVAILABLE: No

POTENTIAL CHILD OR BABY HAZARDS: Some drop-offs, but easy to see where they are

GEAR SUGGESTIONS: Good rain layers

With a name like the "Hobbit Trail," how can this not be a childlike wonder of an adventure? There are two ways you can go about this hike. If you aren't up for a long one, consider parking on the road and hiking the 0.5 mile out to the beach through the tree tunnel section known as the "Hobbit Trail." Make sure you map the parking before arriving because this part is just a pull-out on the side of the road. There's no true designated spot to park, so be aware that you are also getting out on the side of the highway. There is a small sign marking the Hobbit Trail, but you will miss it if you blink.

The more adventurous way to explore the Hobbit Trail is to start by parking at Heceta Head Lighthouse and hiking up to the lighthouse. Stop for a quick tour and a history lesson on lighthouses in the Northwest. The 56-foot-tall Heceta Head Lighthouse was built in 1894 and for many years had the strongest beam in Oregon, shining out for 21 nautical miles. The lighthouse was renovated and reopened in 2013, so it's worth a quick visit.

Heceta Head was named after a Spanish explorer; however, it was originally home to the Siuslaw Indians who hunted sea lions and scavenged sea bird eggs from the rocky shores. In the late 1800s, it was homesteaded, and the lighthouse was erected to help ships traveling north to deliver goods to ports in the north. When you leave the Heceta Head Lighthouse, you climb a set of railroad tie stairs up the hillside. Stop and look out over the lighthouse for a spectacular view down the coastline.

From this point, you crest the hill and begin traveling down. Remember, you will have to hike back up, and while it's not a particularly steep hike, it's long and gradual. If you

have a little walker who runs down the trail, you might be carrying him up. The trail meanders 0.7 mile through the Sitka spruce trees and eventually meets up with the Hobbit Trail.

This last section down to the beach is so much fun for small children with big imaginations. Have a troll in the forest story ready to tell them as you wind down through the tunnel of trees. At the bottom, the trail opens up to a beautiful golden yellow sandy beach. Plan to picnic there. Interestingly, if you hike this in the spring, there are often ladybugs flying around, landing on rock, sand, and little hands. Keep an eye out for these magical little bugs that always delight toddlers. If you hug the edge of the beach toward the trail, there are little trickles of water spilling down that are fun to play in as well.

If you're wanting to add more distance to this hike or are staying a few days, you can also do the 3.5-mile China Creek Trail Loop. This is a lollipop loop hike that starts just across the road from Hobbit Trail. Make a weekend of it by camping in the Carl G. Washburne Campground just down the road.

WHY IT'S A FAVORITE

"We really enjoyed this trail because it feels like you are in a fairytale storybook as you head through the thick overgrowth tunnel down to the beach. The beach is open and fairly empty because it requires a short hike to it, so it never feels crowded." —MARK HODGES

INSIDER'S TIP

The Oregon coast is a magical place with windswept Dr. Seuss–like trees, white sand dunes, and miles of quiet coastline that takes a beating from storms, but this also keeps away the crowds. On a sunny weekend, expect the masses; but if city folk are unsure of weather conditions, you can find yourself on trails alone for hours. Consider waiting for one of those on-and-off days, and you will get the entire beach to yourself. Often there will be sunny days on the coast in the cooler fall months when it's raining inland. Also, it's always 10 to 15 degrees cooler at the coast in the summer, so beat the heat and head out. The majority of this trail is in the shade, so it's a good one to visit on a hot summer day.

MOUNT HOOD NATIONAL FOREST, OREGON, **MIRROR LAKE**

ACTIVITIES: Hiking, splashing, fishing, camping

LENGTH OF HIKE: 4.2 miles

OUT AND BACK OR LOOP: Out and back

DIFFICULTY OF TERRAIN: Moderate

ELEVATION GAIN: 672 feet

PARKING FEE/PASS: Yes

TOILETS: No

CHANGING TABLE: No

NURSING BENCHES: No

DOGS ALLOWED: Yes

BIKES/HORSES/MOTORS ON TRAIL: No

CELL RECEPTION: Spotty

DRINKING WATER AVAILABLE: No

POTENTIAL CHILD OR BABY HAZARDS: Lake

GEAR SUGGESTIONS: Hiking poles, bug spray

Just one of the many beautiful hikes in the Mount Hood area, Mirror Lake is an excellent choice with toddlers and babies because of both the shorter distance and the reward of the mountain and lake views. Here's the warning we will give about this hike: It's a butt burner on the way up. There are some bridges to cross and a point where you'll reach some solid switchbacks, but that said, most of it can be hiked by a little one who is used to hiking. If you're a flatlander, plan to take it slow because this hike is at 4,000 feet above sea level.

What we like about this trail is that it's fairly wide, and once you reach the lake, the 0.5 mile around the lake is completely flat and will give you a lot of picture-perfect moments of Mount Hood and Mirror Lake. You'll also enjoy the boardwalks around the lake that help preserve the landscape and keep hikers in the area on trail.

Wildlife you can expect to see here are black-tailed deer, chipmunks, squirrels, maybe red foxes, coyotes, gophers, mice, and maybe even black bears if you are lucky. They keep themselves pretty well hidden in this area, though.

If you're feeling up for another climb, head up Tom Dick and Harry for an additional 1.8 miles and an even more impressive view of the area. This is not very kid friendly, and there is some scrambling at the top, so you might consider leaving one parent and kid behind for the quick climb. Or consider spending the weekend here and camp at Mirror Lake Campground.

If you choose to camp, bring your bug spray because as the temps cool, the bugs come out fiercely due to the proximity of water. There are six campsites scattered around the lake, so they can fill up quickly on a weekend. It helps that they are walk-in and that the Mount Hood area has plenty of dispersed free camping.

A pass is required for parking at this location, so make sure you have either a Northwest Forest Pass or a National Parks Pass displayed in your window. Rangers do frequent this spot and will ticket. Make sure to note that Mirror Lake Trail is closed from November 1 to April 30.

WHY IT'S A FAVORITE

"Mirror Lake is special because it gives you so much! You start out in the woods where the trees tower above you, then you get to this rocky wonderland where, if you are lucky to see one, pica are squeaking. The hike continues, and just when you think you've had enough of carrying the baby on your back, you get to the lake. You take a breather and stare at Mount Hood in all of its majesty" —LYDIA AGUNDEZ

INSIDER'S TIP

If you like huckleberry milkshakes, head up the road into Government Camp and look for the Huckleberry Inn. Also consider making a quick drive up to Timberline Lodge if you are there in the summer. The beautiful old lodge was built in 1937 as part of a Conservation Corps project during the Great Depression. It's also the building you see in the classic Stanley Kubrick movie featuring Jack Nicholson, "The Shining." Hiking around the lodge is fun for kids, and if you look up on the mountain, you can see skiers and snowboarders shredding the glacier in the summer.

SILVER FALLS STATE PARK, OREGON,
TRAIL OF TEN FALLS

ACTIVITIES: Hiking, nature play area, camping, splashing

LENGTH OF HIKE: 7.8 miles

OUT AND BACK OR LOOP: Both

DIFFICULTY OF TERRAIN: Moderate

ELEVATION GAIN: 700 feet

PARKING FEE/PASS: Yes

TOILETS: Yes

CHANGING TABLE: Yes

NURSING BENCHES: Yes

DOGS ALLOWED: No

BIKES/HORSES/MOTORS ON TRAIL: No

CELL RECEPTION: Spotty

DRINKING WATER AVAILABLE: Yes

POTENTIAL CHILD OR BABY HAZARDS: Steep drop-offs on parts of the trail

GEAR SUGGESTIONS: Hiking poles, sunscreen, bug spray, towels if splashing in water

Why Silver Falls isn't recognized as one of the "Seven Wonders of Oregon" is beyond us. With 10 waterfalls to view in one park, outside of the Columbia Gorge, this is where most Oregonians (and 1.2 million visitors annually) go to get their waterfall fix. With easy, very family-accessible trails, this one is a winner if you want to keep the kids entertained and excited about waterfall wandering. What makes this area amazing is that while you can do a big loop and see 10 waterfalls on the one main trail, you can also just do some out and back on either end of the trail to view a few waterfalls whether you go clockwise or counterclockwise.

The hike has a few climbs, so expect to climb some stairs, but most of it is very doable by children who are comfortable hiking. If you choose to do the entire 7.8 miles, you'll probably end up carrying, but it will be worth it. Chances are with how many exciting waterfall viewings there are around every bend, your little one will want to do a lot of up and down again by the next waterfall.

You can hike this one both clockwise and counterclockwise, with similar climbing in both directions. If you want to start off with a big bang right up front, head by the Visitor Center (great bathroom stop there) and head out to the Upper South Falls and then Lower South Falls. There is a place here where you can turn this hike into a loop and head back uphill. This shorter version is stroller friendly as well with a little pushing uphill if you just stay on the Maple Ridge Trail.

It's easy to see why the original inhabitants, the Kalapuya and Molalla, chose to live in this beautiful region beginning nearly 14,000 years ago. At its peak time, this area was home to around 15,000 indigenous people until disease brought in by people of European descent caused the original inhabitant population to decrease to 600 people. Those left were displaced by homesteaders in the 1800s and sent to live on reservations in eastern Oregon.

There are so many reasons to love this well-maintained Oregon State Park, from the beautiful waterfalls that are up to 177 feet tall cascading down rock walls to the thick forest that is one of the last remaining low-elevation old-growth forests west of the Cascades. This 9,200-acre forest of Douglas fir, hemlock, and cedar is as peaceful as they come, with lush, deep-green, moss-covered trees that are home to woodpeckers, blue jays, robins, and great gray owls to name a few of the birds singing out from high above. On the ground, deer and bunnies are plentiful.

Consider making a weekend out of visiting Silver Falls; individual and group sites are available, but you definitely need a reservation. Also look for the unique North Canyon Nature Play Area in this park near the group camping site. Unlike a traditional playground with plastic structures, this nature-based "playground" was designed to teach children how to mimic animals with a "bear den" to climb in and a "giant bird nest" to jump out of.

WHY IT'S A FAVORITE

"I love going behind the falls with my girls when our family is in a rough patch for whatever reason—and we make wishes from behind the waterfall. The negative ions

and energy of the falls are exhilarating and feel cleansing. I love the North Falls trail-head because the views are amazing and it's less trafficked. South Falls boasts the two big waterfalls we walk behind for wish making, so that section is a favorite as well."
—MEGAN LUCAS

INSIDER'S TIP
Not up for the full, big hike? Do shorter hikes out and back to South Falls, North Falls, and Upper North Falls. Upper North Falls is best in the middle of a hot summer because there is a beautiful toddler-friendly pool of icy water to swim in at the base of the falls. This spot also is often shady, so it's easy to cool down here on a hot day.

MAYER STATE PARK, OREGON, ROWENA CREST PLATEAU

ACTIVITIES: Hiking, wildflower viewing, photography

LENGTH OF HIKE: 1 mile

OUT AND BACK OR LOOP: Out and back

DIFFICULTY OF TERRAIN: Easy

ELEVATION GAIN: No

PARKING FEE/PASS: No

TOILETS: No

CHANGING TABLE: No

NURSING BENCHES: No

DOGS ALLOWED: No

BIKES/HORSES/MOTORS ON TRAIL: No

CELL RECEPTION: Yes

DRINKING WATER AVAILABLE: No

POTENTIAL CHILD OR BABY HAZARDS: Cliffs, heavy poison oak, rattlesnakes, ticks

GEAR SUGGESTIONS: Waterproof shoes, boots

If you love wildflowers, this is one of the most toddler-friendly, easy hikes you can do in the Columbia Gorge. Located at the edge of the rain shadow, where the lush green of the gorge meets the desert just past Hood River near Mosier, turn uphill for a short windy drive off of I-84 that leads to an easy pull-off at the Tom McCall Preserve. We are mentioning the windiness of the road here because it's 2.5 miles with eight very intense switchback curves, so if you have a little one who is prone to carsickness, drive slowly.

Once you arrive, you'll notice that there are two trailheads at this location. One has some serious elevation, is about 3 miles, and has a spectacular view but is only baby-wearing friendly. This is called McCall Point Hike and is open from May to October only. If you do Rowena Plateau and have a sleeping baby or are looking for more length in your adventure, this it totally worth doing, though there's a climb.

Rowena Plateau is the friendlier toddler option but not to be missed in the gorge. This hike will give you a spectacular view of the gorge, amazing wildflowers, frogs, and bird-watching galore and a fair bit of muddy puddle stomping around the two little ponds that toddlers can't help but stop to splash in.

The hike is short but perfect for new walkers because it's mostly flat and a completely well-defined trail cutting through the lush fields of green and a brilliant rainbow quilt of flowers. Leaving from the parking lot, head west across a flat, open field toward the cliffy horizon. At about 0.5 mile, you will come to a little pond filled with thumbnail-sized fluorescent green frogs. Definitely stop to play with these little guys. They blend well into the vibrant landscape, but if you pause and look in the pond, you'll see them swimming and hanging out along the edges.

Continue along this trail for another 0.5 mile and you will come to a clear end of the trail. Just before you reach the end, stop at a little flat spot before a rocky patch (completely toddler doable) for a snack and water break. Here you can really take in the magnificent view of the gorge in both directions. This end part is a little cliffy, so be sure to keep an eye on little walkers, especially if they are runners.

Visit this hike earlier in the spring and the landscape is an explosion of tiny yellow flowers that are about the size of a fingernail. As spring progresses toward summer, the landscape pops with deep purple lupine and bigger yellow flowers called arrowleaf balsamroot, also known as the "Oregon sunflower." These golden flowers were used by Native Americans in the area as food and medicine.

Note that there are no bathrooms at this hike, so you will definitely want to bring a toddler potty if you are in training mode. Also, with over 800 wildflower species in the gorge, including a handful found nowhere else, this very accessible spot is definitely well trafficked because of ease of access. But there's plenty of parking and space for all. Try to get to the McCall Preserve early to beat the crowds.

WHY IT'S A FAVORITE
"Rowena Crest was the first hike our family did in the gorge when we moved to Oregon. This easy hike displays the absolutely stunning beauty of cliffs, mountains, foliage, wild-flowers, and greenery in the Columbia River Gorge. A perfect day to me would consist of a hike at Rowena Crest and then visiting a local brewery with mountain views all around in Hood River." —BECCA HARRISON

INSIDER'S TIP

On the weekends in the peak of the wildflower blooms, there's usually a naturalist from the Nature Conservancy camped out by the entrance of Rowena Plateau. Make sure to stop and ask questions because these volunteers are often a wealth of information about the amazing wildflowers in the area. They also lead interpretive walks on the weekends. Plan to hike this in the spring or very early summer before the heat hits, because there is zero shade.

DESCHUTES NATIONAL FOREST, OREGON, **TODD LAKE**

ACTIVITIES: Paddling, splashing, hiking, camping

LENGTH OF HIKE: 1.7 miles

OUT AND BACK OR LOOP: Loop

DIFFICULTY OF TERRAIN: Easy

ELEVATION GAIN: No

PARKING FEE/PASS: Yes

TOILETS: No

CHANGING TABLE: No

NURSING BENCHES: No

DOGS ALLOWED: Yes

BIKES/HORSES/MOTORS ON TRAIL: No

CELL RECEPTION: No

DRINKING WATER AVAILABLE: No

POTENTIAL CHILD OR BABY HAZARDS: Lake, giardia

GEAR SUGGESTIONS: Swim gear, extra shoes for wet feet or water shoes, water filter

The hike around the lake starts out from a small parking lot that can hold about 20 cars. It's flat and well marked with little foot bridges that, in some cases, are just boards across streams trickling into the lake. Come at the right time of year and you will be greeted by hundreds of tiny thumbnail-sized frogs hopping around that will eventually be full-sized Western toads and Cascade frogs, both of which are endangered species due to habitat changes.

This area gets its namesake from John Y. Todd, an early settler in Oregon. The area was originally called "Lost Lake," but the name was changed due to confusion from a few other Lost Lakes that were also in Oregon.

To date, this was one of our favorite hikes in Oregon with Mason. We loved it so much because it was so easy for a 3-year-old to hike the whole thing by himself. We took a long break in the middle, going for a swim, and then had a picnic on the grassy lakeshore. While there definitely were a number of people hiking the area, it never felt crowded because the area is so open and it's easy to hike off away from everyone and sit lakeside or hike up the mountain for a better view.

While there, we saw families fishing, one guy had an easel set up and was painting the spectacular view of the lake and Mount Bachelor towering over, and we saw a group of elderly hikers, as well as a group of solo mamas with their kids. This trail is definitely great for multigenerational hikes because it's so gentle and easy to navigate.

One piece of advice is to bring water-friendly shoes or plan on having very wet feet when you get back. There will be no way to keep your toddler out of all the little stream crossings. It's way too fun to stomp through these!

This area does see a lot of snow throughout the year, so expect to not be able to get out on the roads until June, and usually it's no longer passable by early October. If you do make it to this area between June and early August, expect an amazing wildflower bloom. This area is one of Oregon's designated Pacific Northwest Region wildflower viewing areas.

WHY IT'S A FAVORITE

"Todd Lake is a magical place with everything you could need for introducing an adventuring toddler to hiking. There's a clear lake, easy-to-cross bridges, no elevation gain, and beautiful views of Mount Bachelor over the lake." —SHANTI AND MARK HODGES

INSIDER'S TIP

There is camping in the area, however, it seems to be limited (3 spots), requires a permit, and is closed a good chunk of the year. If you want to camp in the area, we suggest heading about 15 minutes down the road to Sparks Lake. There is also phenomenal hiking in that area and both paid and free camping.

Trail Essentials

While your hike will most likely be short, you'll want to add items to your pack or stroller that you may not have thought of before. Consider all of these things if you are planning to go some distance and be out all day.

1. Small baggie of wipes in a ziplock bag with 2 or 3 extra bags. These come in handy if you have to section off used wipes from fresh ones or need to contain a really serious explosion (sh*t happens!).

2. Benadryl and Tylenol for babies in case an unexpected allergy or fever arises (leave this in the car if doing a short hike).

3. Retractable or small pocket mirror for checking baby or toddler positioning on your back while you are hiking.

4. Dangling rattle or pacifier on a carabiner or clip for trail entertainment and to prevent a meltdown.

5. Safety pin or two in case something needs McGuyver-esque mending on the fly. This can be added to the plastic bags and wipes.

6. Light muslin cloth for shade cover and changing baby on the ground. Can use safety pins to fasten this to a carrier to keep baby covered in hot sun or cover a toddler's legs that are exposed.

7. Small, easy-to-handle water bottle with a sucking straw or mouthpiece for quick sips. Get your child used to using a water bottle that they suck out of when they are young and while still using bottles.

8. Whistle for kids to have fun with and for you to blow in case of an emergency. Some packs have this built in.

9. Trail toys like a small car or plastic bugs for older kids. (Our son loved to have a car in hand on trail. We brought two in case we lost one.)

10. Extra pair of socks, because babies and toddlers always get their feet wet, even with protective boots. A warm, dry pair of socks can also act as mittens on cold hands.

PRACTICE SMART
SUN SAFETY

A FEW MONTHS AGO, MARK CAME HOME FROM a camping trip with Mason, and my little boy was as red as a tomato! Our main issue is that Mason hates wearing hats, and it's a mega battle to get sunscreen on him. Getting him to stay in the shade? No way. Not going to happen. Over the last few years, we've tried everything under the sun, excuse the pun, to keep him covered up. We now have an arsenal of tricks and products that seem to work pretty well. If we can't get one thing to work, we try another.

SUNSCREEN. We have four different types of sunscreen. Spray-on, lotion, a mini stick, and wipes. The spray-on is easiest if you have a kicking and screaming toddler. It's fast and effective. The tricky part is getting it on the face. Spray it on your hands first and then apply to your child's face and hands.

A stick works wonderfully for teaching kids how to put it on themselves if your little one is in that phase of "me do it!" There are a number of brands like Honest Company, Beyond Coastal, Alba, and Avon who make little sticks that fit in the palm of your hand. These are easy to slide into a fanny pack or baby carrier and take along.

Cloths are easy to wipe on while your kiddo is napping on your back. Or you can act like you are cleaning off his face with the cloth. Sometimes that will work better than admitting you are putting sunscreen on him.

HATS. Not all hats are created equal. Sometimes I think we have tried every hat out there! The best advice is to start putting hats on your baby as soon as possible so they get used to the feeling. If your toddler refuses to keep a hat on, try to distract him or tag team with a partner. You can also involve your toddler in the purchase so he feels like he "chose" it (just make sure you are okay with each of the options!). Here are some things to think about when purchasing a hat:

1. Get entertaining hats. We have a crocodile hat that Mason will wear sometimes because he loves how fun it is. While we can't get him to wear it all the time, we can usually get a good hour of wear with this one.

2. Look for something that is made of a nylon material and has a big, round brim with a buckle strap under the chin. Kids can untie bows, but they can rarely unbuckle.

3. Get sunscreen materials in the hat so there is extra protection. Also, nylon dries fast, so they can wear the hat in water.

4. To get your child used to wearing a hat, try to get her to put the hat on in the house before going outside.

5. Get a matching hat. Mason and Mark both have blue, large-brimmed hats, so sometimes we can get Mason to wear it because Daddy is wearing the same hat.

6. Costume hats. If your kid loves being a fireman, policeman, sailor, or fairy, consider getting some kind of themed hat that she is excited to put on.

When hats won't work, consider other options like a muslin cloth cut in half or a bandana. Sometimes kids will wear a bandana if they think it's a pirate hat or it helps get them into character. This will only keep the scalp from burning, but at least it will help with some sun protection. Three brands we've found that work well and kids seem to keep on are: Sunday Afternoons, REI brand hats, and iPlay.

BODYSUITS. Sunscreen isn't always advised for babies, especially those under 6 months old. Body suits, rash guards, and muslin cloths are great options. There are a number of brands that offer one-piece zip-up suits for children as young as 3 months old. Buy them one size up so you can battle growth spurts for a bit. Some of the brands to consider that Hike it Baby families suggest are: Lark Adventurewear, iPlay , UVSkinz, and Oakiwear.

FIND (OR MAKE) SHADE. When Mason was a baby, we were hesitant to put sunscreen on him. Even the natural kinds seemed a little thick and intense for a baby. We opted to use muslin cloths and umbrellas over him. Consider carrying an umbrella on an extra-hot day. Sure, it might look silly, but both you and baby will be covered, whether front- or back-wearing. You will be surprised at how much cooler this will keep you on a hot day.

Frame carriers like the Deuter Kid Comfort are great options once kids are over 6 months old, because they offer excellent full sun protection when they have a sunshade on them. You can additionally cover your baby by putting a muslin cloth over the shade or on their legs if you are walking straight into the sun.

SUNBURN. Sun is not the enemy. It's just another part of getting out there year-round and something to be aware of. If you are prepared with the right gear, your child will be happier at the end of a long summer day. Remember to reapply sunscreen often, and do regular checks every 20 to 40 minutes for how sunbaked your little one is. That said, sometimes burns happen. Keep an aloe vera gel or a live aloe plant at home, and apply as soon as you can after the burn. Then consider taking a day off from summer and, as much as we hate to suggest this, hang indoors. The burn will pass within a day or two, and you can get back out there and try all of the above again.

Tips for Great Trail Photos

1. Get down to their level and show the perspective of a trail for a 2-year-old.

2. Let them explore and have fun and get out in front of you.

3. Make sure kids are interacting with their surroundings versus the camera.

4. Have them play with nature. Show them ferns, sticks, stones, mud puddles—things that they can learn from and engage with as you are shooting.

5. Shoot farther away to show the environment.

6. Be sure to get some in front and behind as you hike.

7. Skip the "say cheese" and try instead to have them tell you about their favorite thing on that trail. Or tell them a joke to make them laugh.

8. Capture connection (get those tender moments) between parent and child.

9. Capture emotion (don't stop shooting when a kiddo's crying!); these can be great shots.

10. Change your perspective. Lie down in the mud and get that puddle stomping close up!

11. Be creative and play with light. Of course, look for that golden hour, too!

12. Have fun! Be silly. Laugh, and children will laugh with you.

HIKE IT BABY **PHOTOGRAPHERS**

LAURA CASTRO

My husband was deployed as an army soldier, and I started taking pictures to capture every moment of our daughter, who was ever changing and growing. I didn't want him to miss anything. Later, I started a 365 Challenge to document each aspect of our daily lives. This is the approach I bring to my photography on the trails: I don't pose or say much; I try to follow and capture the emotion, connection, environment of each hike. I try to be like a fly on the wall (or tree). I always say it was a good hike when the kids come back covered in dirt or mud and if I got to climb a tree or lie in a puddle. I've been shooting professionally for 6 years, and I take at least one course every year to keep up my knowledge and grow as a photographer.

ASHLEY SCHEIDER

I started taking photos in high school for a digital photography class. It was mainly focused on how to use Photoshop, but I knew I'd want to shoot photos forever. Seven years later, my husband bought me a very expensive camera for Christmas and said as a joke that I'd have to earn back the cost by getting really, really good. He didn't realize I would take that challenge to heart. I started getting into family photography because I loved taking photos of my son, and then I found Hike it Baby. Seeing my friends explore outside with their new babies and seeing my own child's eyes light up with every newfound treasure became an absolute joy. Being able to share and capture my love for nature and these moments outside with friends is an extremely humbling experience.

HIKE IT BABY **PHOTOGRAPHERS**

JENNIFER CAMPBELL

I have always had an interest in photography, but I never committed to actually learning it until I took a road trip with my kids. The early part of the year had been rough, and I really needed a creative outlet. Being in nature is both calming and inspiring. I love photographing children in their natural element, just being kids, exploring, playing, and getting dirty. My favorite way to take photos of kids is by standing back and capturing what and how they choose to explore and follow their imagination. If I am trying to get some intentional shots, I will say, "Hey, look at that [thing]; that looks really interesting. Should we check it out?" Or, "Can you show me that really neat [thing] that you found?" Children enjoy taking the lead on discovery and exploration. Sometimes they just need a few little "seeds" of ideas planted to get them going. And when that doesn't work, a lollipop always does!

Over the years Hike it Baby has had many amazing photographers help tell our story and encourage many families to get on trail. We've found that photos of babies and young children help inspire and remind us that it's totally possibly to do it whether you have one child or five in tow. These are just a few of the photographers who have helped encourage the Hike it Baby community to get out there.

PINE GROVE FURNACE STATE PARK, PENNSYLVANIA, **TOM'S RUN CREEK**

ACTIVITIES: Hiking, camping

LENGTH OF HIKES: 2 or 4 miles

OUT AND BACK OR LOOP: Out and back

DIFFICULTY OF TERRAIN: Easy

ELEVATION GAIN: No

PARKING FEE/PASS: Suggested donation $3

TOILETS: Yes

CHANGING TABLE: Yes

NURSING BENCHES: Yes

DOGS ALLOWED: Yes, on leash

BIKES/HORSES/MOTORS ON TRAIL: No

CELL RECEPTION: No

DRINKING WATER AVAILABLE: Yes

POTENTIAL CHILD OR BABY HAZARDS: Ticks, poison ivy

GEAR SUGGESTIONS: Hiking poles if child carrying

You don't have to be a thru-hiker to enjoy the Appalachian Trail, but if you want to learn more about it all, consider visiting Pine Grove Furnace State Park to get the flavor of the AT experience. There's a perfect toddler out-and-back trail that you can do as either 2 or 4 miles, depending on what your legs are up to. Then visit the Appalachian Trail Museum, which sits near the midway point of the 2,186-mile trail. The museum pays tribute to trail pioneers like Early Shaffer, Grandma Gatewood, Gene Espy and Ed Garvey, whose blood and sweat went into helping make the trail what it is today.

There is also a Children's Discovery Center if you find you're just having one of "those" days when your little one has decided heading to the trail is just not going to happen.

The reason this is a Hike it Baby local favorite in the summer is because it's an easy no-elevation-gain journey with a nice end reward of a general store. "There are tons of stinky hikers stopping by the general store for their half gallon of ice cream to celebrate hiking half of the Appalachian Trail, which is why we call it the half-pint hike. We like to do the same after our modified version," explains Hike it Baby Gettysburg branch ambassador Liz Knapp.

The short version starts at Bunker Hill Road and is about 2 miles round trip. About 0.5 mile in, the trail meets up with the midway point of the Appalachian Trail, where you can snap a few pictures. The terrain can be rocky in parts, so consider a carrier for smaller kids. Dogs may also have trouble, so keep that in mind if you bring your four-legged friend.

Another nice thing about this hike is that there are wood shelters erected for backpackers traveling through the area who camp and stop to picnic on the tables. If you need an outhouse, this is also available, which is great if you are potty training a little one. Consider this hike for a backpacking trial if you are interested in testing these waters. The close proximity to civilization makes it an easy escape if backpacking doesn't work out.

If you consider making a weekend out of this spot and get a campsite, be sure to explore other nearby trails like the Pine Grove Furnace hike (2.5 miles) from Fuller Lake to Laurel Lake. This is a paved/gravel hike that's popular for Hike it Baby families because parents can push strollers there and back and get 5 miles on trail after work. Half the trail is part of the Appalachian Trail (then it loops up into the woods to Pole Steeple). Be aware that half of this trail is "hiker biker trail" accessible to bikes and motorized vehicles (so a ranger can drive down the road). There is swimming at both Laurel and Fuller Lakes and canoeing/kayaking at Laurel if you make it there in the summer. There is also a spring to refill water bottles along the way. Parking is easy at either end of the hike.

Finally, try to get a hike in at Pole Steeple (1.5 miles), which is a little tricky for toddlers to hike, but it's a short carry. There's a scenic rocky outcropping that has one of the best views in the area with Laurel Lake down below.

WHY IT'S A FAVORITE

"I love hiking on the Appalachian Trail and meeting thru-hikers, hearing their stories, and imagining what it's like to hike for 2,000+ miles. Hiking to Tom's Run is a quick and easy taste of the AT. I love that it can be a day hike or an overnight backpacking excursion depending on how adventurous I feel. There's just an energy in these woods that draws me in! You're likely to meet other hikers, but it is not an overly trafficked area, so you still get that backwoods feel." —LIZ KNAPP

INSIDER'S TIP

"Our preferred hike is to park at the end of Old Shippensburg Road. This exact spot is known on Google Maps as Sunset Rocks Parking Area. This is not the official pink "P" on the DCNR map! (This hike starts at the Tom's Run Creek.) The shortest hike you can do here is Bunker Hill Parking Lot on Bunker Hill Road, across from an abandoned POW interrogation camp. This is noted on the official park map with a pink P."

CAW CAW INTERPRETIVE CENTER, SOUTH CAROLINA, CAW CAW INTERPRETIVE CENTER

ACTIVITIES: Hiking, boardwalk

LENGTH OF HIKE: 2–3 miles

OUT AND BACK OR LOOP: Loop

DIFFICULTY OF TERRAIN: Easy

ELEVATION GAIN: No

PARKING FEE/PASS: $2/person

TOILETS: Yes

CHANGING TABLE: Yes

NURSING BENCHES: Yes

DOGS ALLOWED: No

BIKES/HORSES/MOTORS ON TRAIL: No

CELL RECEPTION: Spotty

DRINKING WATER AVAILABLE: Yes

POTENTIAL CHILD OR BABY HAZARDS: Ticks, mosquitoes, alligators, poison ivy, roots

GEAR SUGGESTIONS: All-terrain strollers preferred, baby/toddler carriers encouraged, bug repellent

Every adventure has something special, but Caw Caw has a unique phenomenon you probably won't see anywhere else. Every February when the water is cold and dense, oils released from the decomposing cypress trees float to the top and, when hit by sunlight, create what's called "Rainbow Swamp." The surface of the water in the swamp becomes a blend of pinks, purples, and blues that is hard to describe and has to be seen in person to believe. Local Lauren Adams describes it as "magical," especially if a young child is observing it.

What Lauren likes about this hike beyond the Rainbow Swamp is the fact that it's easy to let a 16-month-old toddle around and not worry. While most hikes in this book give you a specific trail to adventure on, in this chapter, we are going to suggest you make a decision based on what you are interested in seeing in this park, because all of the trails are all very family friendly. Meandering through the boardwalk in the middle of the swamp offers up a beautiful display of the cypress trees and a constant soundtrack of birds singing for you to try and identify their species. Visiting the paddy fields will give you a different perspective. Hiking around the whole outskirts of this preserve will take you through hardwood forest and tidal marshes and give you 3.6 miles. It's all good no matter where you choose to hike.

In the fall, this park hosts "fairy house building" where the children are encouraged to look through the woods for broken and fallen plant matter to construct their very own

fairy house. They have to "check in" with the contractors and are given a building permit and a lot number. This is definitely a favorite event to attend in Charleston if you're a hiking family with little ones.

One thing to remember is that Caw Caw is located on a swamp, as well as old rice fields (paddies). These are prime habitats for alligators, and there are a lot of them at Caw Caw. While there have been no reports of any problems with them from Hike it Baby families, those who are uncomfortable with this should be aware that you are almost guaranteed to see at least a few alligators if you choose the trail through the rice paddies. As for other wildlife, expect to see eagles, barred owls, yellow-throated warblers, lizards, and skunks.

If you don't love snakes, remember the warmer months are popular for our slithering friends, so be on the lookout. The rangers who work there will readily hand out warnings about any snakes that have been spotted to help raise your awareness.

The only season to avoid Caw Caw is the heat of the summer. The swamp lends itself to high humidity and mosquito populations, and as much as the locals love Caw Caw, even they stay away during this time. Fall, winter, and spring, however, are all wonderful times to visit Caw Caw.

WHY IT'S A FAVORITE

"Caw Caw is quite literally my happy place. It is a beautiful nature reserve where they have done little more than clear a path for you to walk and enjoy. This is a place to view nature in a very raw form while also being safe enough to let your little ones enjoy and take it all in. We always come away having learned or seen something new. There is a nice balance of shade and sunshine, and if you avoid the hottest months of the year, you could spend hours there. If I'm having a particularly rough parenting week, Caw Caw has a way of allowing me to press the "reset button" and bring peace to my heart and my mind. When you have finished your hike, they have a wonderfully educational Interpretive Center where the kids can get some hands-on learning about the many animals they may have come across on the trail. The people who work there are always friendly and excited to answer any questions you may have." —LAUREN ADAMS

INSIDER'S TIP

The Interpretive Center is very popular with the kiddos. They also have rocking chairs, benches, and shaded picnic tables just outside, where Hike it Baby families often have a picnic lunch. This is a great place for a nursing or bottle-feeding parent to take a rest and get comfortable.

CONGAREE NATIONAL PARK, SOUTH CAROLINA, **BOARDWALK LOOP**

ACTIVITIES: Hiking, birding, paddling, camping

LENGTH OF HIKE: 2.4 miles

OUT AND BACK OR LOOP: Loop

DIFFICULTY OF TERRAIN: Easy

ELEVATION GAIN: No

PARKING FEE/PASS: No

TOILETS: Yes

CHANGING TABLE: No

NURSING BENCHES: Yes

DOGS ALLOWED: Yes

BIKES/HORSES/MOTORS ON TRAIL: No

CELL RECEPTION: Yes

DRINKING WATER AVAILABLE: Yes

POTENTIAL CHILD OR BABY HAZARDS: Wildlife, uneven path, possible flooding

GEAR SUGGESTIONS: Baby carrier preferred

There are many reasons to visit the Congaree National Park, especially if you love big old trees mixed with wet marshlands. While it's tempting to call this park a swamp because of how much water there is in it, this area is actually technically called an old-growth bottomland hardwood forest due to the flows of water flooding and drying out.

Definitely one of the most popular trails in the park is the Boardwalk Loop, which begins just behind the Harry Hampton Visitor Center. This is a great introduction to all the

27,000-acre Congaree National Park has to offer. Wander through some of the tallest recorded cypresses, loblolly pine trees, sweetgums, swamp chestnut oaks, and cherry-bark oak trees; and enjoy one of the largest old-growth bottomland hardwood forests in the southeast.

It's easy to see that the park has done an excellent job protecting 12,000 acres of old-growth forest that still looks as it looked when Congaree Indians first came to the area. Unfortunately, there are no longer any Congaree living in this area because, according to history records, most of the tribe was more or less wiped out in the late 1600s from smallpox. The remaining tribe members were said to have merged with the Catawba people of this area.

As you leave the Harry Hampton Center, look for American holly trees lining the edges of the boardwalk. In fall and winter months, these trees are easy to identify, as the female trees display clusters of bright red berries in addition to their pointed leaves. From the boardwalk you can jump off on other trails like the Bluff Trail and get a few more miles in if the initial boardwalk hike isn't enough.

The boardwalk is both stroller- and wheelchair-accessible, making this an excellent choice for the whole family. One thing to note is if the water conditions are high, a stroller can be hard to get through parts of the trail, so make sure you check the well-maintained Facebook page for the park to get the most up-to-date conditions. Another side note is that this park has "water trails" where you can canoe or paddle through a marked trail. There are both guided and self-guided options. Keep in mind this trail can look different depending on water heights and time of year, so markers may not always be as visible.

Want to learn more about the wildlife in this area? Look for zebra swallowtail butterflies and pileated woodpeckers flitting about. On the boardwalk, keep on the lookout for beautiful nonpoisonous golden silk orb weaver spiders hanging alongside the trail as you meander through the majestic pine, beech, and bald cypress. You can also see red-shouldered hawk and barred owl nests in the trees and might even catch one of these predators swooping across the water to snap up a crawfish in its talons. Bigger animals roaming about include bobcats, deer, feral pigs, feral dogs, coyotes, armadillos, turkeys, and otters.

Want to have a go at camping with your little one? Try the Longleaf Campground. This is a primitive campground, but the walk-in is less than 200 feet, so it's easy to do with a baby or toddler in tow. Campsites are $10 for a single family and $20 for a group site.

If you want a longer hike, add the Weston Lake Loop Trail onto this hike for a total of 2.5 more miles. This will take you off the boardwalk and put you on trails.

WHY IT'S A FAVORITE

"Pretty unique scenery close to the city and free! It includes a learning center and restrooms." —JILL ISER

INSIDER'S TIP

Every year in late May for a few weeks, the fireflies put on an incredible display of synchronized lighting, where thousands of fireflies light up at the same time in the forest. This is thought to be a mating ritual where this species of fireflies works together to find mates, but this is just a hypothesis. Either way, locals describe this show as spectacular, and every summer the park readies for the hundreds of people who visit every night to watch this natural show. There are only a few spots in the world where synchronous fireflies can be found. Those spots include Great Smoky Mountains National Park in Tennessee, Allegheny National Forest in Pennsylvania, and a wildlife management area near Oak Ridge, Tennessee.

BADLANDS NATIONAL PARK, SOUTH DAKOTA, DOOR, WINDOW, AND NOTCH TRAILS

ACTIVITIES: Hiking

LENGTH OF HIKE: 2.5 miles round-trip total if you do all three of the easy routes described. Add an extra mile round trip if you venture to the end of the Notch Trail.

OUT AND BACK OR LOOP: Out and back

DIFFICULTY OF TERRAIN: Easy

ELEVATION GAIN: No

PARKING FEE/PASS: Park entrance fee

TOILETS: Yes

CHANGING TABLE: No

NURSING BENCHES: Yes

DOGS ALLOWED: No

BIKES/HORSES/MOTORS ON TRAIL: No

CELL RECEPTION: No

DRINKING WATER AVAILABLE: At Visitor Center only

POTENTIAL CHILD OR BABY HAZARDS: Rattlesnakes, cactus plants, strong sun exposure, easy to get lost if you go off trail

GEAR SUGGESTIONS: Lots of water, sunblock

With this area we are suggesting a few different trails because they are all very doable for families and start in the same area. The short and relatively flat nature of these trails makes this a great place for toddlers. There are no big drop-offs or water hazards to worry about, and you are allowed to wander off trail. Each trail has its own unique character that you will not find anywhere else in your travels and that will fascinate both kiddos and adults. The overlook points on the Door and Window Trails have benches available.

Starting off with the Door Trail, this hike begins from the far north trailhead. The first 0.25 mile is on flat boardwalk and leads to an overlook with benches and interpretive signs that look out across the badlands. From the end of the boardwalk, there is a step down to the hard cracked mud of the badlands and the start of the best part of the trail. From here, numbered markers lead you out through the badlands and away from the crowds for another 0.5 mile. The Door Trail provides a door out onto the badlands you can walk through to get the full on-the-moon experience.

Feel free to wander off trail, none really exists here anyways, but always keep at least one numbered marker in sight and bring plenty of water. It is very easy to get lost here. After the first couple markers, you may notice that even all sound has dropped away. The badland formations are very efficient at blocking sound, making it really feel like you are walking on the moon. Jennifer Bradwin said her kiddo was endlessly fascinated with the cracked mud and all its colors on this trail. "He was thrilled that he could get up close and literally dig his fingers in."

Returning to the parking lot, the Window Trail is the next in line. This very short, 0.25-mile round trip, flat boardwalk leads to an overlook peeking through an opening in the rock wall, the "Window," looking out over a canyon and the craggy formations of the opposite wall. Benches are available here for resting, nursing, and snacking. It's easy to see how this one got its name.

The third and final trail from this parking lot is the Notch Trail. The Notch Trail leads to a notch in the rock wall for a view across the White River Valley. This one is moderate and includes climbing up a steep wooden ladder; however, you can make the base of the ladder your turnaround point for an easy and still worthwhile hike. The first section of this trail follows a creek bed that has water in the rainy season, making a small oasis with the most plant life of the three trails. At the base of the ladder is an open area with some great large rocks for toddlers to climb on. "Our almost-2-year-old walked all of it; however, we did not continue beyond the base of the ladder on the Notch Trail. I would carry if you choose to continue to the end of the trail," says Jennifer Bradwin.

This spot is a perfect turnaround point for those afraid of heights like me or if you fear a meltdown coming. If you continue up and beyond the ladder, you are rewarded with views out over the White River Valley from a notch in the rock wall. Getting to the notch involves hiking along a ledge and does have drop-offs. If you continue up this way, it is probably a good idea to put the kiddo up in a carrier. Hiking all the way to the notch is 1.5 miles round trip; to the base of the ladder, it is just shy of 1 mile round trip.

There is ample opportunity to see wildlife throughout the park. Hike it Baby ambassadors reported seeing bighorn sheep, bison, pronghorns, rabbits, birds, and of course lots of prairie dogs, like most of South Dakota and Wyoming. Signs warn of rattlesnakes, but people rarely encounter them here.

These three trails share one very large parking lot. We have been there in May and August and never had any problem finding plenty of parking. The boardwalk section of the Door Trail and the Window Trail do attract some tour bus attention; however, this is not a tour bus–heavy park, and you can quickly get away from the infrequent crowds by taking the Notch Trail or going beyond the boardwalk on the Door Trail.

Two campgrounds are available in the park, one near the main Visitor Center and the other down Sage Creek Rim Road, which is a gravel road. The main difference between the two is convenience versus solitude.

One thing to keep in mind is that the entire park is hot, dry, and fully exposed. Plan ahead with lots of water, sunblock, sunglasses, and coverage for your body. While you are allowed to wander off trail almost anywhere in the park, it is extremely easy to get lost. Bring a good map, the 10 essentials, and tons of water if you choose to wander out of sight from the main trail.

The park is open year-round, but spring and fall are the best times to visit. It gets extremely hot in summer, and snow can sometimes close roads in winter. May is pretty much perfect there.

WHY IT'S A FAVORITE

"The Badlands is one of our favorite destinations. It is compact and accessible enough to be a great half-day detour on a road trip and varied enough to be worthy of a longer stay. Wildlife and overlooks are plentiful, and many of the trails are great for toddler legs. If you venture far enough, you will feel like you have been transported to the moon or Mars, and you do not have to go far to find solitude with an eerie quiet. If you have the chance to camp here, the night sky is not to be missed." —JENNIFER BRADWIN

INSIDER'S TIP

One last trail to note in this park is the Fossil Exhibit Trail, another easy, short, flat, interpretive boardwalk trail that is fully accessible if you have family needing wheelchair or stroller accessibility for hiking. If you have the time and are up for a gravel road, drive the Sage Creek Rim Road. You can find solitude, prairie dogs, views, and bison here.

It's not much of a secret, but a stop at Wall Drug as you exit the park is pretty much required.

APPALACHIAN TRAIL ,TENNESSEE, CARVER'S GAP TO OVERMOUNTAIN SHELTER

ACTIVITIES: Hiking, camping, wildflowers

LENGTH OF HIKE: 11 miles

OUT AND BACK OR LOOP: Out and back

DIFFICULTY OF TERRAIN: Easy

ELEVATION GAIN: 1,500 feet

PARKING FEE/PASS: No

TOILETS: No

CHANGING TABLE: No

NURSING BENCHES: Yes

DOGS ALLOWED: Yes

BIKES/HORSES/MOTORS ON TRAIL: No

CELL RECEPTION: Spotty

DRINKING WATER AVAILABLE: No

POTENTIAL CHILD OR BABY HAZARDS: Stinging nettles, ticks

GEAR SUGGESTIONS: Hiking poles, sunscreen, sun shade if using carrier

Ready to dive deep into the Appalachian Trail and visit two states in one day? Carver's Gap to the Overmountain Shelter is a perfect jumping-off point for a backpacking trip with the baby. Start off in Tennessee, end up in North Carolina, and take in views of Round Bald, Jane Bald, and Grassy Ridge Bald along the way.

While we don't normally hand off this long of a hike to Hike it Baby families, this is an easy one without a lot of elevation and mainly just distance. If you start out early in the day, this is an easy one for the whole family to accomplish. Just keep in mind that you will want to attack this one only if your little has spent some time hiking and you know they can do half a day on trail. Consider doing a 6-mile hike leading up to this so you have tested time. Also, make sure you stop every few hours and let your little one down to crawl around and get circulation moving again. You can also do just 4 miles of this hike by going 2 in and turning around and still getting an amazing experience.

What makes this trail unique is the Overmountain Shelter, which, out of the 250 shelters on the 2,200 miles of trail, is one of the Appalachian Trail favorites. A big red barn built in 1970, the shelter was originally built for farming needs; but in 1983, it was renovated, allowing thru-hikers a nice reprieve from camping outside if the weather turns. The bonus is the barn holds up to 30 overnighters.

If you love wildflowers and rhododendrons, come in the spring. If you're looking for blueberries, visit in the summer. The hike starts out in a small fir forest for the first 0.5 mile. Be sure to watch the trees; you'll often see tween and teen kids sitting in them because they are perfect for climbing. From there, most of the hike is along the ridge above the treeline. Every now and then, the trail drops back into the trees, where you'll see flat open campsites that make for nice breaks whenever you (or baby) decide it's time to call it a day. This is a better adventure when you have lighter babies who are easier to carry, but the elevation gain isn't so significant that you can't hump a bigger kid in or walk slowly with a toddler who is used to doing more miles.

The most standout things on this hike are the grassy meadows of wildflowers, the old giant fir forest, and the natural tiny springs bubbling up everywhere. Make it a day trip by just heading out to Yellow Mountain with a 4-mile out and back, or turn it into 12 miles and take in all of the highland bald with epic 360-degree views. Sunrises and sunsets are amazing in this location thanks to 1,000 acres of grassy rolling fields. This is a year-round hike that may see a dusting of frost in the winter but is usually passable.

"What I love about this trail is you feel something special hiking such an old and famous trail," says Sierra Patterson. "Climbing the same climbs that so many before you have. Imagining the thru-hikers who made it that far. Hiking past and taking breaks in the campsites so many have taken refuge in. It's magic!"

What should you look out for on this hike? Ticks, poison ivy, and stinging nettles. Yes, these are all possible. There are also black bears in the area, although it is uncommon to see them on this part of the trail. Prepare to bring a jacket even in the summer. Those peak winds can be much colder than the valleys below. There are a few areas where you'll want to carry your walking young toddler but no major cliffs.

While this is definitely much longer than a normal Hike it Baby adventure we would send families on, this is one where you can just hike as far as you want and still feel like you really enjoyed the trail. "This is one that my family frequents," says Sierra Patterson.

"The distance is perfect for kids of all ages. It's challenging, but absolutely doable and worth it. It's the perfect full-day hike." We suggest using this one as a trial for how far your little one will adventure. Also, consider making it an overnighter so you can see the Overmountain Shelter, and try backpacking with your baby!

WHY IT'S A FAVORITE

"Carver's Gap to the Appalachian Trail's Overmountain Shelter is an epic day hike traversing multiple balds, which are some of the highest on the AT. We like it because there are multiple flat campsites along the entirety of the trail, which are safe spots to stop for diaper changes, snack time, nursing sessions, and little ones getting some time out of the carrier! The whole hike is around 12 miles. You could also easily backpack it and camp at the shelter, which offers a fire ring, a privy, flat grassy meadows for tent camping, and bunks within the barn!" —SIERRA AND RICHARD PATTERSON

INSIDER'S TIP

The Roan Highlands are known for their views and wildflowers, especially rhododendron. This means things can get crowded! Be warned, a yearly Rhododendron Festival happens in June at Roan Mountain State Park, so cabins and campsites as well as airbnbs are hard to come by.

GREAT SMOKY MOUNTAINS, TENNESSEE, CLINGMANS DOME

DISTANCE: 0.5 mile up a steep ramp to viewpoint

LENGTH OF HIKE: 1 mile

OUT AND BACK OR LOOP: Out and back

DIFFICULTY OF TERRAIN: Moderate

ELEVATION GAIN: 332 Feet

PARKING FEE/PASS: Park entrance fee

TOILETS: Yes

CHANGING TABLE: No

NURSING BENCHES: No

DOGS ALLOWED: No

BIKES/HORSES/MOTORS ON TRAIL: No

CELL RECEPTION: Spotty

DRINKING WATER AVAILABLE: At Visitor Center only

POTENTIAL CHILD OR BABY HAZARDS: Steep trail

GEAR SUGGESTIONS: Carrier, water, binoculars, light jacket

While paved trails don't usually signify adventure, this one felt a little different. At 6,643 elevation, Clingmans Dome is the highest point in the Great Smoky Mountains National Park. It's a steep climb, so expect to go slowly with toddlers walking or get a butt burn carrying (it's too steep for strollers), but the view will be worth the grind. On a clear day, you can get a 360-degree view of the Smoky Mountains and can see as far away as 100 miles.

There are plenty of bathrooms at the base before the hike up to the dome, but remember if you have potty-training littles to check in with them. The hike up to the dome is paved but not recommended for those in wheelchairs because it's very steep. If you need to stop and rest, there are benches all along the climb.

Clouds, fog, and colder temperatures are common at Clingmans Dome. Expect it to be 10 to 20 degrees cooler than the lower areas. Bring a light jacket. You may not need it on the climb, but after sweating on the way up, you could get chilly on the way down.

A lush spruce-fir forest surrounds the dome thanks to all of the moisture, and if you want to hike beyond the 0.5-mile haul up to the lookout of the dome, dip into the forest and hike along the Appalachian Trail or find the Forney Ridge Trail that leads to Andrews Bald, a high-elevation grassy bald.

WHY IT'S A FAVORITE

"The views were spectacular but it was a clearer day which helped! Toward the end of the trail near the parking area or kids enjoyed climbing on a large boulder area. There is also an area across from that with lots of benches and great views. There are great views from the whole area including the parking lot." —JENNIFER CAMPBELL

INSIDER'S TIP

There is plenty of parking which is great! However, this is a very steep trail so once you park, even though it's paved, plan on walking slowly. Bikes or wheelchairs are not allowed on the trail due to it's steep nature, so skip the stroller. Jennifer suggests taking a carrier in case your kiddos needed a ride. "They walked up and down a good part of it but got did get tired as it got steeper. A hiking harness would have helped!"

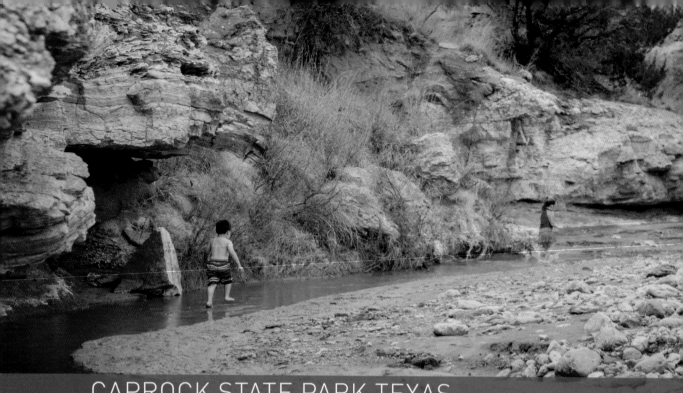

CAPROCK STATE PARK, TEXAS,
CAPROCK CANYONS UPPER TRAIL

ACTIVITIES: Hiking, birding, splashing

LENGTH OF HIKE: 7.2 miles

OUT AND BACK OR LOOP: Both

DIFFICULTY OF TERRAIN: Moderate

ELEVATION GAIN: 880 feet

PARKING FEE/PASS: No

TOILETS: Yes

CHANGING TABLE: No

NURSING BENCHES: No

DOGS ALLOWED: Yes

BIKES/HORSES/MOTORS ON TRAIL: No

CELL RECEPTION: Yes

DRINKING WATER AVAILABLE: No

POTENTIAL CHILD OR BABY HAZARDS: Cactus along trail

GEAR SUGGESTIONS TO BRING: Towel, spare set of clothes for kiddos

For this hiking adventure, we are going to share the Caprock Canyons Upper Trail, although we would highly advise making a weekend out of this and spending a lot of time just hiking out of the campground. Kids can play in the creek for hours at the campground, and there are easily accessed trails right there. For hiking, the Upper Canyon Trail is a bit long, and there are some challenging points where you will want to carry your toddler; but you can also really enjoy a section of this trail and just do an out and back, turning around when you feel you've had enough. The trail starts low in the canyon, with about 1 mile of mellow terrain through deep red earth before you start to climb. It's not steep climbing, but it's steady, so bring lots of water and snacks, and consider hiking poles.

Throughout the park there are around 25 miles of trails to explore. This area hosts freely roaming plains bison, always an exciting and very large animal for kids to see. Expect mesquite, cacti, and junipers covering the landscape, as well as tallgrasses and cottonwoods. Hiding in the grasses, you'll find raccoons, white-tailed deer, roadrunners, foxes, and porcupines.

Jennifer Campbell said her family camped in the Wild Horse Equestrian Loop, a primitive but nice, small camping area that is fenced in (thus keeping larger animals out). They discovered a short, kid-friendly trail right next to their campsite, which was convenient for quick explorations. This trail connected with other trails like the Upper Canyon Trail you can take to go farther. What Jennifer liked about the Upper Canyon Trail was how flat and wide it was for an early stage of walkers. You could even take an off-road-style stroller on it at least for the part they hiked.

Another point of interest that is kid friendly in this park is the beginning of Eagle Point Trail to the Natural Bridge point of interest. Your kids will enjoy rock scrambling to get under the bridge like a cave.

The sun is hot here. By midday, plan on being back at camp playing in the water. Your best bet for a visit is spring because it's cool at night and not too hot in the day.

WHY IT'S A FAVORITE

"We loved this state park! The wildlife is what makes it extra special for the kids. There are bison throughout the park that freely roam and quite often end up close to where you are. There are also a lot of groundhogs that are very visible and fun to watch. The views of the canyon as you drive into the park are beautiful, especially at sunset. The Little Red River Camping Area creek that we hiked 0.25 mile to was by far the kids' favorite part. They spent hours running up and down the creek; it was only about ankle deep and had a sand-based surface. They dug holes, splashed, and climbed on rocks. It was safe for the kids and made watching them very relaxing. Be prepared for all of their clothes to be stained red from the sand and dirt, though." —JENNIFER CAMPBELL

INSIDER'S TIP

Park in the Little Red River Camping Area. There is an excellent unmarked toddler trail here that starts at the end of the parking lot to the right of the campsite. You will walk right next to a campsite picnic table, and then the trail is obvious.

MONAHANS SANDHILLS STATE PARK, TEXAS, **SANDHILL PICNIC AREA**

ACTIVITIES: Hiking, paddling, sledding down dunes

LENGTH OF HIKE: Variable

OUT AND BACK OR LOOP: Hiking up and down the dunes

DIFFICULTY OF TERRAIN: Difficult

ELEVATION GAIN: Variable

PARKING FEE/PASS: $4 adults/Free kids under 12

TOILETS: Yes

CHANGING TABLE: Yes

NURSING BENCHES: Yes

DOGS ALLOWED: Yes

BIKES/HORSES/MOTORS ON TRAIL: No

CELL RECEPTION: Spotty

DRINKING WATER AVAILABLE: Yes

POTENTIAL CHILD OR BABY HAZARDS: No

GEAR SUGGESTIONS: Sunscreen, sun hat, carrier

With 4,000 acres of land, Monahans Sandhills State Park is a fun hidden gem in Texas that people might not think to visit for hiking; however, with little ones, this is a perfect landscape to play in because it's a giant sandbox. This is not your typical hike; it's more of an adventure. Plan to meet up at the picnic pavilion if you have others joining you, and encourage people to bring sand toys (digging toys, buckets, sleds). You can also rent sleds and some other toys at the park headquarters if you forget. As a group, you can hike around the dunes, but there is no official trail here, so your distance will have to be based on what your little hikers are up for. Sand can be challenging, so this hike requires carriers for nonwalkers or early walkers. Children can walk up the dunes but might need a hand here and there to get around.

Kids will love experimenting with the sleds, seeing how high they can go on some of the dunes. In the summer, you might catch a lightning storm in the distance, which you'll be able to see well because there is very little pollution to interfere with the light. You will love the great views from the tops of the dunes.

WHY IT'S A FAVORITE

"My younger child loved just sitting and playing in the sand. I was able to go up and down the dune with my other child while being able to watch my younger child playing in the sand. Once we figured out the best way to sled down, which seemed to be in more compact sand where we really smoothed it out by repeatedly going down the same path, we had tons of fun." —JENNIFER CAMPBELL

INSIDER'S TIP

If you are coming from a distance in the summer, consider staying overnight at a hotel in Odessa or Midland, and visit the dunes first in the morning. It can get really hot in this part of Texas in July and August.

GARNER STATE PARK, TEXAS,
OLD BALDY TRAIL SUMMIT

ACTIVITIES: Hiking, camping, water play

LENGTH OF HIKE: 0.53 mile

OUT AND BACK OR LOOP: Out and back

DIFFICULTY OF TERRAIN: Moderate

ELEVATION GAIN: No

PARKING FEE/PASS: $6 adults/Free kids 12 and under

TOILETS: No

CHANGING TABLE: No

NURSING BENCHES: No

DOGS ALLOWED: No

BIKES/HORSES/MOTORS ON TRAIL: No

CELL RECEPTION: Spotty

DRINKING WATER AVAILABLE: No

POTENTIAL CHILD OR BABY HAZARDS: Ticks, snakes

GEAR SUGGESTIONS: Hiking boots, small daypack filled with water, snacks, sunscreen, first-aid kit. Floaties, water safety gear.

Looking for a fun hike with a lot of diversity in the terrain and some shade? This park is filled with trails that are great for the whole family. For this particular adventure, we are going to suggest the Old Baldy Summit for the beautiful views. While it's steep, it's also a short hike. It will require a spotter or a hand here and there if you are carrying a little one, and you will really want to spot new walkers.

Shade is key in Texas because there are so many hot days in the year. Fortunately, this park has many shaded spots to sit in and relax. If you are camping, bring a hammock and you'll find many spots to unwind.

"We loved meeting other campers and hearing about their traditions of returning to this park each year. Garner State Park truly has a family environment,which kids of any age would enjoy," said Lauren of their camping trip in this park.

If you love wildlife, there is plenty to be viewed, including Rio Grande turkeys, mourning doves, black and turkey vultures, Eastern bluebirds, and several species of migratory birds. Two endangered species of birds also nest here: the golden-cheeked warbler and the black-capped vireo. Look for black rock and fox squirrels, white-tailed deer, and raccoons as well.

It's definitely crowded in the peak season, so if you plan to camp at Garner, you will want to book a spot many months in advance, and especially if you are planning on visiting during a holiday weekend. This park has been one of the most popular parks for camping in Texas since it opened in 1941.

After hiking, you will find a large playground within the park; the playground is next door to a volunteer ranger shop and nature garden. There are endless things for kids to do here!

WHY IT'S A FAVORITE

"There are endless adventures to have within this park, and the different elements of hills, forests, and clear, beautiful water really provide an experience that meets any outdoor need." —LAUREN YELDELL

INSIDER'S TIP

The park rangers offer junior ranger coloring books in the ranger station. During the summer months, there is an evening dance held at the dance hall with a good old-fashioned jukebox and country dancing. It's a ton of fun! www.garnerstatepark.com/the-dance.html

About 45 minutes or so down the road is an awesome restaurant in Utopia called the Lost Maples Cafe. They have a wonderful menu for the whole family and excellent coffee. The Utopia Library is also a precious refuge when the weather isn't ideal and a beautiful, serene garden located behind the library that is open to the public.

ENCHANTED ROCK STATE NATURAL AREA, TEXAS, **SUMMIT TRAIL**

ACTIVITIES: Hiking

LENGTH OF HIKE: 1.3 miles

OUT AND BACK OR LOOP: Out and back

DIFFICULTY OF TERRAIN: Moderate

ELEVATION GAIN: 425 feet

PARKING FEE/PASS: $7 adults/Free kids 12 and under

TOILETS: Yes

CHANGING TABLE: No

NURSING BENCHES: Yes

DOGS ALLOWED: No

BIKES/HORSES/MOTORS ON TRAIL: No

CELL RECEPTION: Spotty

DRINKING WATER AVAILABLE: Yes

POTENTIAL CHILD OR BABY HAZARDS: Slippery surfaces, steep inclines, vertical drops

GEAR SUGGESTIONS: Comfortable hiking shoes, carrier, water, sunscreen

The name Enchanted Rock well suits it. From afar, it's a giant pink granite rock that protrudes from the landscape as if from nowhere. But what's truly amazing about this 425 feet of rock is that actually it spans 62 miles below the surface of the earth, so really you are just seeing the tip of the mountain.

This short summit is a definite butt burner that's equivalent to hiking 40 floors of a building. On the Summit Trail, you can see a different view of the surrounding area. As you travel up, you'll notice different parts of the rock formation and how the landscape changes to pink. There are places to rest as you climb, small rocks to sit on, and places to have a picnic.

"I love how rewarding it is to climb this trail. It was amazing to us that our then-20-month-old daughter was able to climb it. There is never a point where the incline is too steep; it's the perfect challenge for little ones as long as parents are closely spotting or holding their hands. We saw other parents who had their babies in carriers, so that is also an option," says Lauren.

The gentle climb means you will see people of all ages hiking this area. Trail, cave, and rock conditions are inherently hazardous depending on the conditions, so hikers may encounter slippery surfaces, steep inclines, vertical drops, and other hazardous conditions if weather comes in, so make sure you are aware of the latest forecast.

That said, it's Texas, so other than the occasional storm, it's pretty much perfect all year-round. Due to exposure of the area and few trees, you will want to avoid the hottest or coldest days of the year, and definitely don't go when it's raining or if there's a high chance of rain. October and November are beautiful months to visit.

This park tends to fill to capacity as early as 11 a.m. If you get there and the park is closed to additional guests, don't turn around immediately. Often, as campers from the previous night are leaving, the park attendants will open the park to allow others to enter. Also, nearby places of interest include the quaint and adorable town of Fredericksburg, which has an amazing brewery called the Fredericksburg Brewing Company. There are also tons of kid-friendly options in Fredericksburg, including candy stores, toy shops, and so on.

At Enchanted Rock, you will see the usual animals found in central Texas, like rock and fox squirrels, armadillos, rabbits, and other small animals. You frequently see white-tailed deer grazing about. Look for lizards and vultures on and above the summit year-round. The park also contains over 100 archaeological sites at which various Native American artifacts have been unearthed.

WHY IT'S A FAVORITE

"The view from the top of Enchanted Rock's Summit Trails offers 360 degrees of the beautiful Texas hill country. The rock's name "enchantment," is derived from thousands of years of human inhabitants. Arrowheads dating back 10,000 years have been found on the property, and the local tribes of Tonkawa, Apache, and Comanche used the rock and surrounding areas for tribal traditions. It's an amazing thing to behold the magnitude of beauty and history in this location." —LAUREN YELDELL

INSIDER'S TIP

Make sure you have plenty of water and probably some snacks when you scale the dome or surrounding outcroppings. Wearing comfortable hiking shoes is also encouraged— this is not the place for flip-flops or regular walking shoes. Lauren said they had baseball caps and sunglasses for the hike and just packed a small backpack for water, reapplying sunscreen, and snacks. She brought the toddler carrier in case her daughter got tired; but they managed to climb the whole thing, although it's definitely a push at the end.

POTTY ON THE TRAIL
WHEN NATURE CALLS

One of the things every parent dreads hearing on a hike is "Mommy, I need to poop!" It's especially inconvenient when you're midhike, in the middle of the woods, and with the nearest restroom a half mile or more out! When you have to address those quick-I-gotta-go-right-now potty emergencies, there are a few things to know about relieving yourself while also observing "Leave No Trace" trail etiquette.

PACK A PROPER POOP KIT. When I pack for hikes, I also pack for a possible trail crisis from my older two. The things we keep on hand are toilet paper or napkins, ziplock bag (for the toilet paper), plastic shopping bag (for the ziplock bag), and hand sanitizer. We don't always do this, but if you have room in your pack, you can add a trowel for digging.

STAY OFF THE TRAIL. Search for a spot at least 200 feet away from the trail to do your business. When you stay a good distance from the trail, it ensures privacy for you so you don't get stage fright when other hikers walk by. This also helps you avoid that really awkward moment if you run into them again on the trail. It also guarantees that hopefully no one accidentally steps on your gift to nature if they take a few steps off the trail. For kiddos, it's easy to hide behind big rocks or downed trees while Mommy or Daddy keeps a lookout.

DIG, POOP, AND PACK IT OUT. After you find a secret hiding spot (stay away from any water source to avoid runoff), it's time to dig. If you don't have a trowel, a sturdy stick makes a great substitute. Dig a hole at least 6 to 8 inches in the ground, then squat and drop. If you use toilet paper, store it

in the ziplock bag, and toss that in the trash bag to carry with you until you can properly dispose of it. If you had to grab the closest natural materials in lieu of toilet paper, add those to the hole and stir in some loose dirt to jump-start the decomposition process before you completely fill in the hole. Then grab nearby leaves or rocks to cover the pile so it looks like part of the natural landscape. Finally, don't forget to sanitize those hands like crazy.

Vong Hamilton lives a busy life with her husband and three kids, but she makes it mandatory to spend weekends on the trails to recharge and spend quality time together as a family. She's the editorial coordinator for the Hike it Baby blog in her "spare" time.

DEALING WITH BLOWOUTS
SH*T HAPPENS

IT HAPPENS TO ALL OF US. The dreaded blowout on trail midway through a hike. Hopefully, you are close to the car, but usually it's the case that you're not. A blowout can make for a very unhappy child. It can also lead to rashes if your child has poop drying on them for too long, so it's good to clean them up quickly.

While there's nothing you can do to prepare for the up-the-back, destroy-your-entire-outfit blowouts that occasionally happen, here's what you always want to have with you to deal with those more manageable ones.

1. Always carry at least one or two plastic bags to be able to tuck messes away. Thin, small doggy bags can be a great option because they are super packable.

2. Consider purchasing a small portable mat for changing on if you are in wet, mucky, sandy areas. When hiking, there won't always be a nice surface to lay your child on the ground. There are some that are smaller than a squeezie pack of applesauce that work really well.

3. Have a toy ready for trail changes. Kids might be fussy and squirmy, especially if it's cold, so get something ready to distract them.

4. Look for shelter. Under a tree or, even better, a real shelter. This is one good reason to hike in parks with shelters in weathery months.

5. Keep wipes in a ziplock bag, and replenish that bag every hike so you always have a lot on hand. A big blowout takes a lot of wipes, so be prepared.

6. Carry a small hand sanitizer wipe or travel spray for yourself for after you clean up. You might need to give snacks or breast feed post-poopy cleanup, so it's good to make sure you are clean.

7. Don't forget you have water. If it's a really bad mess, use some water to do a preliminary cleanup. Then go at it with wipes. Just don't use up all of your water if you have a long hike.

8. Have a change of clothes in the car for afterward. While you may change on the trail, there are those times when it spreads up the back. Be ready with clothes back at the car. No need to pack them along, but it's great to have them after the hike if you want to continue with your day.

HIKE IT BABY **AMBASSADOR**

SOLO PARENTING ON TRAIL

CHRISTEL PETERS

Finding a village to help support you in parenting can make all the difference, especially when it comes to getting out and adventuring with a baby in places like Alaska or South Dakota. Christel Peters felt this was especially true as a single parent from birth raising a son with little support around her. "I had no mommy friends, and most of the people I knew did not have children," she says. It's not that the support wasn't there if she asked for it, but she just felt alone as a parent because she had chosen to have a child alone. This was especially true in the beginning. "I walked almost everywhere with Sebastian because I was too terrified to drive my manual-drive vehicle on the icy hills of Anchorage! I found that we both were so calm when we were outside, so I didn't mind. I just bundled us up and adventured out. So, it started from necessity and then evolved into fun."

She learned about Hike it Baby from a new mom's group at the local hospital, which was a relief because hiking in Alaska can sometimes be a bit daunting solo. While it's beautiful and trails are plentiful all around town, it's not uncommon to spot mama grizzly bears and cubs or a giant moose ambling down a city path.

Large wildlife spottings and empty trails can be a bit unnerving when carrying a new baby, especially for a mom who never really saw herself as an "outdoorsy" person. In spite of this, Christel quickly found that she and her baby connected better in the outdoors. Sebastian did not have to be taught to love the outdoors—it just came naturally, as it does for so many babies. And as they spent more time on trail, Christel's love of the outdoors grew as well.

When Sebastian was a week away from his first birthday, Christel decided to move to South Dakota and go back to school. She also started a Hike it Baby branch upon arriving. Through this, she found a group of like-minded parents who became her community in her new city and helped her discover trails in their area. "I realize my parenting style is not as conventional as others. That's okay. When others see me as being 'crazy' for taking Sebastian out when it's dark or freezing, I stay open-minded and question: Are we happy, healthy, safe, loved? If we are those four things, then it's okay if I'm crazy. We win."

FAVORITE TRAIL:
Roughlock Falls, Spearfish Canyon, South Dakota. This trail is only 2 miles total—an out and back—and is mainly flat. It's great for small feet with an awesome payout at either end of the trail. Christel likes to start at the lower point of the creek and hike up to the waterfalls.

TANDEM-WEARING ON TRAIL
COMFORT IS KEY

Getting comfortable with two kiddos in carriers can be a little tricky at first, but once you get the hang of it, you'll load up and go! Tandem-wearing can look different for everyone, but the best practice is to keep each child secure in their own carrier. The reason for this is fairly logical—in the event one carrier would fail, both children would not be injured. Here are common suggestions for various ages:

- **NEWBORNS:** Because newborns have no head control, you should consider a stretchy wrap of some sort with both children in the front.

- **INFANTS:** Tandem hip carry in a wrap.

- **BABIES:** Once they can sit up unassisted, you can move to soft-structured carriers front and back. Put the larger child on back. Also consider moving on to a frame on the back to carry items and a soft-structured carrier on the front.

- **INFANT AND AN OLDER CHILD:** Wrap or ring sling on the front, soft-structured carrier or frame on the back. Always keep the smaller baby on front, larger child on back.

You want the carrier to act like your arms, to support your baby or toddler in their natural body position. Usually, you aim for what is referred to as the optimal position: baby's weight sitting on their bottom, legs in a spread-squat position, with spine supported. In addition, baby should be upright and secure against your body. Do not use any baby carrier in a way that is not intended. If you have questions about proper use, please contact the manufacturer directly. Here are some general rules to keep in mind regardless of the carrier type or brands:

- Each carrier should be secured independent of the other unless it was specifically built for tandem-wearing (check out brands like Twingo carriers).

- Neither carrier should impede the functions and use of the other.

- Neither carrier should impede either child's natural movements.

- Make sure the child is the proper size for the carriers (we often see people on trail with a baby that's too young for a frame carrier because people are excited to use that new, fancy piece of gear!)

- Make sure you can quickly and easily see both children's faces and airways to ensure safety. There are great retractable mirrors you can clip on a carrier to look behind you.

Practice using each carrier separately and then together before you leave the house. Then take a small stroll around the neighborhood to make sure everything fits and feels right. There are a few things you can do to make sure you have few troubles on the trail:

- Make sure you can physically carry the combined weight of both children. Practice on flat ground first.

- Ensure you can see the path in front of you and behind you.

- Make sure you can get both children on and off by yourself.

Once you pick the appropriate carriers for you and your children's needs, there are a few logistical things to keep in mind as well:

- If your carriers have waist belts, stagger the waistbands so neither one is impeding the function of the other.

- Keep in mind that most carrier waistbands are designed to be the most comfortable sitting just on top of your hips, so there might be some adjusting. Keep buckles and knots separate so you do not confuse them and accidently take the wrong carrier off.

- If you have a front carrier that crosses over your back, put that carrier on first.

- If you are doing a wrap carry that crosses over your chest, then put the woven wrap on your back first, and use a front carrier that does not cross over onto your back.

- Overlapping shoulder straps are safe as long as both can be tightened down all the way and are not slipping off.

Finally, consider how you'll store and carry other gear while tandem wearing.

- Some carriers have built-in storage.

- Consider a light shoulder bag that you can easily wear while carrying.

- Check out baby-wearing backpacks.

Samantha Reddy is a certified babywearing educator and consultant with the Center for Babywearing Studies. She is the mother to two little ones and an ambassador for Hike it Baby Portland. When not teaching babywearing, she can be found hiking the numerous trails throughout Oregon and Washington around the Portland area. Follow her blog at www.veganbabymama.com/.

Hiking at Night

There are some evenings when your kiddo just won't sleep. We've all been there. Whether they are 3 months or 3 years old, night hiking can help. If you're using a carrier, they may be rocked to sleep in the fresh air. If they are walking, a little time outside under the stars (away from screen time and the chaos of the stacks of laundry and dishes!) may be just the thing to wear them out. Obviously there are limitations to when you can night hike—think middle of winter—but if conditions are right and you are able to slide outside past bedtime, it will likely be a memorable experience.

1. Bring a headlamp even if you don't think you'll need it. This allows for easier exploration and finding hidden things in the night (like raccoon eyes) even on a lit path.

2. Give your little hiker her own headlamp so she can learn about it and play with it. You may not even need to go further than a local park for it to seem like a huge adventure, and it's good for her to get comfortable turning a headlamp on and off.

3. Flat, wide, well-marked trails are the obvious easy go-to. However, if you know of an easy single-track trail that you've been on a fair bit and you have a headlamp, consider exploring it a little, even if you don't go deep into it.

4. Hike to a meadow so you can lie down together and watch the stars. This might mean carrying your child home if he falls asleep, so bring a carrier and not too much else. There are also apps you can download to help identify the stars. Yes, this means screen time, but older toddlers will be fascinated to learn more about the night sky.

5. Do you have a black light? This can be a fun way to spot phosphorescent rocks and other things like scorpions that glow under the light. Sing songs on trail. When Mason and I night hike, we sing "We're Going on a Bear Hunt." This is a way to keep your child focused and not worried, if he or she has any fears of the dark.

6. Move slowly and stop to listen for things like owls, mice, and raccoons moving through the woods.

7. Take a book, sit at a trailhead, and read about nocturnal animals so your child can learn about animals that roam in the night. This will also help keep the bedtime routine somewhat intact even if it's late.

8. Go somewhere just before sunrise and watch all the changes from night to morning and hear the forest waking up.

9. Look for organized night hikes at local arboretums and nature centers. Usually you can find at least one in the summer. It will be one of those things both of you will never forget and will learn from.

CAPITOL REEF NATIONAL MONUMENT, UTAH, **CAPITOL GORGE TRAIL TO THE TANKS**

ACTIVITIES: Hiking, rock scrambling, birding

LENGTH OF HIKE: 4.4 miles

OUT AND BACK OR LOOP: Out and back

DIFFICULTY OF TERRAIN: Easy

ELEVATION GAIN: 100 feet

PARKING FEE/PASS: $10/vehicle

TOILETS: Yes

CHANGING TABLE: No

NURSING BENCHES: No

DOGS ALLOWED: No

BIKES/HORSES/MOTORS ON TRAIL: No

CELL RECEPTION: No

DRINKING WATER AVAILABLE: No

POTENTIAL CHILD OR BABY HAZARDS: Scorpions and snakes in the hotter season

GEAR SUGGESTIONS: Good sun hat

This hidden gem of a park, recognized as the least visited of the big ones in Utah, often gets overlooked because it's so close to the famous national park attractions like Zion (5 million visitors), Bryce (2.3 million), and the Grand Canyon (6 million). However, with toddlers, this is a not-to-be-missed stop in Utah. There are two reasons: great flat, wide, accessible trails for kids to run wild on with easy-to-climb sandstone and awesome apple pie. Yes, apple pie!

Inside the park is a little pioneer town called Fruita, once a Mormon homestead with around 10 families or so at a time living and farming in a fertile little valley in the middle of Capitol Reef. The park has preserved the old one-room school and the farmhouse, and if you wander around the grounds, you really get a sense of what it was like to live in the area in the late 1800s and early 1900s. The farmhouse is now a quaint gift shop offering fresh pies every morning that you can purchase warm with a scoop of vanilla ice cream. Eat them on a picnic bench while looking up at the red sandstone walls all around. Not a bad breakfast option if you are camping in the park for the weekend. If it's hot, you can meander down to the creek afterward and dip your toes in before heading out to hike.

This park is filled with easy-access trails for toddlers, whether you choose to walk on an interpretive boardwalk and look up at petroglyphs carved into the walls, hang out at the pioneer homestead and ranch, or head down the road and hike out through one of the flat, meandering, dry creek beds.

Geologically, this is a fascinating park because it's a 100-mile-long Waterpocket Fold, which is a buckling of the earth that looks like the spiny ridge of a dinosaur as you drive down into the area. There's a mix of traditional red rocks jutting up out of the park, but white Navajo sandstone "domes" also mark the terrain. These are the result of erosion from the uplift of the Colorado Plateau sometime within the last 20 million years, with most of the formations occurring between 1 million and 6 million years ago.

What also makes this park interesting is all of the petroglyphs that were likely carved into the rocks in this area by Fremont culture Native Americans who lived in the region around 1000 A.D. These early humans in the region apparently farmed lentils, maize, squash, and grain. In the 13th century, the Native American culture in this region abandoned the area, most likely due to a long drought, which prevented farming; and it wasn't until the Mormon settlers returned to the region in the 1800s that it was once again a small but thriving community.

One of the park favorites for toddlers (which was specifically recommended for 3-year-olds by an employee in the gift shop whose family had been there for three generations) is the Capitol Gorge Trail—a bit of a drive down to the end of the park to where the concrete ends and the road turns to dirt. This is best accessed with a 4X4 but is doable in a car. When arriving at the trailhead, there is a small parking lot with an outhouse (try to use it before you begin your hike, as there isn't a lot of privacy once you get into the hike). The trail is flat and wide, an easy trail for any child to negotiate and would be fairly passable for those with all-terrain wheelchairs and even strollers. Hiking sandals can actually be worn on this one if you are just hiking the flat arroyo. If you chose to climb up to the Tanks, you will find yourself on more of an upward trail, hiking over flat rocks and sandy trail, but it is still doable with sturdy shoes. Toddlers might get annoyed at the small pebbles that can accumulate, though, so keep this in mind.

As you walk through the flat, open, sandy canyon, you'll notice smooth, round pockmarks in the high Navajo sandstone walls. These have been worn in over thousands of years of flash floods and wind filling the canyon and then drying out again. Inside these round openings, birds' nests can be found and are fun for kids to explore.

Pass by pioneer "graffiti" on the walls, where past inhabitants of the area left their names and the year they were there high up on the sandstone walls. Farther along this trail, look for a trail up to the left that will take you to the Tanks. These were waterholes that pioneer travelers used for restocking water supplies when traveling through the harsh desert.

WHY IT'S A FAVORITE

"In May 2016, our family did a little tour around southwest Utah. Capitol Reef was an unexpected surprise for us. After being awe-inspired with Zion, Bryce, and Escalante Grand Staircase, we thought this little park would seem sort of boring. Wrong! Mason did one of his longest hikes here at almost 3 years old, and we even managed two

hikes in one day. The first was a small, interpretive boardwalk trail where we just happened to walk on when a huge hatching of furry caterpillars was happening. There were thousands of them crawling around, and Mason was totally wide eyed as we walked along the boardwalk watching them. We then followed this up with the great hike to the Tanks (natural waterholes in the desert), and that night he slept better and harder than he had all week." —SHANTI AND MARK HODGES

INSIDER'S TIP

This is an out and back, so plan on taking it as far as your child can manage. It's worth trying to get to the Tanks for a quick visit up to the Tank Bridge, a small rock arch that's clearly marked just off of the Tanks. To get to this, you will hike 0.2 mile up at the end of the trail. After viewing this, there isn't much else other than scrambling around rocks in the area, so this is a good turnaround spot to head back to the car.

SNOW CANYON TRAIL, UTAH,
JENNY'S CANYON TRAIL

ACTIVITIES: Hiking, bird watching, rock climbing

ROCK CLIMBING

LENGTH OF HIKE: 0.3 mile

OUT AND BACK OR LOOP: Out and back

DIFFICULTY OF TERRAIN: Easy

ELEVATION GAIN: 42 feet

PARKING FEE/PASS: $6

TOILETS: No

CHANGING TABLE: No

NURSING BENCHES: No

DOGS ALLOWED: No

BIKES/HORSES/MOTORS ON TRAIL: No

CELL RECEPTION: Yes

DRINKING WATER AVAILABLE: No

POTENTIAL CHILD OR BABY HAZARDS: Sharp rocks

GEAR SUGGESTIONS: Water

Southern Utah is known for its "Mighty Five" national parks and monuments, so Snow Canyon often gets overlooked. What we love about this spot, however, is visitors get the same red rock feel as in Arches and Zion but without the crowds. Jenny's Canyon is a very short hike, suitable for all ages, that ends with a short slot canyon. It is a sandy trail, so kids also enjoy playing in the red sand. Hike it Baby member Katie Rains said she was able to hike it with her 2-year-old, while 8 months' pregnant.

While this is a very short hike and maybe even one of the shortest in this book, it is a hike anyone can do to get a sampling of what slot canyons and Utah deserts feel like. However, this is just a slight taste of what Snow Canyon has to offer, so don't be afraid to venture farther. Your little one will love the very large rock toward the end; they'll need help climbing over it, but it is very doable.

Plan on spending a day venturing deeper into this park, where you'll find numerous toddler-appropriate slot canyons with high walls lined with petroglyphs and beautiful rocks that look like frozen layers of orange ribbon laying across the landscape. There are at least four main petroglyph areas throughout the park and then single petroglyphs around the park. If you are up for more adventuring, try the Petrified Dunes Trail and get 1.5 more miles in.

Kids will love collecting moqui balls, which are small, marble-shaped, colorful rocks that are fun for kids to collect. (Please don't take them home, though, as we adhere to Leave No Trace!) This is also a giant sandbox, so the kids can play for hours if they bring toys. Find a shady spot on the trail while the kids play in the cool sand. Keep an eye on the rock walls because sometimes you'll see climbers hanging off of them, which is entertaining to watch.

Wildlife lovers may see coyotes, kit foxes, quail, roadrunners, leopard lizards, gopher snakes, canyon tree frogs, falcons, desert tortoises, and gila monsters.

Summer months are very hot, with temperatures regularly exceeding 100 degrees. Be very careful if you head into the slot canyons, especially in these hotter months. It's very easy to get turned around and lost while searching for petroglyphs, and a 1-hour hike can get much longer. The parking lot is small, so visitors may have to walk from a lot farther away to this trailhead. If the lot is full, park at the Sand Dunes Picnic Area and hike to the trailhead. It's a great place to have lunch and play in the giant sand dune.

Fall through spring are the best months to hike in this park due to lower temperatures. The trail is closed annually from March 15 to June 1 because of the migratory birds inhabiting the area.

WHY IT'S A FAVORITE

"Snow Canyon has a huge amount of diverse areas. It has various types of petrified dunes that any kid can climb on. There are epic panoramic views in every direction. There are red dunes, white dunes, slot canyons, and petroglyphs everywhere." —HEATHER BRADEN

INSIDER'S TIP

Don't miss the petroglyph rocks and the moqui marbles. These are a bit deeper in the park and not on this trail.

QUECHEE STATE PARK, VERMONT,
QUECHEE GORGE DEWEY POND TRAIL

ACTIVITIES: Hiking, swimming

LENGTH OF HIKE: 1.4 miles

OUT AND BACK OR LOOP: Out and back

DIFFICULTY OF TERRAIN: Moderate

ELEVATION GAIN: 154 Feet

PARKING FEE/PASS: No

TOILETS: Yes

CHANGING TABLE: Yes

NURSING BENCHES: Yes

DOGS ALLOWED: Yes

BIKES/HORSES/MOTORS ON TRAIL: No

CELL RECEPTION: Yes

DRINKING WATER AVAILABLE: Yes, at the trailhead

POTENTIAL CHILD OR BABY HAZARDS: Deep water

GEAR SUGGESTIONS: Carrier, water, change of clothes

Want a hike with a great view from the top as you head down? This is it. Carved out by glacial melts 13,000 years ago, this is Vermont's deepest gorge. What's great about it for parents, though, is when you get to the viewpoint, there's a huge fence that you can see through to the bottom of the gorge, but your toddler won't run off the ledge. This allows little ones to run and explore and you can feel safe. This is exactly what Hike it Baby means when we say "family friendly."

Keep on hiking, and at the bottom you'll be rewarded with little pools to splash in and a gorgeous river running through. Take a moment to look back up to the top of the gorge and you'll feel so small.

Dewey Pond gets its name from A.G. Dewey, who owned a wool mill in the area from 1869 until the 1960s. The mill used the pond water for manufacturing, and if you look for it, you can see remnants of the old mill on the trail.

This is a great place to visit all year-round, but local Hike it Baby ambassador Natalie Kendrach suggests summer and fall for the most dramatic scenery. This hike is good for little walkers, but remember as you go down, you might need to help on the 0.2 mile uphill, where it gets a little rough. There are great nursing benches for new parents as well as tired little kids to stop and rest.

Expect to see many birds around Quechee State Park, including the yellow-rumped warbler, Canada goose, mallard, Northern goshawk, bald eagle, golden eagle, red-tailed hawk, Northern harrier, veery, red-shouldered hawk, osprey, black-throated warbler, scarlet tanager, white-throated sparrow, blue jay, and mourning dove. There is a bird rescue at the Vermont Institute of Natural Science, so your toddler can meet the local resident raptors.

No need for heavy-duty hiking shoes; runners will do just fine. Want to spend the weekend? There is a campground if you plan ahead and make reservations. There are 45 tent/RV spots and 2 bathrooms with showers.

WHY IT'S A FAVORITE
"The gorge is an impressive sight from the top. The trail is an easy walk down to the bottom. We loved that the trail was wide and had a fence to keep our toddler safe. If it is warm out, you can swim in the river at the bottom of the gorge. The view from the bottom is beautiful too." —NATALIE KENDRACH

INSIDER'S TIP
Down the road is a place to get free cheese tastings at Cabot Creamery. Also consider visiting Woodstock, a super-cute little town nearby.

SHENANDOAH NATIONAL PARK, VIRGINIA, **BLACKROCK SUMMIT**

ACTIVITIES: Hiking, camping, cycling, horseback riding

LENGTH OF HIKE: 1 mile

OUT AND BACK OR LOOP: Loop

DIFFICULTY OF TERRAIN: Easy

ELEVATION GAIN: 175 feet

PARKING FEE/PASS: $25/car to enter Shenandoah National Park; an annual pass can be purchased for $50, or entry is included with a national parks pass.

TOILETS: No; closest toilets at Loft Mountain Campground, 5 miles away on Skyline Drive

CHANGING TABLE: No

NURSING BENCHES: No

DOGS ALLOWED: Yes

BIKES/HORSES/MOTORS ON TRAIL: No

CELL RECEPTION: Very limited

DRINKING WATER AVAILABLE: No

POTENTIAL CHILD OR BABY HAZARDS: Large rocks, wildlife (including bears)

GEAR SUGGESTIONS: Snacks, water, camera, sunscreen, hats or shades

Ease, short distance, and a great natural play area at the top make this a perfect Hike it Baby family day on the mountain. While we love this hike for little ones, there are also a lot of learning opportunities on this trail for slightly older children because the trail follows the Appalachian Trail on the way up. Hike it Baby's Stephanie

Jacobsen told us she used their time on the trail to teach her 4-year-old daughter about the Appalachian Trail and to explain what thru-hiking is. "I explained how long it is, and about the different color blazes and what they mean," she says. "We also saw a small clearing that had recently been used for camping, and talked about backpacking, which my daughter calls "camping hikes."

From the back of the parking lot, start on the AT/white blazes heading west. Continue on a gentle uphill for around 0.5 mile until the trail winds around a huge talus slope of giant rocks. From here, you can turn right at the trail marker if you want to add the additional mileage of the Trayfoot Mountain spur. To stay with Blackrock, stay left at the trail marker, curve around the rocky slope, and follow the Blackrock Hut Road back down to the parking lot.

The rocks are easier to climb just past the intersection of the Trayfoot Mountain spur and will be easier for small legs to do on their own, but there is no wrong way up them.

If you want to get a little more distance in, Trayfoot Mountain spurs off the Blackrock Summit Trail to add 1.6 miles. Nearby on Skyline Drive are the Jones Run and Doyles River Trails—each can be done as a 3-mile out and back, or they connect to form a 6-mile trail leading from one parking lot to the other. Another bonus of this amazing web of trails is that there are swimming holes along each trail, and Doyles River has a couple of waterfalls. Keep in mind that Jones Run has a steep hike out, so don't do it if you have tired kids.

Independent walkers who are a little older can do this entire trail on their own. Tod-dlers can definitely walk, but they will need close supervision around the rocks. Stephanie said she chose to wear her little one while picking through rocks, as most of them were spaced too far apart for toddler legs.

While there are no nursing benches on this hike, the rocks are plenty large enough to comfortably sit for nursing or lunch/snacks. Also, there are usually clear stopping points where people have camped, so these make for a good spot to sit down and picnic.

While there are no huge hazards on this hike, some of the rocks have large drops of about 10 feet, so depending on how adventurous your little one is, you might want to keep an eye on him or her if scrambling around. Also, there are ticks with Lyme disease in Shenandoah National Park, so take precaution against bugs.

Another thing to note in this park is that you need to keep an eye out for black bears. They are well known to approach hikers as they look for food in some areas. The noise kids makes scares them off, but they are out there.

As for sun exposure, a lot of the trail is very shaded, but as you enter into the rocky area, you will be exposed. Sunscreen for all and hats/sunshades for younger babies should be used.

Considering camping? Loft Mountain Campground is nearby. This is a large family campground with both RV and tent-only sites, including walk-in sites. The campground has a camp store, bathrooms, potable water, and showers and has a fee of $15 per night. There is also backcountry camping available, though a (free) permit is required that can be obtained through the National Park Service.

WHY IT'S A FAVORITE

"This is a pretty straightforward trail that leads to a phenomenal rock scramble with amazing views of the Blue Ridge Mountains. It's a perfect trail to add to a camping trip because it is so short. The payoff from the views make a drive worthwhile if you want to spend just the day. There are a lot of gorgeous places on Skyline Drive where you can pull off and look over the valley and onto the various mountain peaks; but this trail gets you very wide panoramic views without the sound of cars passing behind you and with the feeling of accomplishment that comes from hiking to the views. The rocks are also really fun to climb for adults and kids alike!" —STEPHANIE JACOBSEN

INSIDER'S TIP

The Loft Mountain Campground wayside is only 5 miles north on Skyline Drive, and there is a small cafeteria there that sells hot food and ice cream. Nothing beats lunch looking out at the views from a mountain you just hiked, but the wayside is a good stop for bathrooms, and ice cream is always a fun posthike treat!

5 EASY TRAIL GAMES
FOR TODDLERS

With toddlers, you never quite know what you're going to get on the trail. Some days, they may hike several miles on their own like it's nobody's business, and you congratulate yourself on successfully having raised an outdoorsy child. But the next time you head out, they're in a different mood altogether. Fortunately, preparing a few simple games and activities can make the outing more fun for everyone and help keep little hikers happy and attentive on the trail any day. And on those most challenging days, they could even mean the difference between finishing the hike or turning around and going back home.

BE A TREE HUGGER. Trees have a way of invoking a sense of wonder in children, so take advantage of it by getting to know some of the trees along the trail a little bit better. Choose a tree to embrace while closing your eyes and staying completely silent for a minute. Can you hear the leaves rustle in the wind? Can you feel the trunk swaying? How does it feel to hug a tree? After you've tried hugging a few different trees, challenge your child to find a tree whose girth perfectly matches the length of his arms, so that his fingertips touch when embracing the trunk. If you have more than one child, have them try to find a tree with a trunk so thick that they all need to hold hands to reach around it.

WALK LIKE AN ANIMAL. This game is a perfect way to change things up when your child is starting to show signs of hiking fatigue. Have your child choose an animal that she would like to emulate. Keep moving down the trail and guess which animal your child is trying to be by watching the way she walks and acts. Is she creeping like a leopard, flying like a bird, or jumping like a kangaroo? After you make the correct guess, switch roles so that you're doing the charades and your child is trying to guess which animal you are.

MAKE A JOURNEY STICK. A traditional journey stick is a memento from a hike that kids can make by collecting natural items that they find along the trail—for example, leaves, flowers, grass straws, tree nuts, twigs, feathers, and pieces of bark—and attaching them to a stick using a piece of string. While older children can try making their sticks the traditional way, it's easier for toddlers to attach the items to a piece of cardboard with double-sided tape (use industrial adhesive tape if available). Prepare the journey stick ahead of time by cutting out a 12-inch by 2-inch piece of cardboard and attaching the tape to one side of the "stick." Leave the protective backing on the tape until you start the hike, then peel it off gradually as your child adds items to the journey stick. Before you head out, make sure to go over which items are fine to pick and which ones may be off limits.

WHAT'S IN YOUR HAND? Ask your child to put her hands behind her back, palms facing up. Place a small natural object in your child's hands—for example a rock, pine needle, shell, or a tree nut—and let her feel it without looking at it. Ask your child first to describe what the object feels like (hard or soft, rough or smooth, heavy or light, etc.) and then guess what it is. If you have several children with you, just let the child with the object in her hands describe it, then have the other children guess what it is based on the description. Take turns until all children have had the chance to hold an object and make guesses.

COUNT TO 10 WITH NATURE. Challenge your child to count to 10 using the natural features that you see along the trail. Start by finding something that there's only one of, for example, a creek or a lake, then gradually make your way up to 10 by counting 2 butterflies, 3 birds' nests, 4 beetles, and so on. Mix things up by using actions as well, such as making 8 laps around a tree or standing on top of a rock for 5 seconds. You can either make up a list in advance or just improvise by choosing things to count as you go.

Linda Åkeson McGurk is the author of There's No Such Thing as Bad Weather: A Scandinavian Mom's Secrets for Raising Healthy, Resilient, and Confident Kids. *Visit her blog for more tips for getting outside with kids of all ages: www.rainorshine mamma.com.*

30 THINGS TO DO WITH YOUR KIDS OUTSIDE

Look at a cloud and say what you think it looks like.

Make a wish on a dandelion.

Explore a cobweb and make spiders cool.

Hug a tree.

Build a house for fairies.

Read a book in the woods.

Fill a basket with nuts, leaves, and sticks that have fallen from trees.

Pick up 3 pieces of trash from outside.

Identify 3 birds.

Throw rocks in a river, pond, or puddle.

Plant wildflowers.

Build a rock cairn.

Slide down a sand or grassy hill.

Explore a trail you have never been down.

Draw pictures in the dirt.

Paint rocks with water and see what colors arise.

Splash in a big puddle.

Put bugs in a bowl and observe them.

Work in a garden or explore a public garden.

Pick out how many shades of green you see on a trail.

Look for something prickly.

Sing in the rain. no rain?? stick your head in a fountain or waterfall and sing!

Plant a seed that you find on the trail. i.e. acorn, pine cone, willow fuzz

Have a picnic.

Find a trail with a creek and look for the animals that live in it.

My Trail Name a trail with your own special name.

Make binoculars out of toilet paper rolls and spy something through them.

Make a new friend.

Walk like a duck, a deer, or a bear.

Find different items that are your child's favorite color.

HIKE IT BABY

OLYMPIC NATIONAL PARK, WASHINGTON,
SECOND BEACH

ACTIVITIES: Hiking, camping, water play

LENGTH OF HIKE: 2 miles

OUT AND BACK OR LOOP: Out and back

DIFFICULTY OF TERRAIN: Easy

ELEVATION GAIN: 80 feet

PARKING FEE/PASS: No

TOILETS: Yes

CHANGING TABLE: No

NURSING BENCHES: No

DOGS ALLOWED: No

BIKES/HORSES/MOTORS ON TRAIL: No

CELL RECEPTION: No

DRINKING WATER AVAILABLE: No

POTENTIAL CHILD OR BABY HAZARDS: Steep, switchbacks, stairs, possible large driftwood.

GEAR SUGGESTIONS: Sand toys, flashlight if hiking out late

Deanna Curry picked this trail for Hike it Baby families because it was her first backpacking trip with her 4-year-old daughter, and she said it couldn't have been more perfect. Second Beach is in an area called La Push, which is a remote beach in northern Washington and home to the Quileutes. This was also the rumored spot where the movie Twilight took place, but only select shots were filmed here and in the nearby town of Forks. The movie was actually filmed in Portland. But what this area is most known for is as a popular "secret" surf spot for those brave enough to wear a 4-millimeter wetsuit and paddle out in cold, dark, sharky water. But if you're not a surfer, this is still an excellent adventure to check out.

Why we are recommending it for backpacking is there is less than a mile hike to the beach, with some stairs to switchback down, but an easy enough trail for toddlers to hike and then traverse down the beach until you pick the perfect camp spot. This is a great distance for novice backpackers wanting to get their feet wet, literally. Set up camp and enjoy splashing in the surf on a warm summer day.

If you don't plan on camping, this is also an excellent day hike. Hike down past a porta-potty and a fence into the beginning of the trail, which travels up and downhill until it reaches the stairs. After the stairs, you'll come to a tree that a number of people have left little "surprises" on. Check it out, but please don't add to the pile as we believe strongly in Leave No Trace with Hike it Baby.

One of the things we love about this beach is how peaceful and scenic it is. This might be one of the most beautiful stretches of coastline in the Northwest. Look for the small islands off in the distance, Crying Lady Rock, and the Quillayute Needles archipelago, home to 14 species of seabirds, sea lions, harbor seals, and sea otters. This area is a critical wildlife protection area that was set aside especially to protect sea otters, which almost became extinct in the early 1900s due to being hunted for fur.

Once you pick a campsite (don't forget about tidal changes, so pick accordingly), you'll be able to easily find driftwood for a fire (make sure there isn't a fire ban in effect). Before the sun sets, head to the north side of the beach to look for a giant natural arch. After dark, you'll find yourself in awe of the incredibly pitch-black sky thick with stars. If it's a moonlit night, you'll see the sea stacks ominously towering over the water just off of the beach.

Throughout the day, keep your eyes on the sky and out toward the ocean. Bald eagles and seals, seagulls and crabs are everywhere. Whale migrations occur in March, April, and October, so if you visit during this time, keep your eyes on the horizon and look for spouts. Bears and raccoons are often out and about in the summer, so make sure you keep your food contained and hung in a tree.

Wake up early in the morning and catch the tides right and you will be able to walk between some of the sea stacks, but pay attention to tides coming in! Also look for tide pools to explore when the tides are low. This is one adventure that will feel like it's truly a far-out journey but really is just a quick jaunt back to the car if you forgot anything. This can definitely be done as a day trip as well.

WHY IT'S A FAVORITE

"Falling asleep to the sound of the waves was so relaxing. We loved every minute of our trip building sand castles, exploring the beach, and playing Frisbee. When we got back to the car, we asked our daughter what she liked best about the trip, and her response was, 'Everything!' I want to go again!' Even if you can't camp here, it's a great hike and beautiful beach." —DEANNA CURRY

INSIDER'S TIP

Yes, you can backpack here, but you need to get a permit at the Wilderness Information Center in Port Angeles. It's $8 per person (15 and younger are free) per night. A bear canister is needed, and you can get one from the center or rent them at REI and other outdoors stores. If camping, plan to bring a thick sleeping bag as the ocean breeze can get chilly at night.

MOUNT RAINIER AREA, WASHINGTON,
GROVE OF THE PATRIARCHS

ACTIVITIES: Hiking, wildflower viewing, splashing

LENGTH OF HIKE: 1.5 miles

OUT AND BACK OR LOOP: Loop (once you get on the boardwalk) Lollipop

DIFFICULTY OF TERRAIN: Easy

ELEVATION GAIN: 50 feet

PARKING FEE/PASS: Park entrance fee

TOILETS: Yes

CHANGING TABLE: Yes

NURSING BENCHES: Yes

DOGS ALLOWED: No

BIKES/HORSES/MOTORS ON TRAIL: No

CELL RECEPTION: No

DRINKING WATER AVAILABLE: Yes

POTENTIAL CHILD OR BABY HAZARDS: Tree roots, river

GEAR SUGGESTIONS: Camera (amazing views!)

If you have ever wanted to wander amid 1,000-year-old trees, this is your chance. A short hike with a boardwalk, a river to splash in, and a fun suspension bridge to cross help make the adventure even more appealing. Grove of the Patriarchs has huge trees that are hard to visualize. Some are more than 40 feet in diameter and 300 feet tall, which makes this hike a crowd pleaser for all little explorers.

Considered one of the easiest hikes in the Mount Rainier area, it's definitely worth a visit because little legs can hike this one year-round rain or shine. The thick overhead tree coverage helps keep you somewhat protected on a rainy day and shaded in the sun.

As you hike, look for a huge fallen tree along the trail with massive weathered roots that create a type of "tree cave" toddlers will love to climb in and explore. This tree makes you feel so small when you stand in it no matter how big you are. Be sure to take your time on the suspension bridge. The turquoise green color of the Ohanapecosh River will take your breath away!

Another thing that makes this hike special is the fact that the trees are surrounded on both sides by the Ohanapecosh River, which is part of the reason these trees have grown so massive. The river has protected this area from natural forest fires that usually sweep through most forests having such large trees at some point in history.

Expect to see the typical Douglas firs, hemlocks, and Western red cedars typical of most of the Mount Rainier area. In the trees, woodpeckers, blue jays, ravens, caterpillars, beetles, and spiders crawl about. Licorice ferns cover the landscape, and squirrels and chipmunks sit watchfully waiting for any morsel of snack you might drop.

The distance is perfect for toddlers and little kids with barely any elevation gain. Deanna Curry said her daughter loves reading the signs and learning about the different trees and plants (or loved having Mommy read the signs to her).

This hike can get busy especially when wildflowers are blooming or leaves are changing colors. In a pinch, you can park on the shoulder of SR 123 outside of the park entrance, but please support our national parks by purchasing a park pass.

Want to make a weekend of it? Ohanapecosh Campground is about a 2-mile walk from the trailhead, and you pass the gorgeous, equally toddler-friendly Silver Falls Loop Trail, which you can also do to add 2.8 more miles onto your hike and make a full day of it (Silver Falls Loop to Eastside Trail, crossing Stevens Canyon Road).

WHY IT'S A FAVORITE

"This is an easy hike with beautiful, big Douglas firs, hemlocks, and cedar trees! My daughter loves to give the massive trees a hug; she says they're magical. The suspension bridge and river are also highlights of the hike. We always take a break and play in the river and eat lunch before finishing the hike." —DEANNA CURRY

INSIDER'S TIP

You can follow the Eastside Trail south across the Stevens Canyon Road to the Silver Falls Loop Trail and visit a spectacular waterfall for extra bang for the hike. Consider really exploring the other trails in this area because there are numerous toddler-friendly options. This trail leads all the way back to Ohanapecosh Campground, a great place to stay in the park overnight.

ACTIVITIES: Hiking, caving

LENGTH OF HIKE: Upper Cave 1.5 miles, Lower Cave 0.75 mile

OUT AND BACK OR LOOP: Out and back

DIFFICULTY OF TERRAIN: Lower easy; Upper difficult

ELEVATION GAIN: 460 feet

PARKING FEE/PASS: $5

TOILETS: Yes

CHANGING TABLE: No

NURSING BENCHES: No

DOGS ALLOWED: No

BIKES/HORSES/MOTORS ON TRAIL: No

CELL RECEPTION: No

DRINKING WATER AVAILABLE: No

POTENTIAL CHILD OR BABY HAZARDS: Large rock piles, low ceilings (when carried), 8' vertical wall (if attempting Upper Cave), the trail is usually wet and slippery

GEAR SUGGESTIONS: Hiking boots, carrier, at least two light sources per person, helmets for children, warm and waterproof clothing (the cave holds a temperature in the low 40s year-round).

We have to get a cave in our adventures, so Ape Caves seemed like a good one to share. Located just south of Mount St. Helens in the Gifford Pinchot National Forest, this area has two caves, one of which toddlers to pre-K can walk fairly easily with help. If carried, infants and babies can enjoy a ride through this amazing cave as well. The other is for more advanced hikers who are comfortable babywearing.

"Personally, I love the feeling I get every time I descend the staircase into the cave. The sunlight doesn't shine far into the cave. When you get to the bottom of the metal staircase, it is cold and dark. This was exactly where we thought our oldest (now 4 years old) was not going to let us continue on last year," she said. Once you get to this point in the cave, there is no plant life or natural light. For some kids, this can be scary, so once you get 100 feet or so into the cave, shut off your lights for a moment to experience the complete darkness. That will help kids adjust to the change in scenery.

Another thing to note is that there are smaller branches off the main lava tube. Most are not large enough to explore, though there is at least one small branch in the Lower Cave that is fun to climb in and explore especially for little kids.

The majority of the hazards are in the Upper Cave. However, there are some things to be aware of in the Lower Cave as well. The cave is usually wet, so any stairs or rock formations you'll be climbing will be slippery. The ceiling can be a bit low in areas, too, so make sure you are aware of that when babywearing. In the Upper Cave, be aware of the large boulder piles, holes in the floor, low ceilings, and the 8-foot wall. Also, to exit the Upper Cave, you need to ascend a metal ladder. This may be difficult for young children and possibly slippery as well.

When you see pictures of Ape Caves online, you'll usually see the "skylight" where the cave ceiling has caved in. The sunlight shining into the rocky cave, with the plants dangling from above, is a beautiful contrast between the barren cave below and the flourishing forest growing just a few feet above.

The only wildlife you can expect to see are birds, chipmunks, and golden-mantled ground squirrels, but this will usually be outside of the cave. There are probably bats in the cave, but it's highly unlikely you will see them. We've also heard that this is a good area to look for Bigfoot, whether you believe in that or not.

Ape Cave is open year-round (though the parking lot may be closed in winter). The experience is always the same because it's a cave. Sometimes in deep winter there can be a lot of snow at the entrance of the cave, making it more difficult to get down into the cave and very slippery and icy. If there has been snow in the area, consider waiting until it clears. Also avoid visiting during holidays. The cave can be very busy during the summer, and parking fills up fast.

WHY IT'S A FAVORITE

"No photograph can possibly capture the challenge you face or the awe-inspiring views. Our oldest is a bit afraid of the dark. He was very uneasy the first time through the Lower Cave last year. With a little coaxing and assurance that there were no monsters living in the cave, he let us carry him to the end of the cave. By the end of the cave, he was walking with little assistance. This year, he walked on his own, only requesting assistance in areas his short little legs couldn't scale alone. His brother (20 months at our last visit) did well, as I carried him down the cave. On the way back, I let him walk until the trail got rough near the entrance. Both boys loved the experience, and we can't wait to go back next year!" —STEPHANIE NORBY

INSIDER'S TIP

Turn off your headlamps when you get about 100 feet into the cave to help your kids adjust to the darkness. Make sure they have a light, too, so they feel in control of their own lighting situation. There are some really great headlamps for kids out there.

GIFFORD PINCHOT NATIONAL FOREST, WASHINGTON,
FALLS CREEK FALLS TRAIL

ACTIVITIES: Hiking

LENGTH OF HIKE: 3.4 miles

OUT AND BACK OR LOOP: Out and back

DIFFICULTY OF TERRAIN: Easy

ELEVATION GAIN: 650 feet

PARKING FEE/PASS: No

TOILETS: Yes

CHANGING TABLE: Yes

NURSING BENCHES: No

DOGS ALLOWED: Yes, on leash

BIKES/HORSES/MOTORS ON TRAIL: No

CELL RECEPTION: Spotty

DRINKING WATER AVAILABLE: No

POTENTIAL CHILD OR BABY HAZARDS: Some steep areas

GEAR SUGGESTIONS: Hiking poles, good rain jacket

The trail starts off from the trailhead on a flat and wide section in a forest of Douglas fir, great for walking toddlers to run around and explore. After a little while, the trail parallels the creek and starts to climb moderately. Almost the whole hike follows the creek on one side and has a lush forest on the other. When it does not follow the creek, the hike takes you through old-growth forest with a lot of great sights.

The hike's terrain ranges from well-packed dirt to large rocks, so hiking shoes are recommended. "We love this hike because it has everything that is great about the Pacific

Northwest—trees, moss, a creek, two bridges, and a waterfall!" says Katherine Takata. "The other reason we love this hike is its sense of seclusion, yet it is not that far of a drive from town."

Whether hiking this in the spring or during the changing of the seasons, it's a gorgeous and very moderately trafficked hike. The creek provides a wonderful soothing sound while you check out all the moss, trees, and wildflowers. Also in the first 10 to 15 minutes of the hike, you can find points where it's easy to hike down to the creek bed and splash in the creek. Smooth rocks and small pools of water are easy to enter and frolic, but the water is ice cold year-round.

If you like suspension bridges, you will cross one and look for the hollow tree trailside that Melody reports her kids use as a "boat." The climb for this hike is gradual, so you won't notice the elevation gain for most of the hike. When you get to the waterfall at the end of the hike, there's no question that the reward is totally worth it, especially with how easy the trail is. The trail comes to a natural stopping point at the thundering falls, and large boulders scattered around the area are great for resting to picnic. Keep in mind that there are drop-offs here, though, and it's important to watch that your toddler doesn't get too close to the edge.

The trail continues; however, an out and back might be the best way to go. To make it a loop, there's a steep climb and the hike is already a fairly long one, depending on how far your child hikes. Also, the upper trail is not as toddler friendly, with steeper drop-offs.

WHY IT'S A FAVORITE

"This is such a pretty forest hike with plenty of moss along the way. It is flat and nice for kids who are just learning to hike, with an amazing destination. The waterfall at the end makes a 360-degree cathedral of water on top. While enjoying the view of the waterfall, there are big rocks that are fun and safe to climb, so everyone is happy. It is not usually super crowded and feels much wilder than the Columbia River Gorge." —MELODY GEORGE

INSIDER'S TIP

Note with this hike that you have limited access and the road is only open April 1 to November 30.

STEIGERWALD WILDLIFE REFUGE, WASHINGTON, **GIBBONS CREEK WILDLIFE ART TRAIL**

ACTIVITIES: Interpretive trail, wildlife viewing, birding

LENGTH OF HIKE: 2.8 miles

OUT AND BACK OR LOOP: Both

DIFFICULTY OF TERRAIN: Easy, ADA accessible

ELEVATION GAIN: None

PARKING FEE/PASS: No

TOILETS: Yes

CHANGING TABLE: Yes

NURSING BENCHES: Yes

DOGS ALLOWED: No

BIKES/HORSES/MOTORS ON TRAIL: No

CELL RECEPTION: Yes

DRINKING WATER AVAILABLE: No

POTENTIAL CHILD OR BABY HAZARDS: No

GEAR SUGGESTIONS: Binoculars

This is one of those rare hidden gems easily missed as people hastily speed out to catch the waterfalls and wildflowers in the Columbia Gorge. If you have a toddler, it's completely worth stopping for a quick walk. The reason: Wildlife viewing is phenomenal and up close and personal. On any given day, you can expect to see deer grazing alongside the trail, beavers swimming across the stream past ducks and blue herons, and hawks diving from high in the sky to grab fish in their talons and swoop away.

The trail is a gravel out and back, so it's doable with a wheelchair or walker. The path is lined with fun interpretive art and music elements that you can tap on to hear different sounds. Pay close attention to all of the details on the trail. The first time we visited, we missed the hollowed-out tree that had a giant beetle statue inside it. Later we found it when Mason poked his head into the hollowed-out tree. Your toddler will love the bridge crossing and the way the trail meanders through the wetlands. This park was established in the late '80s after the dam was resurrected in the '70s and early '80s. There was concern for animal habitats in the area, so the goal of Steigerwald was to help provide a home for animals displaced by the industrialization of the area.

The art and interpretive portion of the trail opened in 2010 but rarely has more than a few cars in the lot, so don't worry about visiting it throughout the year. The hike is partially exposed, so on a hot summer day, there is limited shade.

WHY IT'S A FAVORITE

"The first time we hiked this trail, Mason was just starting to walk, so we loved that the ground was very even and it was easy to let him run and play. We were with another friend whose son was the same age, so they were able to adventure and explore without any warnings from us." —SHANTI AND MARK HODGES

INSIDER'S TIP

Please don't feed the animals at this park. We know that goes without saying, but it can be tempting when you see so many ducks floating about and crossing the trail. If you visit between May and September, you will notice a big, artsy, wrought-iron door that is open. This is closed the rest of the year to protect wintering birds.

LAYER UP!
IN COLD WEATHER

ONE WINTER I WENT TO ANCHORAGE TO VISIT FAMILY, and once I got there, everything I brought seemed all wrong. Temperatures were in the teens and twenties, and my then-toddler Mason hated everything I tried to put on him.

"No hat, Mommy. No jacket," he screamed at me as I tried to dress him. "No outside. No snow."

I felt like a total mommy failure. Dressing for "outdoor fun" seemed impossible, and I had wasted time and money on expensive gear that we weren't even using! While I can't help you convince your kids to actually wear the right layers, I can help you find the right gear (at the right price) once the tantrum's over and they're ready to get outside.

BRANDS MATTER. Look in your closet, and if there is a brand you like, chances are they also make great gear for kids. I am a big fan of Columbia, Patagonia, and North Face. If you don't want to pay full price, there are some great used sites like Hike it Baby's buy and sell forum (www.buynsell.hikeitbaby.com) and Threadlyte (www.thread-lyte.com), where you can find quality used outdoor gear for the whole family.

SHOP OFF-SEASON. There are many ways to get discounted high-quality gear. Look for sales in the off-season or at the end of a season for the following year. Last year I purchased 2T and 3T long underwear from REI for Mason that was normally $21 for $4. I bought ahead and put them in a box for this year so I knew where to find them when winter rolled around. That was the one thing Mason wore every day while in Alaska.

TOASTY HANDS. We often get so caught up in jackets, pants, snowsuits, and rain suits that we forget what's going on a baby's hands. Think about what your little one has right now. Big, bulky gloves aren't necessarily warm. Put a finger in there and think about how those gloves feel compared to yours. Remember, if you have a crawler, they will have very wet hands. Waterproof/water-resistant gloves matter. If you have fleece gloves, you can wash them in products like NikWax to make them more water-resistant. Fleece picks up dirt, mud, and water, so add a shell if in damp, mucky weather. Look for a few different gloves depending on conditions. If you have a very fussy kid who won't wear gloves, look for gloves with "action" details on them. Sharks, superheroes, and bright colors are winners.

SOCK IT TO YA. In winter, cotton is not a good choice on a child's foot for many reasons. Kids often take boots on and off repeatedly. They run around in a wet hallway then put their boots back on and head outside with wet feet. Think wool and polyester blends. Double up the wool or wear tights under the wool socks. Any way you can keep those little feet from getting cold is important.

BOOT CHOICES. My suggestion is to have one good pair of solid rain boots. Once you have rain covered, think seasons. If you plan on being in snow a few times, plastic boots without liners will be cold. Look for something that is rated for cold, and even if you only get a few wears out of them, you can resell them at a premium price. Again, this is a great thing to look for in the off-season for the following year. Or ask friends with older kids if they want to unload their previous year's boots. Look for a soft fleece or felt liner inside a good rubber boot. There are even boots that can be worn in both rain and snow with a removable liner.

HEADWEAR. If your little one hates hats, look for something like a balaclava, where they can't pull the hat off of their head. A tie under the chin can also be great. Sometimes Velcro works, but my kiddo tears that off. Look for hats with animal ears on them or other things that might be fun for them to put on. Strangely enough, my son seems more excited to wear my hats than his own, so I always travel with two in case he is in one of those moods.

LAYER IT ON. Full-body rain suits can double as snowsuits with the right layers underneath. Look for brands like Oakiwear, Tuffo, and Columbia. The nice thing about a full-body rain suit is that when the weather shifts from snow to rain, you can zip them in and send them out to swim in mud puddles without concern. The downside to rain suits is that you have one piece, so when it gets wet, that's it. It will need to dry out. This is where I honestly think if you can pull it off, consider one full-body rain suit, a pair of rain pants, and a shell jacket. This will leave you with a lot of optionsfor multiple days of outdoor play.

BASE LAYERS. Long underwear is key. Tights can go over them, then socks over the tights. They make tights for boys, too. If your child can do wool, there are some excellent brands out there for base layers for little people. Polyester is possible, too, but I haven't found many brands that make base layers for littles. They are spendy, but honestly, base layers have been one of my best investments. Try brands like Ella's Wool, Patagonia, Simply Merino, or Wee Woolies.

TOP-SHELF BUYS. Pick and choose what you buy at a premium. For us, that was a down jacket. I came home from my Alaska trip and bought a down jacket for Mason. We had owned one previously that lasted from when he was 6 months to 24 months (that was pushing it). It was one of our most expensive but best purchases made for getting him outside. Mason loved this jacket so much he often slept in it for naps because I couldn't get him out of it after coming inside. Think about what pieces you are willing to buy at full retail and look for sales on the brands you prefer. Remember that good-quality products mean you can resell them or gift them to another parent who will be super-stoked to get that expensive item.

ASK AROUND. What is working for your friends and hiking buddies? While there are lots of brands that are popular, make sure they aren't just popular because they are cheap. Find out why your friend bought something. Did they buy it based on price or quality? Assess how much time they spend outside and if that product would really work for you.

Cold Weather Tips for Baby

There are a few things to think about when keeping your littlest hiker warm. While you don't want your baby to be cold, more is not always best. Infants can't regulate their temperature like adults can. If they are too hot, they will overheat and dehydrate quickly. Watch for signs of fussiness and flushed skin.

• For new babies, use fleece onesie PJs as one of your first layers. You can put socks under them and then the fleece zip-ups and then put your own wool or cashmere socks over baby feet and legs for an extra layer.

• Socks should be wool, if possible, or synthetic. It may seem shocking to pay adult prices for tiny socks, but this item is especially important when little feet are sticking out of a carrier and not quite at the shoe-wearing phase. Consider two pairs of socks on a baby and a blanket or cover over a carrier to keep little toes warm.

• If you are nervous about pajamas, take an old pair of wool or cashmere socks of yours and pull them up over your baby like leg warmers on top of their socks for an extra layer over their feet and legs.

- Outerwear is important to help keep little bodies safe from the wind, wet, and cold. Get an extra-large jacket for yourself to zip over the carrier and provide a cocoon to keep baby warm. If you have a poncho, you can also use that to protect a baby in a carrier from wind and rain.

- If you don't have a big enough jacket, make sure you have a down or fleece bunting for baby on those cold days. Built-in mittens and hoods are a bonus when they hit toddler phase and try to kick things off. Make sure things aren't too tight on babies because they can't tell you.

- If you are wearing your little one in a Soft-Structured Carrier (SSC), they should be nice and snug against you, soaking up your body heat. The dangling extremities can still get chilly, though. Heavy boots or shoes should be avoided as they can cut off circulation on dangling legs.

- Hats that cover the ears and go under the chin are a must-have for those exposed heads. When wearing a baby, your exhaled breaths can condense on your baby's head and make their head dangerously cold. This also holds true for breathing on cold body parts; the moist warm air from your mouth actually causes the skin to become wet and causes it to be even more dangerously cold.

- If your baby is in a stroller, he or she should be nice, warm, and dry with all of these layers and a weather shield or heavy blanket covering them as well. Consider finding a water-resistant blanket for the top layer. Also, you can get covers for a stroller, which will help keep a baby warm and dry.

Start short and sweet with a walk around the block to see how you both do, then take your adventures further.

WOLF GAP RECREATION AREA, VIRGINIA,
BIG SCHLOSS TRAIL

ACTIVITIES: Hiking, camping

LENGTH OF HIKE: 4.4 miles

OUT AND BACK OR LOOP: Out and back

DIFFICULTY OF TERRAIN: Moderate

ELEVATION GAIN: 1,000+ feet

PARKING FEE/PASS: No

TOILETS: Yes

CHANGING TABLE: No

NURSING BENCHES: Yes

DOGS ALLOWED: Yes

BIKES/HORSES/MOTORS ON TRAIL: No

CELL RECEPTION: Spotty

DRINKING WATER AVAILABLE: No

POTENTIAL CHILD OR BABY HAZARDS:
Falling danger at overlooks

GEAR SUGGESTIONS: Water, snacks, carrier
for small toddlers/babies, hiking boots,
long pants

Located along the ridge of the Great North Mountain Range straddling the border of Virginia and West Virginia, Big Schloss is a popular weekend getaway for families in the Richmond and DC areas. While popular, this hike is in the middle of the George Washington National Forest, a 1.8 million-acre stretch of greenspace with over 2,000 miles of trails, meaning there are plenty of other trails from which to choose all through this region. German settlers gave the hike its name Schloss, which means "castle" because of the dominant rock outcroppings that have a palace-like, towering feel to them.

Start your hike out of Wolf Gap Campground, and head up until everything levels out and you eventually cross a little wooden bridge. Keep in mind that you will break a sweat on this one because it begins with a steep, rocky 0.75-mile climb, but the pain only lasts a little over 0.5 mile with switchbacks leading up the mountain until it plateaus across the ridge. Don't get scared away by that first little climb, however, because this is a good family hike with a slight challenge that's worth the hump. When you reach the top of the mountain, the terrain changes to a grassy environment as the trail narrows. On your right, there are little overlooks to catch a sneak peak of the views from the end of the trail. One-quarter mile from the end, take a right at the sign toward Big Schloss. The terrain differs from the other two sections of the trail; there are lots of evergreen trees. Enjoy the views from the bridge and the rocks on the other side before heading back down the way you came. This hike is a fairly year-round hike, but in the fall you'll look out over beautiful, fiery, fall-colored leaves changing as far as the eye can see.

We recommended this adventure for the great views, varied terrain, and ample parking with a campground if you want to make it a weekend. While the hike can get crowded at the most popular times of year, it's still fairly easy to navigate and get on trail. Keep an eye out for peregrine falcons flying overhead; and if you visit near dawn or dusk, you might hear the hoot of a distant owl.

There are two types of snakes, copperheads and rattlesnakes, that are native to the area but are rarely seen. Wear long pants because the trail is narrow and has high grass and weeds that can be annoying as you hike. Also, there are a lot of loose rocks, so be careful especially when coming downhill and carrying a little one. Hiking boots are advised to prevent slipping on the steep part.

Expect this hike to take between 2 and 4 hours depending on how quickly your family moves. Plan to take your lunch or snacks at the top, where you will have the best views. If you want to make a full weekend of this, you can camp out in the 10 primitive spots at Wolf Gap.

If you are looking for another hike in the area, Bucktail Trail is a few miles away on the same road. It's a loop over 10 miles long, so typically with kids this is hiked in just a few miles out and back rather than completing the loop. Horses are allowed on this trail, so be careful. Trout Pond Recreation Area (15 miles away) has a lake for swimming, bathhouse, picnic areas, camping, and a trail loop around the lake (about 1 mile). Lost River State Park (30 miles away) has lots of trails, cabins, bathrooms, and picnic areas.

WHY IT'S A FAVORITE

"Big Schloss is a well-maintained out and back trail near the quaint mountain town of Wardensville, WV. There are breathtaking views at the top of foliage for as far as the eye can see." —STEFANIE OTTENSTEIN

INSIDER'S TIP

If you take an immediate right after crossing the bridge, you can walk up to an area of relatively flat rocks that are great for picnicking or taking in the views instead of limiting yourself to the rocky area straight ahead.

CANAAN VALLEY RESORT STATE PARK, WEST VIRGINIA, **BALD KNOB TRAIL**

ACTIVITIES: Hiking, biking, whitewater rafting, berry picking, camping

LENGTH OF HIKE: 2.5 miles

OUT AND BACK OR LOOP: Both

DIFFICULTY OF TERRAIN: Easy

ELEVATION GAIN: 400 feet

PARKING FEE/PASS: $5/person

TOILETS: Yes

CHANGING TABLE: Yes

NURSING BENCHES: Benches in lodge, one or two at the top of the ski lift; plenty of "comfy" rocks

DOGS ALLOWED: Yes

BIKES/HORSES/MOTORS ON TRAIL: No

CELL RECEPTION: Spotty

DRINKING WATER AVAILABLE: Yes

POTENTIAL CHILD OR BABY HAZARDS: Ticks, poison ivy

GEAR SUGGESTIONS: Blueberry basket in season, bug spray

Bald Knob is one part exciting, one part peaceful, and one part pure beauty and a perfect hike for all ages. The hike climbs a mountain for stellar views of Canaan Valley. Starting at the Canaan Valley Resort State Park ski area, you can either hike the entire time or choose to relax and take in some views on the ski lift for a small fee of $5 per person. Then there is a 1.25-mile hike to Bald Knob, a mountaintop clearing with granite outcroppings. It's worth noting that before beginning the hike, there is a hang glider launch right at the top of the slopes. It offers views of the valley as well, but from the other side of the mountain. If you're lucky, some pilots may be out for a ride.

From the top of the lift, head into the woods following the Bald Knob Trail. About half the trail is in the pines, shaded, but full of rocks and roots. It is not especially treacherous, but watch your step. After the woods, the trail opens up to an open grassy area and shortly after begins the climb. Near the summit is a patch of wild blueberries (called huckleberries by the locals), usually ripening around late July. It's the perfect motivation to get small children up those last hundred yards or so, and we recommend bringing a small container to forage berries to take back or eat at a picnic atop the lookout.

With wild berries, this also means that the area is home to black bears. While not usually aggressive, they should be treated with caution and respect. During prime hiking weather, the trail is generally well trafficked, and bears are not overly plentiful, but look out for them. Other common wildlife you can expect to see are deer, squirrels, chipmunks, and a wide variety of birds (there is a nearby bird sanctuary down the mountain). The tall, grassy area is prime real estate for ticks, so bug spray and thorough tick checks are encouraged. There is some poison ivy along portions of the trail, but it is very easily avoided if you are familiar with the plant's appearance.

At the top of Bald Knob, there are several rocky overlooks from which to view the beautiful Canaan Valley. There isn't much shade, but Baldy Grove, just a short walk to the right, has plenty of shade and a small sitting shelter in case of bad weather. For backpackers, this is an ideal backcountry campsite to use, following state park regulations, of course. When ready to leave, the ski lift on the way down offers even better views, or you can opt to walk the full trail to the bottom. Be sure to bring

a map for both trail options, and pay attention to closing time for the ski lift (usually around 4 p.m.).

The Canaan Valley area offers no shortage of outdoor recreation adventures from kayaking to whitewater rafting, hiking, skiing, mountain biking, caverns, and camping. There are plenty of public lands to explore: Canaan Valley State Park, Blackwater Falls State Park, Canaan Valley National Wildlife Refuge, Dolly Sods Wilderness, and Monongahela National Forest, to name a few.

WHY IT'S A FAVORITE

"I always hiked Bald Knob with my grandparents as a kid on our family vacations to a ski resort in August. As a teen, I ended up throwing a routine hissy fit at how "boring" the vacation was and how uncool it was to hike the same mountain every year and ride a ski lift with no snow. My dad pulled me aside one year to point out how the shadow of the clouds could be seen along the mountain ridge, and I still remember being in awe (even though I pretended not to care). Now, I take my son with his grandparents, and we do the same hike every year. It's such a special place for my family and comes with a spectacular view. Hopefully, my son skips the temper tantrum/hating hiking phase! I love the hike because ski lifts are exciting and relaxing and beautiful, and climbing mountains is fun!" —ELIZABETH KNAPP

INSIDER'S TIP

Stop in one of the nearby towns—Thomas and Davis—to chat with the locals about their favorite spots to explore, and you're bound to find something new and exciting. If making a weekend visit, I highly recommend stopping by the Purple Fiddle in Thomas for a bite to eat and ice cream, live music (every day), and maybe a local beer. This venue is for all ages and advertises that you'll never need a babysitter. There are plenty of camping options at the state parks and national forest or free camping on CVI grounds outside of Davis.

KETTLE MORAINE STATE FOREST, WISCONSIN, **PIKE LAKE TRAIL**

ACTIVITIES: Backpacking, hiking

LENGTH OF HIKE: 4 miles

OUT AND BACK OR LOOP: Out and back

DIFFICULTY OF TERRAIN: Easy

ELEVATION GAIN: Moderate

PARKING FEE/PASS: $8/day

TOILETS: Yes

CHANGING TABLE: No

NURSING BENCHES: Yes

DOGS ALLOWED: Yes

BIKES/HORSES/MOTORS ON TRAIL: No

CELL RECEPTION: Yes

DRINKING WATER AVAILABLE: Yes

POTENTIAL CHILD OR BABY HAZARDS: Ticks, mosquitoes, roots, rocks, street crossings

GEAR SUGGESTIONS: Backpacking gear, bug spray, bathing suit, towel

Ready for miles and miles of trails that weave in and out of beautiful forests and up and down the moraines and eskers? The Kettle Moraine State Forest covers 56,000 acres and is divided into two large forests and three smaller units. On the eastern side of Pike's Lake, one of the smaller regions of this park, you will find the perfect training ground for backpacking with your little ones. This route along the Ice Age National Scenic Trail allows you a bit of burn in the legs, perfect for beginning to build muscles while wearing a pack, but it isn't so demanding that you will be wiped out when you hit the campsite.

The hike in has some hills, but it isn't too difficult for little ones. If you want to add a bit of mileage and get a view, you can take a spur path to head up to the tower. From the top of the tower, you get an excellent view of Pike Lake, a 522-acre spring-fed kettle. According to the Ice Age Trail website, a kettle is "a surface depression formed by large, detached blocks of melting ice that were buried with sand and gravel. As the ice melted, the other material collapsed, leaving a crater-like depression. Some kettles are more than 100 feet deep. Kettles can be found in many places along the Trail." This is a great view of how the Wisconsin landscape was shaped by the glaciers receding in the last ice age.

The camping season is the best time of year to visit because you can reserve a walk-in site. Since these sites are on the Ice Age Trail, they go quickly, so plan ahead!

The camping spot is well secluded and decently sized. Campsite 3 is the largest and has a little rock wall that makes a fun play area for the little one. Keep in mind that there are ticks during the warm months, so please check your little ones regularly. Since there are port-a-lets for restrooms next to the campsites, there's no need to dig a cathole in the middle of the night if a toddler or little one needs to use the restroom. Each campsite also has a fire ring, and the office is within walking distance if you want to buy firewood for the evening.

WHY IT'S A FAVORITE

"A great way to try backpacking is a moderate out and back on the Ice Age Trail at Pike Lake. The walk-in sites are only about 2 miles from the beach parking area, making it a decent walk for a little one but not so far if you need to go home right away. It's a great way to test gear for a longer trip and make sure you are ready to roll for big adventures. The sites are decently sized, allowing you to have multiple families on the trip."
—JESSICA FEATHERSTONE

INSIDER'S TIP

You can park at the lake/beach area. If someone needs to quickly grab the car, there is a parking lot about 0.25 mile from the camping area. This makes it easy for one party member to get the car while the other packs up camp.

It's also easy to keep the kids moving back toward the cars since that's the same direction as the beach. Pack a bathing suit and towel for your return so you can play in the water before loading up for the drive home.

COPPER FALLS STATE PARK, WISCONSIN, **COPPER FALLS TRAIL, DOUGHBOY LOOP**

ACTIVITIES: Hiking, walking, birding, playground

LENGTH OF HIKE: 1.7 or 3.1 miles

OUT AND BACK OR LOOP: Loop

DIFFICULTY OF TERRAIN: Easy

ELEVATION GAIN: 257 feet

PARKING FEE/PASS: $8

TOILETS: Yes

CHANGING TABLE: Yes

NURSING BENCHES: Yes

DOGS ALLOWED: Yes

BIKES/HORSES/MOTORS ON TRAIL: No

CELL RECEPTION: Excellent

DRINKING WATER AVAILABLE: Yes

POTENTIAL CHILD OR BABY HAZARDS: Bridge

GEAR SUGGESTIONS: Soft carrier, hiking boots, camera, swimming gear

Looking for an easy hike that's not mobbed with people? Try this hidden gem in northern Wisconsin not far from Lake Superior. Copper Falls State Park offers waterfalls and well-maintained bridges and overlooks, making it easy for new walkers to hop off your back and get some toddle waddle time and a bit of stair climbing to tire them out.

"A 3-year-old can totally finish this hike with breaks. There are benches for resting and places to run wild and throw rocks," says Hike it Baby ambassador Dineo Dowd.

New walkers are safe here with lots of space to roam and shade to sit under and take a break. Enjoy the bubbling sound of the waterfall, and look for butterflies flitting through wildflowers in this beautiful park.

The nice thing about this hike is both the shade and the fact that it's relatively bug-free in the summer. It's an easy loop trail and kids will enjoy climbing the stairs and crossing bridges. You can wear any comfortable shoe without much concern of rough terrain.

Go for the short loop, or extend out and make it a 3.1-mile journey. It's easy to make the call on this decision after the hike begins, because there are a few options for extending the loop along the way.

While in the park, look for deer, skunks, raccoons, red squirrels, chipmunks, and even gray wolves. Also look for black bears and porcupines, frogs, wood turtles, and snakes (none are poisonous). There are also over 200 species of birds, so expect to see everything from woodpeckers to chickadees to eagles.

While in the park, you might notice a mine shaft in the southeast corner of the picnic area. According to the region's history, there is evidence of Old Copper Culture Native Americans who mined the flowing rivers in this area from 3000 B.C. to 1000 B.C. But it wasn't until the late 1900s that a miner named Wells Ruggles, who was in search of ore, attempted to build a larger-scale mine in the area and failed miserably. The mine was continually flooded by the river; and in 1902, he blew rock to divert the river, but the mine was still a failure. The land officially became a park in 1929.

Want to stay over? The 55-unit campground offers wooded sites, including 13 with electric service, showers, and both flush and vault toilets. There is a full-service dump station for RV campers. If you come in the summer, bring your swim gear because there is excellent swimming in the clear, spring-fed Loon Lake.

WHY IT'S A FAVORITE

"We hiked along the trails and saw Copper Falls, Brownstone Falls, and the Cascades. Bring your camera for some great pictures! This loop trail is easy to follow, and the kids will enjoy climbing on the stairs and crossing the bridges. You get a better view in the fall with the leaves changing." —DINEO DOWD

INSIDER'S TIP

Much of the trail building you see in the park, from the wooden footbridges and log fences to the log buildings, was constructed in the early 1920s by returning veterans from World War I. More work was done during the Great Depression by the Civilian Conservation Corps. Today, these historic structures add a nice rustic charm to the park and are a great backdrop for snapping family photos. Also look for the huge playground next to the parking lot and restroom for the kids after you hike.

PARFREY'S GLEN STATE NATURAL AREA, WISCONSIN, **PARFREY'S GLEN TRAIL**

ACTIVITIES: Hiking, splashing

LENGTH OF HIKE: 1.7 miles

OUT AND BACK OR LOOP: Out and back

DIFFICULTY OF TERRAIN: Moderate

ELEVATION GAIN: 500 feet

PARKING FEE/PASS: Yes, Wisconsin State Park sticker or $8/day

TOILETS: Yes

CHANGING TABLE: No

NURSING BENCHES: Yes

DOGS ALLOWED: No

BIKES/HORSES/MOTORS ON TRAIL: No

CELL RECEPTION: Yes

DRINKING WATER AVAILABLE: Yes

POTENTIAL CHILD OR BABY HAZARDS: Rocks, water, bugs

GEAR SUGGESTIONS: Hiking poles, sandals, waterproof boots, carrier, bug spray

At first, Dineo Dowd was nervous about moving from Utah to Wisconsin in 2017 because she was just getting comfortable on all of the trails in her area. An active member of Hike it Baby, she was happy to join the local branch in her area and quickly found many hikes, including Parfrey's Glen, one of her favorites. She said, "I like this one because it's a great hike that doesn't take too much time to accomplish, along with beautiful Merrimac scenery."

The trail starts out with a paved path that is short-lived as it turns into an earthen path that's just as easy to follow. For about 0.5 mile, this route seems like a common path with no discernible features. Then a stream appears off to the left, and the scenery starts to change. After this point you realize that you're very slowly ascending. Also about 0.5 mile in is a Parfrey's Glen plaque describing the history of the area. First-timers should take note as the short narrative gives you some neat facts.

While this trail starts out with a very moderate incline on your way in, you'll need to use the rocks in the stream if you want to continue, but it's not too technical. There are some areas you have to navigate by rock stepping if you want to stay dry.

Leave No Trace ethics are particularly important here as the glen has many rare flora that are unique to the ecosystem in this area. Also, you might notice a lot of unfixed damage in this park due to flooding as recent as 2010. The lower part of the park has been flooded numerous times and continues to be at risk, so instead of continuing to add bridges, the park has opted to have people hop over stones to navigate the various trails. Use caution if venturing past the marked trail. You can get close to the waterfall but not around it.

Walking along, you'll notice pebbles of quartzite embedded in the rock walls; they tell the history of once-sandy inland sea beaches 500 million years ago and many floods. The park gets its name "Glen" from the Scottish word for narrow, rocky ravine. When you hop over the creek (that was once a river), look for a rare species of beetle swimming about. There are a handful of rare plant species here, thanks to the shady rock walls and continual flooding of the area. Also lining the trail are yellow birch, mountain maple, and red elder trees.

This trailhead will lead you to a segment of the 1,000-mile Ice Age National Trail. If you want to venture farther, you can continue on from this park for 4 miles and an elevation gain of 775 feet deeper into Devil's Lake State Park.

As you move along, proper hiking shoes are necessary. Be aware that temperatures drop in the gorge because the walls are over 100 feet high and moist with moss and lichen. Expect your feet to get wet on this hike no matter how deep you go. When you get to the area with a lot of boulders, don't turn around; keep going because the reward is worth the effort. Consider bringing a hiking pole to help you navigate through the creeks and climbs.

WHY IT'S A FAVORITE

"This hike is equally fun for kids and adults. It's a gorgeous shaded trail in the summer that's beautiful, with amazing bluffs, rock formations, and a nice, flowing stream. The watering hole was really pretty." —DINEO DOWD

INSIDER'S TIP

Parfrey's Glen is one of the most visited areas in Wisconsin, so it's advised to get there before 10 a.m. if you really want to enjoy all that the park has to offer, (the park is open from 6 a.m. to 8 p.m.) Keep a spare pair of socks and shoes in the car for after this hike because you will have wet feet!

GRAND TETON NATIONAL PARK, WYOMING, **JENNY LAKE TRAIL, TAGGART LAKE**

ACTIVITIES: Hiking, water play

LENGTH OF HIKE: 3.3 miles

OUT AND BACK OR LOOP: Out and back

DIFFICULTY OF TERRAIN: Easy

ELEVATION GAIN: 466 feet

PARKING FEE/PASS: Park entrance fee

TOILETS: Yes, an outhouse

CHANGING TABLE: No

NURSING BENCHES: No

DOGS ALLOWED: No

BIKES/HORSES/MOTORS ON TRAIL: No

CELL RECEPTION: Spotty

DRINKING WATER AVAILABLE: No

POTENTIAL CHILD OR BABY HAZARDS: Bears

GEAR SUGGESTIONS: Bear spray

Since we have offered up more toddler-friendly hikes in Wyoming, we thought we would throw this one in for the simple beauty factor. It's not long but does have some bridges to cross and is far enough that you will probably be carrying for part of the hike. It's also a trail that is usually busy and has common bear spottings, so bear spray is advised. Aside from all of that, this is a not-to-be-missed hike if you are in Grand Teton National Park.

Located underneath the stunning 13,000-foot peak of the Grand Teton, this 305-acre glacially carved lake was named after an assistant geologist who surveyed the area in 1872. William Rush Taggart and his boss, Frank Bradley, were among the party that attempted to climb Grand Teton during that expedition, a feat that is hard to imagine even now in modern times. When you see the massive jagged peak, you will understand what we mean. The best time of year to visit is July or August. You can visit in June, but expect it to be chilly. Consider hiking with the ranger (who will be carrying bear spray for you), and plan to arrive an hour early so you can find a parking space and make a quick restroom stop.

Like many paths in this park, the trail is well groomed with small rocks and pebbles but mostly dirt. There's enough room for people to walk single file in both directions. Taggart Lake starts with a little bit of a hill toward the beginning, but then it's mostly flat the rest of the way. As you head out, you will cross a bridge toward the beginning of the hike and walk alongside a creek. No need to stop and play because you can splash in Taggart Lake at the end of the hike, although it is glacier water, which means it's always cold.

"My young 3-year-old and I did it in 2015," says Maribeth Davidson. "We went back in 2016 when she was 4 and we had a 4-month-old baby. It would be a good hike to carry and let a toddler walk for little parts. Most of the hike is open and not in the trees. We saw tons of families with all ages of kids hiking in when we were leaving, so it seemed like this was a good one for the whole family."

Maribeth said she picked this trail because you can do it as a ranger-led hike, which can be good for novice hikers who aren't used to bears, moose, and big mountains. "Rangers carry bear spray, and that gave me a peace of mind since I was going to be hiking alone with my 3-year-old. The ranger would also stop and point things out to us along the way. We stayed with the group for about 30 minutes before we switched to toddler pace."

You'll often see moose and elk foraging in the woods and bald eagles and hawks flying overhead. Toddlers will love spotting the tiny fish in the lake and climbing on the rocks and fallen trees surrounding the lake. Basically, this park is a magical animal wonderland that looks like it's straight out of a Disney set, but the best part is it's all real.

Can any child walk a good part of this adventure on his own? Amelia says yes. "My 3-year-old walked the entire trail. It did take us over an hour to walk one way, but I went at her pace." Plan for it and take your time!

"My kids love the scenery, the bridges to cross, and playing at the lake at the end. We could have easily spent hours at the lake and will next time!" says Amelia.

WHY IT'S A FAVORITE

"This is our favorite local hike. It's especially busy in the summer, so go early to avoid the crowds. It's fairly flat, so even toddlers can hike most of it. The views are fantastic and the lake is perfect for spending the whole day there!" —AMELIA MAYER

INSIDER'S TIP

Get to the park about 30 to 45 minutes before the ranger hike starts so you can secure a parking space and guarantee you have a ranger with bear spray to lead you to the lake. The lot fills up quickly.

DEVILS TOWER NATIONAL MONUMENT, WYOMING, **JOYNER RIDGE TRAIL**

ACTIVITIES: Hiking, camping

LENGTH OF HIKE: 1.5 miles

OUT AND BACK OR LOOP: Loop

DIFFICULTY OF TERRAIN: Moderate

ELEVATION GAIN: 230 feet

PARKING FEE/PASS: Park entrance fee

TOILETS: No

CHANGING TABLE: No

NURSING BENCHES: Yes

DOGS ALLOWED: No

BIKES/HORSES/MOTORS ON TRAIL: No

CELL RECEPTION: Yes

DRINKING WATER AVAILABLE: Yes

POTENTIAL CHILD OR BABY HAZARDS: Ticks, mosquitoes, poison ivy

GEAR SUGGESTIONS: Hiking shoes, sunscreen, poles, carrier, water, binoculars

The terrain changes from meadow to forest, to rock, and back again throughout the hike. Be sure to wear appropriate footwear with good tread. Sun protection is important for the areas where you'll be exposed to sun and heat. If babywearing, poles are helpful for balance during elevation changes but are not necessary. Bring plenty of water as there is no potable water available at the trailhead. There are also no bathroom facilities, so be sure to go before heading to the trailhead. You will find a garbage can available, but be prepared to pack out in case the can is full, especially if toting diapers, which can take up a lot of space. Binoculars are fun to have so you can zoom in on the Tower or gaze for animals like deer or birds.

At the trailhead, you can choose to follow the path up and to the left or down and to the right. The local suggestion is to head up to the left and follow the path through some trees (this way you aren't climbing up at the end of the hike). On this route you will find yourself descending on switchbacks and natural rock steps until you reach a meadow, where you may just spot some hungry deer! This is where the trail meets with another popular park trail. From here, follow the trail to the right and you'll be immersed in the shade of a small forest. The Tower is directly above/behind/to the left of you at this point. The final stretch is a wide-open meadow. This is a great meadow for enjoying a picnic with the Tower looming in the distance.

If you come at sunset, follow the path a short distance up and to the left of the trailhead to find a perfectly placed bench to sit on and enjoy the show that the sunset brings as it lights the Tower with amazing colors. You can also watch from the parking lot!

Devils Tower is a remarkable place that can be enjoyed as a day trip or a weeklong camping adventure! Keep in mind that there is a significant elevation change that requires climbing down natural steps (or climbing up, depending on your direction). There are steep places that can be dangerous if people venture too close to the edge, so be especially vigilant with your walking little one.

The park itself is open year-round, but the trailhead cannot be accessed when heavy snows cover the road that leads to it. You can access the trail by hiking from another longer trail. Consider a visit in the fall, when temperatures are cooler and there are more colors to see.

This trail has ample opportunities for stopping to rest. Little hikers can manage the whole trail on their two feet with some assistance at the rocky elevation change portion. After you finish the hike, a visit to the Visitor Center is always a treat!

On your drive in, you will go through Prairie Dog Town. Pause and watch the prairie dogs roaming everywhere. There are pull-outs and a parking area near the campground if you want to get out and say hello to them. Other wildlife you can expect in the area are deer in the meadow and large birds like red-tailed hawks and eagles flying overhead. Of course, the Tower itself is in view most of the time, and you can sometimes spot the climbers who adventure up the sides to the top.

WHY IT'S A FAVORITE

"We enjoy all of the trails at Devils Tower, but this one is a favorite because it is less traveled, takes you through changing terrain, and is an amazing spot to watch the Tower change color as the sun sets in the evening." —CHRISTEL PETERS

INSIDER'S TIP

Don't forget your personal water container. The Visitor Center is located up the road and does not sell bottled beverages due to the unfortunate consequence of people leaving used bottles on the trails. There is a water fountain available to fill water storage containers near the pavilion at the base of the Tower.

LAURANCE S. ROCKEFELLER PRESERVE, WYOMING, **PHELPS LAKE LOOP (WOODLAND TRAIL OR LAKE CREEK TRAIL)**

ACTIVITIES: Hiking, splashing, birding, fishing

LENGTH OF HIKES: 3.1 miles or 7.2 miles

OUT AND BACK OR LOOP: Both

DIFFICULTY OF TERRAIN: Easy

ELEVATION GAIN: 260 Feet

PARKING FEE/PASS: Park entrance fee

TOILETS: Yes

CHANGING TABLE: No

NURSING BENCHES: No

DOGS ALLOWED: No

BIKES/HORSES/MOTORS ON TRAIL: No

CELL RECEPTION: Spotty

DRINKING WATER AVAILABLE: Yes, at Visitor Center

POTENTIAL CHILD OR BABY HAZARDS: Water, bears

GEAR SUGGESTIONS: Bear spray

Some days hiking with your little ones is easy, and other days you just aren't going to be able to go far. This is a great hike for either scenario. Amelia Mayer, blogger of Tales of a Mountain Mama, as well as mother to five kids who are all under 10 years old, knows what to look for in a good family trail. You can either keep it relatively flat and easy with a 1.5-mile hike out to an overlook above the lake, or make a day of it and go for the entire loop.

Wildlife is plentiful here, from elk ambling through sagebrush meadows, to bears snacking on huckleberries and blueberries in the summer, to moose bugling in the distance in the fall. The lake sits at 6,633 feet. Just above that, bald eagles and pelicans fly over the crystal clear waters as they scan for cutthroat trout. Bears are common, so spray is recommended. However, in the height of the summer, this part of the trail sees quite a bit of human traffic, which will usually scare off animals. NOTE: In the fall, sometimes a bear closure is in effect with a detour away from the preserve that adds about a mile.

The serene beauty of the lake makes it easy to see why this was once a retreat for the Rockefeller family, whose name is in the park legacy through the nature center they built and the over 34,000 acres they donated throughout the years. The most recent donation of 1,100 acres happened in 2001 and included the building of an impressive nature center that's open and staffed with rangers from June through the end of September.

We recommend that you start hiking in this area early in the morning for two reasons: It takes half a day to trek it if you are going slowly and enjoying the scenery. Also, by noon the parking lot is full and there is no overflow, so you will have to wait for a parking space! This is stressed over and over in online reviews of the location. Other than this minor inconvenience, there are so many more reasons to visit this area if you have the opportunity.

The hike begins at the Laurance S. Rockefeller Preserve off the Moose-Wilson Road. From the parking lot, hike a short ways to the Visitor Center. From there, stay on the Woodland Trail, which is the most direct route to the lake (about 1.2 miles). You can also take the Lake Creek Trail, which is a bit longer (about 1.6 miles) and goes directly to the overlook mentioned below. Connecting the two makes a great loop for families. At one point, you do cross over the Moose-Wilson Road, which is narrow and winding though easily crossed. (Just be sure kids are looking for cars!)

It is about 1.6 miles to the lake overlook via the Lake Creek Trail. Right before the lake, there is a very nice bathroom perfect for pit stops or changing a baby. The overlook is a man-made rocky point that allows for great views of the lake. Go a little farther down the trail to access the lake. The majority of the hike is shaded, and the terrain changes enough to keep interest.

If you are feeling more ambitious, you can continue circling the entire Phelps Lake for about 7 miles and even add on an out and back spur to Death Canyon. This is the much more advanced version of the visit, though it's not recommended for those with inexperienced little hikers or a baby who hasn't spent a lot of time in a pack or carrier.

The reward, whether you hike the 1.5 miles or do the whole loop, is a fairly quiet lake, thanks to the limited parking, which keeps the crowds at bay. This adventure is for sure a pleaser for the whole family with minimal effort for those with multiple kids.

WHY IT'S A FAVORITE

"We love this hike because it's an easy 3 miles and the elevation gain is fairly minimal. There's a great end point perfect for picnics. While there are a few different trail options, we recommend taking the Lake Creek Trail going and the Woodland Trail back for a good loop with kids. Our kids love to jump off the rocks and play around the trees, and the preserve is gorgeous!" —AMELIA MAYER

INSIDER'S TIP

There are numerous nature programs offered at the Laurance S. Rockefeller Preserve Center. Make a reservation for the 9:30 a.m. hike with a ranger, or just show up at the Preserve Center Porch for a 30-minute "Critter Chat" demonstration and learn about animal safety in the forest. It's offered on Sunday, Tuesday, Thursday, and Saturday at 3:30 p.m. If you have school-age kids along, check out a Nature Explorer's Backpack. This is a pack with a journal full of activities to guide them through the park. This is best for children 6 to 12 years old.

Healthier, Homemade Energy Bars and Trail Cookies

Dr. Erika Siegel is a mom, physician, health educator, and wife: by nature, a juggler of life's abundance. She has the honor to practice and preach naturo- pathic medicine in Portland, Oregon, where she focuses on family medicine. Try her kid-friendly superfood product, Nourish Me, in your smoothies! Check out her website at www.nourishme.com.

These treats are fun to make with kids as they can help with every step. You can nibble on these energy snacks fresh from the fridge or freezer and pack them to go in lunches or backpacks on the trail. They are packed with healthy fat, protein, and fruit, fueling you with balanced nutrition any time of the day.

Fig-Almond Energy Bars with Cranberries

There are too many "health" or "energy" bars to choose from—and most are processed with hidden, unhealthy ingredients. This recipe is based in whole foods with dense, efficient nutrition. It calls for dried fruit, which should al- ways be purchased without preservatives (sulphur dioxide) because many people are sensitive to these preservatives, and it really changes the flavor of the fruit. It's also best to choose raw unsalted nuts for maximum freshness and health. You can soak the nuts first for better digestibility (see below).

INGREDIENTS:

2 cups raw almonds

¼ cup whole flaxseeds

1 ½ cups dried cranberries

1 ¼ cups dried figs, destemmed

1 tablespoon organic orange zest

3 tablespoons tahini

1 tablespoon almond butter

2–3 tablespoons maple syrup

¼ teaspoon salt

DIRECTIONS:

Soaking the nuts first will make them easier to digest. If you do this, cover the nuts (not the flaxseeds) in a few inches of water with $\frac{1}{2}$ tablespoon of salt for 12 hours. Then rinse, drain, and spread the nuts on a cookie sheet. Bake at 150°F for another 12 hours. You can bake them longer (24 hours) for crispy nuts to munch.

Line an 8 x 8-inch-deep pan or dish with plastic wrap or waxed paper. (You can use a different shape pan as long as it's close to the same size.)

In a food processor, pulse the nuts and seeds until they are well broken down but still chunky. Do not overpulse or it will turn into nut butter. Then transfer this nut and seed mixture to a large mixing bowl.

Roughly chop the dried fruit on a cutting board and add it to the processor. Pulse until broken down into small chunks, but be careful not to let this turn into mush. If at any point during the process your food processor seems to be straining, add just a splash of water. A little bit of water goes a long way, and you don't want to end up with sticky, wet bars.

Add this mixture to the mixing bowl with the nut and seed mixture.

Add the remaining ingredients to the large mixing bowl with the chopped-up fruit and nuts, and slowly add the sweetener and salt. After everything is combined, taste the mixture to see if you want to add some more of either.

Then, with your hands, dig in! Mush and mix all of the ingredients together until everything is well incorporated. When the mixture sticks between your fingers, you're done. You can do this step in the food processor, but it may require a lot of stopping, scraping the sides, and adding a bit more water. We find it works best when done by hand.

Put the mixture into the plastic-lined pan, pressing firmly to even it out. Cover and refrigerate for at least 1 hour to let it harden and for easier cutting. Finally, cut into desired-size bars and seal in an airtight container for up to 2 weeks or freeze for up to 2 months. (We keep ours individually wrapped in the freezer.) *Makes 16–20 snack-sized bars.*

Chocolate-Chia Trail Cookies

The nutrition in these little cookies is so impressive you may decide to eat them for breakfast without an ounce of guilt. They are really a superfood disguised as a treat. Cacao powder is rich in antioxidants, providing minerals and producing happy hormones. The chia seeds are rich in calcium, magnesium, omega-3 fats, and protein—helping to sustain energy for hours. These cookies are moist with a fun, brownie-like texture. Enjoy them on the trail or anywhere!

INGREDIENTS:

1 cup chia seeds

1 ½ cups almond flour

⅓ cup unsweetened cocoa powder or raw cacao powder

¾ cup coconut palm sugar

Scant ½ teaspoon salt

½ teaspoon baking powder

2 eggs

½ cup coconut oil or organic butter, melted

2 teaspoons vanilla extract

½ cup tightly packed dried cherries or cranberries, chopped (optional)

20 liquid stevia drops to desired sweetness

DIRECTIONS:

Preheat oven to 350°F.

Grind the chia seeds in a coffee grinder or high-quality blender until it is a fine powder. Mix all the dry ingredients in a medium bowl. In a small bowl, lightly beat the eggs. Stir in the melted coconut oil or butter and the vanilla. Combine with the dry ingredients and mix well. Stir in the dried cherries if using. Form the dough into flattened rounds using a soup spoon, and place them on an ungreased cookie sheet at least 1 inch apart.

Bake until the cookies have a soft, brownie-like consistency but are still a bit moist inside, about 12 minutes. *Makes approximately 20–24 cookies.*

NURSING ON TRAIL
COMFORT IS KEY

When my son was born in 2013, I began hiking very regularly. It became an enormous outlet for other stressors in my life. However, the outlet for stress started to become a stressor in itself when it came time to feed. I hiked with other women with children, and they were always very kind and supportive when I said I needed to stop and feed my son. However, it got to a point where I was feeling like I couldn't enjoy the hikes. It felt like I was almost becoming resentful of nursing. That is, until one particular hike when a fellow mother taught me how to breastfeed while my son was in the carrier.

I don't remember the particular hike; I don't even remember who the woman was. I only remember that this was a pivotal moment for my son and me. He was still quite young, maybe 6 weeks old, but this changed my whole mothering world. As I was constantly worried about when I would need to stop for his next feed, I was not experiencing the hike in its entirety. However, I was then able to meet my son's feeding needs while enjoying the beauty around me. Over time, this skill also provided me with the confidence to feed out in more public places as well. It was a liberating feeling.

I won't pretend that it didn't take some practice. I was no master breastfeeder right off the bat. However, I was persistent and kept with it, and soon I found myself eager to teach other breastfeeding mothers the magic of breastfeeding in a carrier. Because of this, and a few other lactation-related aha moments, so began my journey to becoming a lactation consultant.

As a lactation consultant, one of the most rewarding things for me is to see parents feel empowered in their feeding adventure. Having assisted many mothers in learning to breastfeed their child on trail, I've found that learning to breastfeed in a carrier can be a huge turning point for the duration of their breastfeeding journey. Here are a few things to consider if you are taking those first steps in learning how to nurse your child on trail:

- Wear appropriate nursing clothing. Look for shirts with wide openings and zippers in the front that give you easy access and go low.

- Make sure you are comfortable with your carrier and loosening and tightening it when in motion or on trail.

- Think about the bra you are wearing and how easy it is to open and close.

- Consider the weather. Layering is a smart move whether you're hiking with a child or not. However, when you're nursing, remember that you'll have more skin exposed.

- If it's chilly or raining, you may want a jacket or something to zip up around yourself or place over yourself and the carrier to shield you from the cold or rain.

Hiking with a young child, although wonderful, can be stress inducing at times, especially when it comes time to feed the child. Remember, as your child gets older, it's simple to pack them granola bars and apple slices. And that's coming! However, hiking and breastfeeding with a brand-new infant can be tricky to learn how to navigate a latch, but start slowly. Take those first steps while sitting on the couch in the comfort of your own home, and slowly move out to the backyard or up and down your street. From there you'll feel more ready to head out onto the trail. Also remember to not be shy and ask other women around you who you see nursing on trail for tips.

Kristen Mannion is a licensed lactation consultant who lives in Portland, OR. She is also one of the founding members of Hike it Baby. She has taught numerous women how to nurse on trail and while carrying their child.

What's in My Pack?

Large Pack or Stroller (Most Space)

- ❑ 1–2 books (thin paper books are better than board books)
- ❑ Light changing mat
- ❑ Wipes
- ❑ 1 diaper
- ❑ Wet bag
- ❑ Snacks and bribing treats
- ❑ Muslin cloth
- ❑ Flashlight

- ❑ Bubbles
- ❑ Medical kit
- ❑ Tissues
- ❑ Change of clothes
- ❑ Extra socks!!!
- ❑ Water bottle
- ❑ Phone
- ❑ Keys

Backpack (Some Space)

- ❏ Light changing mat
- ❏ Wipes
- ❏ 1 diaper
- ❏ Wet bag
- ❏ Snacks and bribing treats
- ❏ Washcloth
- ❏ Flashlight
- ❏ Bubbles
- ❏ Band-Aids
- ❏ 1 pair of thin pants/leggings
- ❏ Extra socks
- ❏ Water bottle
- ❏ Phone
- ❏ Keys

Fanny Pack or Carrier (Limited Space)

- ❏ 1 diaper
- ❏ Ziplock bag of wipes
- ❏ A few Band-Aids
- ❏ Simple snack
- ❏ Phone
- ❏ Keys
- ❏ Carry water bottle

Todder Pack (Kid Gear)

- ❏ Stuffed animal
- ❏ Water bottle
- ❏ Tiny notebook
- ❏ Pencil
- ❏ Snacks
- ❏ Trail-sturdy toy
- ❏ Walking stick

PHOTO CREDITS

Author's note: a huge thanks to the Hike it Baby photographers and individuals who sent photos to help us tell our story in this book and encourage many more families to get out on the trail. I hope their images have inspired you!

Page 3: Louisa Albanese

Pages 6-7: TK

Page 10: Ashley Scheider

Page 12: Ashley Scheider

Page 15: Laura Castro

Page 17: Krystal Weir

Page 20: Jennifer Bradwin

Page 21: Tais Kulish

Pages 22-23: Kathryn Jones

Pages 24-26: Kristin Hinnant

Page 27: Kathy Rumsey

Page 29: Georgia Kubik

Page 31: Georgia Kubik

Pages 32-33: Amanda Bernard

Page 35-37: Jill Craven

Page 38: Stefie Gold

Pages 40-41: Deanna Curry

Pages 42-43: Annika Mang

Pages 44-45: Ali Chandra

Pages 46: Anka Trifan

Pages 48-49: Xenia Pyne

Pages 50-53: Ryan Idryo

Pages 54-56: Arika Bauer

Page 57-61: Ryan Idryo

Pages 62-64: Vanessa Wright

Pages 65-66: Louisa Albanese

Pages 67-72: Megan Mountain

Pages 73-75: Krystal Weir

Page 76: Kim Ives

Page 78: Krystal Weir

Pages 80-81: Ashley Scheider

Page 85: Jennifer Campbell

Pages 86-88: Lindsay Frost

Pages 89-90: Corey Heacock

Page 91: Abby Czachur

Page 93: Abby Czachur

Pages 94-96: Crystal Osborn

Page 97: Sammy Prugsamatz

Page 98: Ashley Scheider

Page 99: Ali Chandra

Page 100: Dineo Dowd

Page 102: Ashley Scheider

ABOUT THE AUTHOR

SHANTI HODGES is on a mission to build worldwide communities, both online and offline, to help connect people to nature. She is the founder of Hike it Baby (hikeitbaby.com), a nonprofit organization dedicated to helping families with babies and toddlers find each other in the outdoors. Hike it Baby is currently active in over 330 cities and plans 2,500 hikes a month in the calendar.

In addition to her work with Hike it Baby, Shanti also runs women's retreats and guides hike adventures in Southern Utah (hikingmyway.com) and also launched an outdoor family festival (familyforestfest.com) in Oregon.

Prior to founding Hike it Baby, Shanti was a freelance writer and a consultant helping small businesses with their websites and social media, contributing to magazines like *Outside*, *Men's Journal*, *Marie Claire*, *Shape*, and *Self*. She authored a book, *Women Who Run*, in 2007.

Shanti is a passionate outdoor enthusiast who splits her time between Portland, OR and La Verkin, Utah (Zion National Park area) with her husband Mark and son Mason.